Mobility in Space and Time

Contributions to Economics

http://www.springer.de/cgi-bin/search_book.pl?series=1262

Sardar M. N. Islam
**Mathematical Economics of
Multi-Level Optimisation**
1998. ISBN 3-7908-1050-9

Sven-Morten Mentzel
Real Exchange Rate Movements
1998. ISBN 3-7908-1081-9

Lei Delsen/Eelke de Jong (Eds.)
**The German and Dutch
Economies**
1998. ISBN 3-7908-1064-9

Mark Weder
**Business Cycle Models with
Indeterminacy**
1998. ISBN 3-7908-1078-9

Tor Rødseth (Ed.)
**Models for Multispecies
Management**
1998. ISBN 3-7908-1001-0

Michael Carlberg
Intertemporal Macroeconomics
1998. ISBN 3-7908-1096-7

Sabine Spangenberg
**The Institutionalised Trans-
formation of the East German
Economy**
1998. ISBN 3-7908-1103-3

Hagen Bobzin
Indivisibilities
1998. ISBN 3-7908-1123-8

Helmut Wagner (Ed.)
**Current Issues in Monetary
Economics**
1998. ISBN 3-7908-1127-0

Peter Michaelis/Frank Stähler (Eds.)
**Recent Policy Issues in Environ-
mental and Resource Economics**
1998. ISBN 3-7908-1137-8

Jessica de Wolff
**The Political Economy
of Fiscal Decisions**
1998. ISBN 3-7908-1130-0

Georg Bol/Gholamreza Nakhaeiza-
deh/Karl-Heinz Vollmer (Eds.)
**Risk Measurements, Econo-
metrics and Neural Networks**
1998. ISBN 3-7908-1152-1

Joachim Winter
**Investment and Exit Decisions
at the Plant Level**
1998. ISBN 3-7908-1154-8

Bernd Meyer
Intertemporal Asset Pricing
1999. ISBN 3-7908-1159-9

Uwe Walz
Dynamics of Regional Integration
1999. ISBN 3-7908-1185-8

Michael Carlberg
European Monetary Union
1999. ISBN 3-7908-1191-2

Giovanni Galizzi/
Luciano Venturini (Eds.)
**Vertical Relationships and
Coordination in the Food System**
1999. ISBN 3-7908-1192-0

Gustav A. Horn/
Wolfgang Scheremet/
Rudolf Zwiener
Wages and the Euro
1999. ISBN 3-7908-1199-8

Dirk Willer
**The Development of Equity
Capital Markets in Transition
Economies**
1999. ISBN 3-7908-1198-X

Karl Matthias Weber
**Innovation Diffusion and Political
Control of Energy Technologies**
1999. ISBN 3-7908-1205-6

Heike Link et al.
**The Costs of Road Infrastructure
and Congestion in Europe**
1999. ISBN 3-7908-1201-3

Simon Duindam
Military Conscription
1999. ISBN 3-7908-1203-X

Bruno Jeitziner
**Political Economy of the
Swiss National Bank**
1999. ISBN 3-7908-1209-9

Irene Ring et al. (Eds.)
Regional Sustainability
1999. ISBN 3-7908-1233-1

continued on page 235

Nicole Pohl

Mobility in Space and Time

Challenges to the Theory of International Economics

With 37 Figures
and 8 Tables

Physica-Verlag

A Springer-Verlag Company

337
P74m

Series Editors
Werner A. Müller
Martina Bihn

Author
Dr. Nicole Pohl
University of Duisburg
Institute for International Economics
Lotharstraße 65
47048 Duisburg
Germany

Printed with support of the Deutsche Forschungsgemeinschaft, D 464

ISSN 1431-1933
ISBN 3-7908-1380-X Physica-Verlag Heidelberg New York

Cataloging-in-Publication Data applied for
Die Deutsche Bibliothek – CIP-Einheitsaufnahme
Pohl, Nicole: Mobility in space and time: challenges to the theory of international
economics; with 8 tables / Nicole Pohl. – Heidelberg; New York: Physica-Verl., 2001
   (Contributions to economics)
   Zugl.: Duisburg, Univ., Diss.
   ISBN 3-7908-1380-X

Physica-Verlag Heidelberg New York
a member of BertelsmannSpringer Science+Business Media GmbH

© Physica-Verlag Heidelberg 2001
Printed in Germany

Softcover Design: Erich Kirchner, Heidelberg

SPIN 10795704   88/2202-5 4 3 2 1 0 – Printed on acid-free and non-aging paper

Foreword

The pure theory of international economics operates within a methodological framework of (static) equilibrium modelling. This sets a number of restrictions to its capability to explain empirical economic phenomena. A huge part of the scientific discourse takes place within this equilibrium framework. This is also true for new approaches like e.g. the New Economic Geography and models operating with market structures of oligopoly. This is why it is a courageous effort to try to cross the apparently unalterable borders set by equilibrium modelling.

Most certainly this cannot be an end in itself. Especially the pure theory of international economics is still in many fields lacking adequate possibilities to deal with phenomena in space and time. These two dimensions have in common that they make the introduction of specific facets of movement, change, evolution – and therefore "mobility" – possible. Besides this "dynamic" component a point of view that includes space and time challenges us to find new possibilities to model heterogeneous agents.

If these ideas are not so revolutionary in their content, the attempt to introduce them into a formal model is a big challenge. Moreover, it poses the question about the role of a theory of "international" economics in such a wider framework.

Despite these arguments Nicole Pohl has chosen the task to develop the existing theoretical framework into a completely new direction. What is new is that knowledge from economic geography, economic sociology, cultural economics and evolutionary economics is combined. This way, the space and time dimension is enriched with an economically relevant content. The result is a picture that is closer to reality, complex and dynamic. It is based on the pillars agents and their interaction and location in space as well as in time. In such a picture, the nation state is only one aspect that may create distance.

It goes without saying that this complex evolving picture of the spatial economy cannot be modelled by using traditional methods. Therefore, Nicole Pohl suggests to apply new mathematical methods as e.g. used in sociodynamic modelling.

In a discussion with Prof. Masahisa Fujita he stated that the New Economic Geography has been a step forward done by researchers who are however now looking to young economists who are able to develop new ideas. Nicole Pohl's work is indeed a step forward because it introduces knowledge from other disciplines, integrates the objects of interest of international economics into a framework of mobility in space and time and last but not least gives mainstream theory a chance to survive.

Nicole Pohl's dissertation opens the mind for new ways to develop a time-space oriented framework in order to analyze transactions between heterogeneous agents. It may show the way for more than a new interpretation of international economic theory. The combination of heterogeneous agents and heterogeneous locations as well as the introduction of different types of distances and open paths of evolution pose challenges – and offer possibilities – to develop an interdisciplinary research agenda that exceeds the boundaries of the traditional theory of international economics. The most important contribution to the discussion in international economics about how to create progress in narrowing the gap between theory and reality is Nicole Pohl's way to bring state-of-the-art knowledge from different disciplines together. Her approach seems to be a highly promising starting-point for value-adding research of a new generation of open-minded economists.

December 1st, 2000   Günter Heiduk

Acknowledgements

This work would not have been possible without the advice, encouragement and support I have generously received from a number of people and institutions.

First of all I want to thank Günter Heiduk, who has been my advisor for this doctoral thesis. He encouraged me to look beyond the borders of mainstream economics and taught me to develop an attitude towards this discipline that makes it possible at once to estimate given knowledge and to try to cope with new challenges. By introducing me to a number of his friends and colleagues in Europe, the US and Asia, he provided me with valuable academic support. I am sure that this dissertation would neither have been finished in a comparable time, nor would it have read the way it does today without his support.

I also have to thank Prof. Hans-Heinrich Blotevogel for being the second referee of my dissertation.

Moreover, I would like to express my gratitude to Kozo Yamamura, who has become a very valuable advisor for me during the last two years. He never left any doubt about his confidence into my scientific capabilities and he gave me more support than I could ever have expected. The valuable help and above all the dynamic spirit of both, Kozo Yamamura and Günter Heiduk, gave me the drive to realize plans I would otherwise not have thought possible.

A fellowship by German Academic exchange service (DAAD) gave me the opportunity to discuss my topic with a number of colleagues in the United States. I have to thank DAAD for this because it enhanced the progress of my work a lot. Especially I also want to thank Prof. Masanao Aoki, Prof. Nicole Biggart, Prof. Gerald Meier, Prof. Allan Pred, Prof. James Rauch, Prof. Suzanne Scotchmer and Prof. Kar-yiu Wong. Similarly, Prof. Wolfgang Weidlich greatly influenced my scientific work by introducing and explaining new methods of modelling socio-economic phenomena to me. My research benefited a lot from the open-mindedness of these colleagues and their willingness to share their knowledge with me. The network of contacts I have established since then gave me the impression that the global scientific community is really alive.

Moreover, Deutsche Forschungsgemeinschaft (DFG) supported the publication of this dissertation financially.

In a much different way I cannot forget to mention my good friend Nicole de Haan. Without her encouragement and understanding I would frequently not have dared to "go against the tide".

Finally, I have to mention my family who set the foundation for a way I have only started to go.

December 1st, 2000   Nicole Pohl

Contents

1   Introduction: aims and conceptions

"Economic science deals with phenomena that are more complex and less uniform than those with which the natural sciences are concerned; and its conclusions, except in their most abstract form, lack both the certainty and the universality that pertain to physical laws. There is a corresponding difficulty in regard of the proper method of economic study; and the problem of defining the conditions and limits of the validity of economic reasonings becomes one of exceptional complexity." (Keynes 1891/1984: 72)

International economics deals with the causes and effects of transactions and economic relations between nation states as well as with the degree of interdependence (ranging from integration and co-operation to isolation and competition) that is created this way. More precisely, the international economy has its starting-point in the agents pursuing a wide range of economic activities within these nation states. These are on the one hand national or multinational enterprises and on the other hand individuals acting as owners of factors of production and consumers, but also political decision-makers. Implicitly, the term "inter"-national already gives us an idea of the relevance of borders as places where movement can be inhibited or restricted. But what is it that is contained within the borders of nation states, why do borders make a difference and why does the difference "inter" versus "intra" matter? Taken literally, the idea of the nation is related to the common origin of its inhabitants. Having a look at the main approaches of international economics we quickly become aware that

- nations are mostly defined as political entities in the sense of states or countries; sometimes also the term "economies" is used;

- related to this is the idea of territories within which agents and factors of production are mobile, but between which there is immobility.[1]

International economics analyzes what happens between nations that are defined in this way. However, not only intra or inside aspects of nation states are neglected in this framework, but also any other aspect that may be a relevant feature of a nation. Moreover, it is by no means clear why an economy as a relevant entity should be congruent with the territory within political borders. Furthermore, there are a number of other disciplines besides economics that make valuable contributions to the question which elements make up a nation or a relevant entity in space (sociology: societies, cultural areas; political science: supra- and subnational entities or geographical concepts). These starting-points are also relevant from an economic point of view. This leads us to one characteristic all these concepts have in common: They all can be defined as extensions in space. As to the spatial scale that can be taken as a starting-point to structure space, we may e. g. distinguish local, regional and a number of wider spatial scales apart from the national scale. While the latter possesses clearly defined boundaries, this is not necessarily true for the former.

It may be useful to try to understand the international economy on the basis of the commonly used unit, the nation, but this can only serve as a starting-point. National political borders most certainly are meaningful entities and they are important because of their power to inhibit movements and to set rules. Nonetheless, it will be shown that there are a number of other aspects or borders that give a structure to the economic system.

The following chapters will however also show that we do not only need a more differentiated view about borders and boundaries, but also about the ways agents are interrelated. Batten et al. (1995: VII) explain that "what makes a collection of objects a system rather than just a collection of things is that they are connected in some interesting and important way". The "objects" connected in the economic system are agents and decision-makers. Traditionally, economic agents in international economics are connected by price signals on markets. Looking at the aspects underlined by other disciplines we get aware that other types of relationships may be also relevant for the laws and patterns derived in international economics. As interdisciplinary views highlight a broad set of aspects in this field, they are helpful to better understand the topics analyzed traditionally in international economics.

---

[1] These assumptions are most relevant in the pure theory of international economics. This part of the theoretical building is of special importance for the aims pursued here as the focus will be on flows of goods and factors of production as well as locational decision-making rather than financial aspects or the exchange rate.

Among other things the following chapters will strive to shed light on the following subjects:

- Which are the relevant *agents* and how are they *interrelated*? What are their relevant characteristics and capabilities?

- What is the *spatial framework* in which economic action has to be analyzed?

We can start by assuming that the theory of international economics above all has to be interested in the rules governing processes of interaction between different agents in space with nation state borders structuring space. Interaction contains a number of actions that include the exchange of goods, material and immaterial factors of production as well as non-price interaction like exchange of information, mutual learning, imitation and spillovers regarding knowledge, use of common resources or other things. According to Johansson and Westin (1994:247), the formation and restructuring of economic interaction is a basic phenomenon which influences the development of short and long distance flows between regions and the changing structure and renewal of the economy. Flows of goods and factors of production as one visible expression of interaction across space may however not only vary over time in their intensity, but also in their direction. This may be due to the fact that partners of interaction are changing, but also because agents have the ability to change their locations in space. Thus, from an empirical point of view our analysis should be done within a space- and time-related framework. The following question therefore has to be added:

- Can we distinguish temporal patterns of change in the global spatial economy?

The direction of flows is determined by three factors: the location of agents, the way partners of interaction are matched and political decision-making. These aspects – locational decisions and interaction across space - are variables rather than given parameters. Agents and firms are more or less able to choose and change their location. On the other hand, with whom to trade, exchange and interact also is a matter of decision-making. Finally, the two concepts of locational mobility and mobility of flows are interdependent in the following way: Locational choice can be considered a decision about interaction as well. It is at once a decision to engage in small scale spatial interaction with agents at the same location, it is choosing a framework of locational conditions, but it is also a decision about the distances that have to be crossed to reach agents at other locations. Whenever crossing distances involves costs, the question of proximity to others will be decisive. If we accept that decision-making is done under uncertainty and that information in space and about space is not equally distributed, the idea of learning and of evolving capabilities will be relevant. Empirical observation shows that agents differ with respect to the degree they are able and willing to "move" within the relational and spatial framework of the economic system.

These ideas about the premacy of flows across space and locational decisions suggest that basically international economic theory should not be focused on nation state borders as an object of interest. These are only the starting-point to define the international. In contrast, we can plausibly assume that the theory of international economics is in its aims part of a *theory of mobility*. Whether the rigid framework of national borders that has up to now been taken as a starting point is able to fulfill the tasks linked to such a theory may be doubted. Peculiarly enough, thinking about relevant *economic* structures in space leads us to conclude that it is hardly possible to predefine spatial entities that are necessarily also economic entities. Of course, from an economic point of view, we often deal with concepts like centers and peripheries, industrial agglomerations or economic regions, but these terms describe outcomes rather than inputs into the theory. The following chapters will show that besides the concept of political nation states, other disciplines may offer promising ways to define the space in which economic action occurs.

Moreover, it will be assumed that mobility is not an absolute or given characteristic. There is a scope of possibilities behind it that can be shaped by economic agents. Mobility is a capability. This is why the framework to be chosen will have to take up those aspects that have proved to be important elements in a world of mobility: *agents* and their *capabilities* and competences, their *interaction* and of course, *space* and *time*. The causal relationships to be derived from this starting-point are different from traditional points of view because we proceed from mobility to spatial economic structures rather than from given borders to patterns of mobility. These aspects will be explained more fully in the following paragraphs in order to give the reader a better understanding of the aims of this approach.

Mobility therefore means on the one hand *mobility of flows* and on the other hand *mobility of the locations* of at least some economic agents.[2] As is shown in figure 1.1, locational mobility means that agents (individuals as well as firms) are able to decide where to locate, when and if to change their location and whether - as in the case of multinational firms - to have several locations. What makes up a location is both, the number of agents pursuing some kind of economic activity and the flows leaving and reaching it, but also circulating within it – flows that may cross different spatial distances.

---

[2] The following chapters will focus on those flows that are directly related to the activities of firms as productive units. Theories dealing with international capital flows are not the subject here.

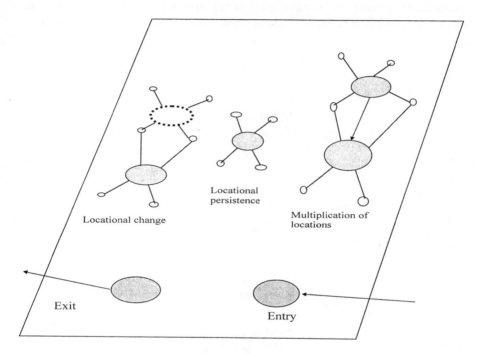

Fig. 1.1: Locational mobility, adapted from: Brockfeld (1997), p. 42

Mobility of flows is based on the ties, relationships and interaction among agents. Ties are created whenever two or more agents transact repeatedly for a certain time and when this has the effect of binding agents together in some sense. Interaction is considered as a very complex concept as it comprises the development of relationships in time, but also the transactions and behaviours resulting from these relationships. Mobility of flows can have manifold facets as regards the type of flows, the intensity of interaction, the direction of the exchange and the strength of ties as well as the parameters that are decisive for its direction. Locational mobility, interaction and mobility of flows have to be considered as interrelated concepts. If interaction across space is costly, locational decisions will to some extent be a function of patterns of interaction. On the other hand, if space itself is not homogenous, there will be good reasons for agents to choose locations carefully. Finally, if ties are weak and space is heterogeneous, the question with whom to interact might follow the locational decision. Flows might in that case also be a function of location.

The following figure 1.2 summarizes the main ideas about mobility. While the relationship between mobility and space seems to be more obvious, the relevance of time will be left to be explained in the following chapters, especially in part C.

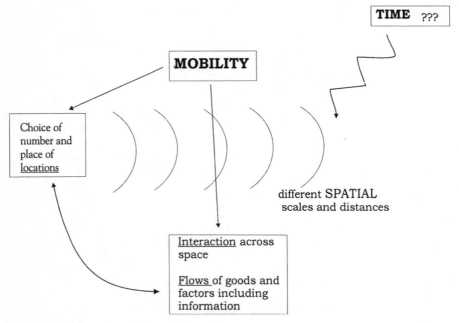

Fig. 1.2: Mobility of locations and flows

The last decade has been characterized by a number of technological and political developments that have in many respects extended the possibilities for mobility. This is especially true as regards the possibilities to interact across space and to exchange goods, factors and especially information. Thus, *distance* from a geographical point of view more and more seems to have lost importance. As a result, the decision where to locate may have become more flexible for many agents. Locational differences and advantages may be exploited more easily because geographical distance no longer creates serious restrictions. On the other hand, many authors stress that in a number of respects intensive and close relationships have gained importance so that ties and proximity may still be important determinants of locational decisions. Thus, the patterns of mobility predominant in this century do by no means simply point toward the extinguishing of distance. They depend on the way agents perceive space with its two expressions of distance and location as well as on the strategies resulting from this. Mobility therefore has to be interpreted within a broad framework of decision-making including decisions with whom to interact how, where to locate, whether to change, multiply (e. g. in multinational firms) or keep a location. We cannot simply assume that those who move more frequently in order to exploit existing locational differences are those that have advantages compared to others. Rather does the proposition hold that those who are able to exploit the set of new possibilities more successfully and flexibly are those who use the capability "mobility" more effectively. Mobility thus comprises elements of immobility (agents being tied to their location or deciding to stay where they are) as well as hypermobility (instantaneous exploitation of advantages in space) without any ranking to indicate which is more valuable.

Immobility means that certain ties (to space, but - as will be explained - also to certain organizational frameworks like firms and others) prohibit motion or make motion unfavourable. This implies that only a small part of the number of objects and individuals we observe as immobile is immobile by nature. There are others who did not try or did not succeed in developing capabilities for mobility or who decided to stay at a location, although they might have been able to move. Immobility therefore is different from inertia. It largely reflects active decision-making. What about those agents that are - at least temporarily - not free to choose their locations? They nonetheless interact with others that may be more mobile. They may have to try hard to attract the attention of more mobile agents into their sphere in order to realize their economic goals. A special type of a spatially immobile agent is that of the political decision-maker. His actions are not only fixed from a spatial point of view, but they strongly influence spatial characteristics and shape the quality of economic locations within a given spatial horizon. He therefore has the aim to direct or influence movements of mobile agents. As the empirical observations in chapter 2 will show, even political borders nowadays are not fixed. Processes of regional integration weaken the importance of national political borders as barriers for mobility and shift political power between different political levels. Together with the notion that immobile resources have in many fields become replaceable, whereas the importance of the principally hypermobile productive factor information is rapidly rising, it is obvious that current developments may have to be approached by the notion that there is mobility nearly everywhere rather than the observation that there are some agents that are immobile and structure the world. We therefore observe a relatively mobile economic system embedded in space and changing in time (=spatial dynamics) – a system however where besides mobility immobility also has its reasons.

Agents have to develop the tool mobility in order to be more flexible in reaching their goals. They have to create the capability "mobility" and they have to decide when to use this tool. To summarize, the last decades have been characterized by a number of developments that reduce the theoretical dominance of an immobile political-spatial framework and favour an agent-oriented view. The reason for this is that there is an ever wider scope for the individual or the firm to use mobility as a tool to enhance success and efficiency. Meanwhile, the restrictions political borders set for mobility are decreasing and within processes of integration borders seem in some way have become more flexible. Thus, there are many reasons why agents' capabilities to develop and use the many facets of mobility that can be available for them today should be the starting-point of theoretical reasoning.

Space is one of the dimensions mobility is embedded into. What are the relevant characteristics of space? The concept of space to be used here is multifaceted and not purely geographical by nature. It is assumed that space and distance are not only absolute, but also relative concepts. Distance is regarded an expression of agents ties and relationships to each other, which may be shaped by a number of variables other than geographical distance. On the other hand, spatial developments can only be derived if we succeed in analyzing agents' relationships towards and their perception of space. Only if we fill space with economic action and interaction, we will be able to give it meaning from an economic point of view.

In traditional international economic theory, space mostly enters models on the basis of an inside-outside view. Only if flows cross national borders, they are recognized as relevant by international economic theory. On the political side, this limits the set of relevant agents to state-level political decision-makers. An analysis of other spatial horizons (cities, regions, agglomerations, cultural regions etc.) may however contribute to our understanding of international economics, although this perspective has up to now not become pervasive in the theoretical field. The significant feature of "international" economics has up to now been its interest in actions that cross borders, neglecting in many cases a detailed analysis of what happens within these borders and ignoring the fact that borders - if we do not reserve the term exclusively for national borders - have a definition that may be as relative as the idea of inside and outside. It depends on where we are standing, how we perceive our environment and what is our spatial horizon to determine whether our position is inside or outside and whether we perceive flows as remaining inside borders or crossing them.

Finally, it will become obvious that space is a hierarchical system of many levels - be it political, economic, cultural, institutional or geographical. Spatial structures resulting from a mobile society can therefore be depicted by "projecting" economic, sociocultural, political and institutional spaces on geographical space (Kamann 1991:39). All these aspects influence individual decisions and thus global spatial structures. However, even if we only enlarge our point of view to regions and cities, there are a number of empirical facts that cannot be explained by market models of international economic theory.

It is a *theory of mobility of agents* (firms and individuals) *in space and time* we need to analyze contemporary empirical developments. Within this theory, international mobility of flows and international locational decisions are only one of the objects of interest. Mobility does not only comprise the decision whether to cross national borders, but it can and has to be applied to a broad range of spatial horizons (local, regional, national, supranational and others). Trying to explain spatial dynamics, we have to operate within a highly complex system of agents that may be mobile or not, of links between these agents that may have different contents (exchange of goods, material and immaterial factors of production, competitive relationships...), intensities as well as flexibilities and a spatial framework that is shaped by an interplay of political and economic decision-makers and different spatial scales.

When introducing *time* in the sense of change (novelty and adaptation) into our spatial framework, we can formulate our questions more concretely:

- What are the driving forces that make agents change their relationships to each other and their spatial locations?

- Are there agents whose development and decisions are critical for the development of the system because they have developed special capabilities for mobility and/ or because they are willing to make decisions earlier than others and take risks?

- Motion once started will cause further motion and change, whose speed and patterns will crucially depend on existing patterns of interaction. How does change - once it has been introduced into the system - diffuse? This question will above all be relevant, if we acknowledge that interaction is not a global, but rather a local phenomenon. Only then can we observe diffusion of change in time.

- How do patterns of interaction and mobility evolve in time?

- How do different political levels shape mobility?

- Are there other criteria besides the political level that structure space in a meaningful way for mobility?

Of the various problems associated with existing approaches in international economic theory the following three aspects are particularly crucial:

- The inadequate recognition of the fact that patterns of mobility are based on individual initiative, entrepreneurial drive and relationships that go beyond market interaction: We have to realize that there is some scope of action and competence behind what we observe as mobile or immobile.

- An often unquestioned restriction of international economic theory to country analysis. Accepting that the theoretical interest is focused on facets of mobility in space, there is no reason to define space exclusively as a given country or national structure. This on the one hand restricts the spatial scale analyzed to the political level of nation-states, but also prestructures space by special aspects of political boundaries and neglects others.

- A lack of consciousness of the fact that mobility is not a timeless concept. Mobility of agents differing in their capabilities and characteristics, learning and evolution leads to complex and dynamic patterns.

Therefore, the aim of the following chapters is to explain international transactions and decision-making within a concept of the mobility of interacting agents. International transactions are understood as a result of a more complex set of determinants than the ideas given by national political borders. This aim will be realized in a stepwise approach: First, chapter 2 will explain how the economic environment is today shaped by a number of developments that have a direct influence on questions of mobility and spatial dynamics. These are technological, political-economic and organizational by nature. Furthermore, it will be explained that the concept of mobility in space and time has many facets and poses as many questions (ch. 3). The main pillars of the following parts – agents, space and time – will be introduced in detail. Afterwards, part B will start with an analysis centred around the question of how far existing theories of international economics contribute to an explanation of this complex system of mobility in space and time. Methodologically, the reader's basic knowledge of the models dealt with will be presumed, so that the analysis can be restricted to pure interpretational work. It will become obvious that questions of mobility are not only of major empirical importance (and thus of theoretical importance as well), but that their theoretical explanation leads us in many ways to the fringe of what is often regarded as feasible in mainstream international economic theories. It will be shown that there are basic methodological restrictions that make it doubtful whether common theories of international economics are able to give a complete image of mobility. This leads us to a search for new starting-points regarding content and methods which offer better ways to deal with mobility and which are at the same time open for an integration of future developments.

The basis of the analysis is therefore the notion that the empirically and theoretically important phenomenon of mobility has to be analyzed within a framework of space and time and that for its explanation we cannot neglect concepts of individual motivation and interaction between economic agents. Part C will present a more integrated approach, taking into account not only political boundaries, but also cultural and organizational structures and special features of agents and their relationships.

Part C will therefore have to deal with approaches that might be able to cope with the problems and open questions described in the chapters before and with the possibility of creating an integrated concept of mobility in space and time. In order to reach this aim, approaches beyond the boundaries of mainstream international economic theory will have to be taken into account and methods from other disciplines may have to be borrowed. It will be shown that it is possible to integrate the many facets of mobility into one conceptional framework that may offer us a better understanding of the relevant interdependencies among political, economic, cultural and institutional determinants of international transactions. It will become obvious that – depending on the specific constellation - foci will have to be set flexibly and different determinants will have to be emphasized.

Part D will draw conclusions about the achievements and will address further questions that remain to be pondered.

Part A   **A concept of mobility in space and time**

2 Mobility in the 21st century: some empirical observations

"The Essence of Life is Change." (Lao Tse)

The following chapter will describe a range of empirical trends that are assumed to influence the possibilities for and expressions of mobility. These are among other things new information and communication technologies, the observation of a globalization of the world economy and increasing tendencies of regional integration. Processes of globalization have in the last decades often led to the conclusion that we are living in a time of rising mobility without any spatial limits and ties. This assumption will be considered critically.

2.1 Mobility and global information

2.1.1 Access to information

Information is in many ways a matter of exchange. Apart from the genuine creation of new information or knowledge we receive information from others or communicate it to them. The possibilities and restrictions in this field are due to the technologies available to gain and exchange information as well as the special features of the productive factor information. As to its influence on mobility we can name above all two aspects:

- information about more or less distant locations as a basis for locational decision-making,

- the exchange of information as an expression of interaction across space.

During the last decades several developments could be observed that shape individual possibilities to interact across space and that may help to render decision-making more efficient.

In general, new technologies have led to decreasing costs of transportation and thereby rising mobility of goods and factors of production. However, this development has already had a long history and is not true for every field of transportation technology (e. g. passenger transportation by car may in the future become more expensive because of several reasons like taxes on fuel etc.). Meanwhile, the tremendous importance information and communication technologies have gained has a major impact on society and economic life. Not only do they constitute an essential industrial branch themselves, but they also create important inputs for other industrial sectors. New technologies change economic and social structures beyond the boundaries of their own industrial branch (Mosdorf 1998: 1). The slogans of global villages, wired societies and electronic highways have become widespread wisdom. They are often considered as the mirror of the spatial organization of societies in the information age.

What do these technologies imply for mobility? On the one hand, their upsurge sheds light on the growing importance of information as a factor of production. Much like highways do for the transport of physical goods, new technologies of information and communication serve as media for the transportation of information. To the degree information is able to substitute physical transportation of other factors, traditional transportation technologies and information and communication media may be substitutional. However, there may be complementary relationships as well. These may be based on the creation of competitive advantages because of a better availability of knowledge. Nonetheless, in all those cases where face to face communication is important the influence of new information and communication technologies may not be that radical. In many cases the growing importance of the competitive advantage information that may frequently be related to tacit knowledge will make proximity a more important aspect of economic activities.

Interpreting these media as transport technologies, their integration into international economic theory might not be that difficult at first sight. Finally, all transport technologies are in some sense "space-adjusting" technologies reducing the meaning of distance and its costs. It is "time-space" or "cost-space" convergence we observe when places get nearer to one another with respect to time or cost considerations (Gillespie and Williams 1988: 1316). However, as regards the exchange of information, these new media do not reduce spatial distances, but they may render them meaningless. This is why many people have argued that space is more and more rendered neutral. According to Sassen (1999a: 1) information is nowadays characterized by hypermobility.

Furthermore, traditional infrastructures of transportation are often considered public goods. Economic theory mostly treats the costs of transportation as a factor that is exogenous to the system and independent from concrete spatial locations. This is not true for communication media. They may have the capability to render space meaningless, but access to them is not spaceless at all. They more or less constitute a net of private roads (Gillespie and Robbins 1989: 13). That means that they do not reduce distance between every region or every individual equally. The meaning of distance may in addition to this be different from what we perceive as physical distance because transactions are shifted into electronic spaces, which can hardly be measured as Euclidean distances (Sassen 1999b: 12). Sassen (1999a: 1) calls this "spatial virtualization".

We therefore have to think about the special character of the productive factor "information" and its relationship to space. Most probably, information cannot be interpreted as purely substitutional to other factors of production, but it is the basis for their efficient use and for economic decision-making. Among other things, this also concerns the decision about where to locate and with whom to interact. Several special features become obvious:

- Information is acquired in a different way than other factors of production: It is most of the time not bought on the market, but created individually or acquired within interaction and exchange that is not based on market mechanisms. This may draw our attention to processes of diffusion of information and imitation of knowledge and to the temporal structures of these processes.

- The pure possession of knowledge and information does not ensure its efficient use.

- In contrast to other inputs information will not be used up: The possession of information and knowledge often even proves to be self-reinforcing; as learning in time and diffusion in space are important features (Mosdorf 1998:1).

- There may be a trade-off between cooperative attitudes to share information and work together in its production and the wish to keep it secret.

- The availability of information will in most cases be incomplete. Although an economy with perfect information may give us the idea of pareto-optimal situations, it is also a highly unrealistic construct. Information can be conveyed

  - by signals that are visible to a broad range of agents,

  - by direct exchange and sharing among a more or less restricted set of agents,

  - by individual creativity and/ or learning.

- The exchange of information seems to be less sensitive to geographical distance than to the availability of adequate channels to transmit it. This is not only true in a technological sense, but also as regards the relationships and ties among agents at different locations in space.

We therefore have to find adequate ways to incorporate information as an input or output into processes of decision-making and evaluate its importance for locational choice and patterns of interaction.

The possession of information may make decisions more efficient. Some of these pieces of information may be related to space and locations and may thus be relevant for decisions of mobile agents. The availability of information may in this way shape spatial dynamics. What is often neglected by economic theory is that economic agents may not only refrain from transacting across space because transaction itself is costly, but also because distance impedes good information about partners and possibilities for interaction. Economic space may be used more efficiently because of better knowledge about locational advantages depending on the way mobile economic agents perceive space and gather spatial information. Progress in the communication and information sector may thus give a new character to space in the eyes of economic agents because it is understood as an opportunity rather than a restriction in the sense of distance. Knowledge about alternatives in space and time can set incentives for mobility. Thus, the idea of individual competences to deal with mobility does not only rely on the ability to move, but also on good evaluations where to move. Rationality in gaining and using information therefore is of rising importance. In the sense of technology it can make the creation of competences for mobility easier.

We finally have to ask ourselves which are the factors that influence the evolution of patterns of interaction, if not geographic distance alone. We may suggest that the possession of information and the knowledge about the level of information of other agents as well as the possibility and willingness to transfer information are important determinants of spatial interaction in our times. Therefore we have to characterize space according to its "informational accessibility".[3] Finally, a decreasing importance of the "natural" barrier "distance" may go hand in hand with an increasing importance of the competitive advantage "access".

Altogether, the question of diffusion of information among agents and the spatial structures that go along with this lead us to approaches that are completely different from the idea of structuring space by transportation costs and geographical distance. It is not the costs of the transfer of information, but rather the access to information and communication technologies and channels, the selection of relevant information and the choice of partners of interaction that are important. The transfer and creation of information in addition to this are often not

---

[3] Nicol (1983) deals with the necessity of "connectivity" to foster regional development.

a bilateral transaction like traditional market transactions, but may be related to a network of agents in space.

2.1.2 Information and organization

Having a closer look at the impact of new technologies, there are further reasons why these developments might reach farther than earlier revolutions in the transport area. These technologies will not only influence the spatial organization of the economy because they change the possibilities of transportation for spot transactions, but in a more indirect way they also shape the structure of industrial spaces because of their long-term influence on intra-firm and inter-firm organizational patterns.[4] Communication media bear great potentials of co-ordination because they are inherently interactive by nature. Better possibilities of interaction may make decentralization and co-operation within and among firms easier. They facilitate control within multinational companies, even if their functional units are spatially dispersed. They may change the importance of economies of scale and scope. The availability and exchange of information are related to matters of organization.

This is why inter- and intra-organizational structures might serve as a bridge between technological change and spatial dynamics. Increased division of labour within and among firms may lead to an increase of transportation of goods and factors so that flows of information, goods and factors would in this case be complementary. However, although economic activities can be dispersed easier because of increased use of new technologies, the importance of central management and co-ordination in few central places may also be rising. Sassen (1999b: 10) therefore describes that these central places are producers of "organizational goods", they are the places where the "work of globalization" is done.

New technologies do not only modify possibilities for spot transactions directly, but they also shape patterns of mobility indirectly by influencing organizational structures in space as well as within and among institutions.

---

[4] For a survey of theoretical approaches see Capineri and Romei (1999:196-200).

2.2 Mobility in space: globalization, regionalization and localization

In a globalized resp. globalizing world, there seem to be nearly no reasons why firms should have a need to locate close to each other. This is why many authors assume that space in the sense of distance has become neutral for economic transactions. However, this may be only one half of the truth. The importance of face-to-face communication is in many fields still high (Blotevogel et al. 1989: 78). Although technically, many of these transactions might be substituted by new media that may render the exchange of information less costly and would not require spatial coincidence, the transactions involved have features that make the application of new technologies inadequate. This is also the basis for the idea of externalities in the form of "spatially mediated knowledge spillovers" (Audretsch and Feldman 1996: 630). Belussi distinguishes two forms of technological knowledge: On the one hand, codified blueprints that are nearly freely available to all economic agents, easily transferable and thus footloose. On the other hand, there is tacit knowledge that is sticky in its place of production, embodied in firms and individuals and therefore localized (Belussi 1999). As Storper supposes, even in a time where transportation costs are decreasing, geographically-constrained untraded interdependencies might have outlived geographically-constrained input-output linkages (Storper 1995: 209).

In addition to this, not only agents' ties among each other may be ambivalently influenced by globalization, but also their ties to certain territories. Many times, the argument that firms have become footloose has been used. If we define a location as a territory of activity chosen for a longer period of time, we may nowadays be induced to describe plants of transnational firms as having no spatial location, but being rather integrated into a footloose intrafirm-network that changes "permanently". Space that is constituted by the behaviour of this type of firms is a space of flows rather than a space of locations (Läpple 1999: 11). In a globalized world, there seem to be no specific ties between firms and regions or nations. However, there are also proponents of the hypothesis of a growing embeddedness of firms into their environment.[5] We thus not only have to ask for the reasons that render firms more mobile, but also for the sources of regional and interorganizational ties.

Globalisation may imply that space becomes a new field of action and that old restrictions rather than the importance of space itself may be decreasing. Altogether, there seems to be a tension between the development logic of a globalized world economy and the phenomenon of territorial embeddedness as well as between a decreasing importance of international borders and an

---

[5] For a detailed discussion see Fuchs et al. (1999).

increasing importance of locally unique features. There may be space-time-compression on the one hand and new needs for local embeddedness on the other hand. Local and global may be interdependent concepts. And although our times may be global, there will also have to be a redefinition of the local. However, "if the 'local' is being redefined, it is in terms of and under the conditions of the forces of globalization. It is global dynamics that now shape the structure and dynamic of localities, regions and nations." (Amin and Robins 1991: 105)

The debate centered around globalization versus localization is strongly related to the question how much distance still matters. However, distance from an economic point of view is not necessarily related to a geographical spatial extension. It can also be created by other borders impeding mobility. Today, "artificial" political barriers to mobility are vanishing because of increasing trends of regional integration worldwide. These are barriers to mobility that can hardly be influenced by single private agents. They are shaped by processes of political decision-making. Depending on the type of integration barriers to mobility of goods and/ or factors are nowadays increasingly erased. As already described above, mobility of flows and locational mobility are supposed to be interdependent, so that complex changes in the behaviour of mobile agents may arise. In addition to this, processes of regional integration may be the basis for realizing the gains of mobility new technologies may offer.[6]

Having a closer look at the aspects that make up the nation state from the point of view of international economic theory, we realize that it is just its mobility-restricting character that is underlined. If borders loose their importance in this respect, the exclusive division of space into national and international or home and foreign may become obsolete for "international" economic theory. As Fischer et al. (1999: 4) explain, the likeliness "that national borders coincide with the significant demarcation line between low and high economic, social and cultural costs of moving" becomes lower the more countries integrate economically. However, we then have to ask which level(s) besides the nation state will be important. How do we have to define the relevant geographical unit(s)? Will we have to emphasize smaller or larger spatial units? May it be necessary to take political influences on various levels simultaneously into consideration? E. g. Ohmae (1993: 78) states that "on the global economic map the lines that now matter are those defining what may be region-states. The boundaries of the region-state are not imposed by political fiat. They are drawn by the deft, but invisible hand of the global market for goods and services." And as Cooke (1996: 312) explains, "historic nation states represent no genuine community of economic interests, define no meaningful flows of economic activity and neglect true linkages and synergies among economic actors." From an economic point of view

---

[6] In this context Maggi differentiates between new borders and old barriers, see Maggi (1994).

we may therefore have to search for some kind of natural economic zones. It becomes obvious that the idea of the nation state as the dominant structural element of the world economy is increasingly doubted.

This idea of decreasing importance of the nation state has recently also been perceived by researchers in international economics who started to focus stronger on regions instead of nations. But: What is a region? How can we define its borders? Can we find criteria that enable us to define regional borders endogenously? How do economic regions interact with predefined political structures? The range of questions is broad.

And finally: The statement that the economic importance of borders is decreasing is one-sided. Political-economic borders may be vanishing to some extent. However, linguistic and cultural differences persist and so do differences in legal systems. Whether these barriers are congruent with national borders may be doubtful. Some of these disparities may decrease in the course of time, others however will probably remain. And we also observe the creation of new borders. A good example may be the fractioning of the old Soviet Union into CIS. The effects of these processes may be able to give a hint on the effects political borders have on economic processes.

Finally, we will have to make up an idea about what the relationship between political institutions and economic developments is regarding their impact on the spatial patterns that emerge out of an interplay of the two forces.

Altogether, we can state that in the last decade we have been observing changes that question many traditional ways of thinking about the importance of space for international economic patterns. The effects of these changes many times can only be assessed taking into account the way agents perceive and deal with space and interact with one another. For international economic theory all these tendencies mean that completely new challenges arise and that new conceptions will have to be found. New spatial structures will be less predetermined by economic and political structures successful in the past. New spatial patterns and processes may be more diffuse and less clearcut, which is among other things due to the fact that firms have become more footloose (Bergman et al. 1991: 3). We have to strive for better knowledge about spatial structures in a global economy, and evaluate critically whether it is a "terra incognita" (Gibson 1997: 5) we have to deal with, a new game whose rules are not known (Thurow 1997: 230) or whether there are patterns of mobility in the global economy.

2.3   Mobility and spatial patterns of development

Finally, regional development is guided by the laws and patterns of individual mobility. Especially in a European context, processes of growth and decline of regions as well as the question of spatial inequalities have received much attention. E. g. Europe nowadays is frequently perceived as a collection of regions that are more or less central rather than as a collection of internally homogenous nations. In a time when globalization is a key concept, the preoccupation with local phenomena is strong. There is a reinvention of the local. In spite of more homogenous space regional differences are reasserted. Meanwhile, local is no longer subordinated to national. There is regional competition that is independent from national borders (Zimmermann 1995: 147).

Spatial structures are characterized in different terms:

- Central regions are understood as those regions that exhibit a higher level of industrialization. In Europe much interest in this context has been paid to two main corridors of economic activity:

  - the "sunbelt"-axis: Paris - Northwest Germany – Scandinavia,

  - the "blue banana" from Southeast England through Benelux along the Rhine valley to Lombardy (Nijkamp 1993: 158ff).

  The configuration of these regions shows that centrality from an economic point of view may be independent from national political borders.

  It is broadly accepted that a vanishing importance of national borders is relevant for spatial development. Discussions about whether central regions will gain more from integration than peripheral ones have therefore been manifold.

- Besides this core-periphery discussion the distinction between city and hinterland has gained importance. One of the main functions of cities is their being a gateway in regional, national and international economic relations. City regions generally are more productive and wealthy than others. Europe is presently characterized by a hierarchy of cities that is growing more and more complex. Cities are nodes in modern networks of transportation and communication. They are places of agglomeration and linkages to the outside world. Sometimes their relationship to their parent nation is weak. Thus, they seem to find their position in a European rather than national context. Recognizing the importance of cities as well as regions, we have to analyze a multilevel spatial system where differences between hinterland and cities in one region may be stronger than differences between cities in different regions.[7]

- Empirically, we often find another ambiguity: On the one hand, the fact that mobility is rising is broadly accepted. This should imply rising instability of spatial structures as well. On the other hand, we observe industrial locations with strong persistence. So, even if potentials of mobility are rising, there may be reasons why these potentials are not in every case used. This was also realized by Markusen (1996) who differentiates between "slippery spaces" and more persistent industrial districts called "sticky places". She acknowledges that the degree to which spatial structures are dynamic or not is a product of different forces like corporate firm strategy, structure of industrial sectors (innovative capabilities, size of firms, linkages between each other, network effects, dynamics), the product life cycle and the role of public institutions as well as policies (the nation-state as rule-maker, part of industrial demand and promoter of innovation...). As a result, different patterns of "stickiness" can be discerned, which shows another time that spatial developments are complex phenomena.

Besides the fact that the influences described will pose many completely new challenges to international economic theory, the next chapters will underline that there are already many basic problems that are difficult to handle.

---

[7] One of the ideas about European structures on the level of the city was brought forth by Kunzmann under the headline of the European Grape Model, see Kunzmann and Wegener (1991: 191).

3   Mobility in space and time - structuring a complex phenomenon

"Nothing in physical world is purely spatial or temporal: everything is process."
(Blaut 1961: 2)

Although mobility is a basic concept in international economic theory, existing approaches are not able to create a flexible framework for an analysis of mobility and the spatial dynamics resulting from it that recognizes the many facets of the phenomenon. Clearly, we cannot expect to explain the whole phenomenon of mobility in its complexity in one theory. However, even the sum of the partial explanations which existing theoretical models offer today are not sufficient. This chapter therefore is to delineate the concrete meaning of mobility as an individual competence and decision that is embedded into space and time. Afterwards different approaches of international economic theory will be analyzed more closely in part B in order to evaluate how they deal with (international) mobility.

3.1   Mobility and agents - microeconomic foundations of mobility

Mobility means motion or the possibility to move. Franz (1984: 24) defines mobility as the movement of an individuum between defined units of a system. Of course, not only individuals may be mobile, but other units like firms or other groups of individuals as well. This abstract definition moreover shows that spatial mobility is only one part of the whole phenomenon of mobility. According to the choice of the systemic categories, different types of mobility that are related to spatial mobility, but focus on different, often apparently "non-economic" phenomena, may be considered: Geographical definitions may be useful for the analysis of spatial mobility, but in other contexts we may speak e. g. of

- cultural mobility: movement of people and firms of a certain culture away from the territory where this culture is rooted or adoption of certain cultural features by outsiders;
- political mobility: shifts in the distribution of power among decision-makers on one level (e. g. regional competition) or between different levels (e. g. from national to supranational);
- social mobility: breaking up old ties, creating new. Social mobility is not to be understood in the sense of social hierarchies, but rather as the mobility and flexibility of ties and relationships. Depending on the strength of ties and their distribution in space, the direction as well as the degree of spatial mobility will be influenced.

We therefore deal with a framework that recognizes that mobility is an important phenomenon with many facets. Of course, for the approach chosen here economic aspects of mobility will be in the center of interest. However, purely economic reasoning may not be able to grasp the many facets of the phenomenon because cultural, political as well as social questions may interfere with economic mechanisms. E. g. cultural, political and social aspects may sometimes be much better reasons to explain why economic action has territorial roots. Economic actions that are considered isolated from political, cultural or geographic aspects often seem to be footloose only reacting to price signals in a global economy. Only when combined with other aspects like political boundaries or geographical distance e.g., will ties to a territory and spatial frictions of movement result.

As described in chapter 2, the relationship between (economic) mobility and geographic distance or even cultural distance is a variable when considering the possibility of creating and using new technologies/ skills. And this is the aspect that makes mobility from an economic point of view different from pure geographic considerations. It is not only the geographical distance between Berlin and Beijing or New York we have a look at. From an economic point of view, this distance is not a given parameter. It depends on the underlying type of economic action as well as the technologies available to cross this distance. Travelling to China from Berlin may from a geographical as well as cultural point of view be far. However, New York is not that much nearer by geographical distance, but from a cultural point of view, it may be much closer. And finally, e-mailing to New York or Beijing makes distance nearly neutral, if technologies are available at all three locations and a common language is spoken. In a broad sense "technologies" to shorten distance may not only be technical appliances, but also individual capabilities to bridge cultural, institutional or other distances.

In addition to this, any of the systems analyzed can be subdivided into smaller units, e. g. a division of nations into regions. Mobility may take place between these units or within them (interregional mobility vs. intraregional). This depends on how small our regional subdivisions are and whether we are able to find criteria to structure space that are relevant for mobility.

As the analysis of mobility that is given here is to be based on the decisions of individual agents, an important aim will be to find out whether patterns of mobility can be distinguished that might offer a microfoundation for models in international economics. Acknowledging that mobility is based on certain capabilities, empirical research will have to find out why some agents develop better competences to deal with mobility than others.[8] Such a detailed empirical analysis however goes beyond the intention of this work. We will have to rely on plausible ideas to be integrated into theoretical approaches. Boschma and Lambooy (1999: 414) call a similar method "behavioural geography".

Apart from the different forms of mobility described above, economic mobility comprises:

- On the one hand, flows of goods and factors across space (space of flows) (Castells 1985: 33): As described above mobility in the form of flows of goods and factors is assumed to be a mirror of interaction between individual agents or organizations. Simultaneously with analyzing mobility, we therefore have to analyze how patterns of interaction based on individual decisions evolve in time. What about the stability of patterns of interaction? What kind of influence (intensity and quality) does decision-making by one agent have on other agents?[9]

- On the other hand, locational mobility (space as a place): This may concern the choice of a location when a firm first enters a market, the possibility to change a location or the possibility to be active at several locations (with similar or different activities), e. g. in the case of multinational firms. If we include the entrance of a firm into the market, we should as well include its exit from the market. Therefore, locational mobility can be defined in a very broad sense or in a way that is restricted to pure locational changes. And of course, we also have to consider the decision to stay at a certain location as an important facet

---

[8] In the following chapters we will use the term agents also denoting firms (agents = decision-making units) about mobility.

[9] Ulrich and Probst differentiate between active, reactive, sluggish and critical units. Active units are those that are not strongly influenced by others, but exert strong influences. Reactive agents underlie strong outer influences, but do not exert strong signals. Those agents that are sensitive in both aspects are critical agents and finally those that do neither receive nor send strong signals are sluggish; see Ulrich and Probst (1988: 143).

of mobility. If agents are mobile as regards their capabilities and decide to stay nonetheless, this also has an important effect on spatial "developments": persistence of spatial structures. From a macro point of view we could include all those alternatives in the definition of mobility that change the spatial density of economic activities or stabilize it.

Furthermore, we have to make a distinction between observed mobility (behaviour), the potentials and capabilities for mobility and the willingness to move (Franz 1984: 28). Sometimes, English literature uses the term motility for the capabilities that underlie mobility. Therefore, microfoundations of patterns of mobility might be based on these three aspects of mobility. We will have to ask why and when motility is transformed into mobility. Is mobility a phenomenon of marginal adaptation to changes or are there thresholds of incentives that have to be passed in order to make agents change their locations? How does motility in the sense of organizational competences and the ability to acquire and use information evolve in time? What impact does this have on spatial structures and political decision-making? How is motility influenced by individual and cultural characteristics as well as social ties? As a phenomenon that has its sources in creativity and learning motility is not only related to space, but is also variable in time. It is the basis for mobility and spatial dynamics. The following questions will be emphasized:

- Why does firms' behaviour in space differ although they are exposed to similar outside stimuli?

- In how far are their decisions interdependent?

3.2   Spatial patterns, interaction and mobility - structuring space by analyzing mobility

This chapter is intended to deal with the way mobility is embedded into space and spatial structures are created. Pred (1969: 7) emphasizes that it is necessary for an understanding of economic phenomena in space to realize that these processes have a behavioural basis. This is also underlined by Nicol who states that economic and spatial structures cannot be analyzed independently from each other. They are different manifestations of one process (Nicol 1983: 24). Thus, we will have to bridge the gap between micro behaviour and aggregate spatial dynamics. This is only possible, if mobility is understood as a process of interaction. Spatial structures are reflected in the intensity and kind of activities at different locations as well as the intensity and type of flows between these locations. Economic theory often starts with exogenously defined geographical aggregates as an input. These are traditionally defined in national categories, that is political units. At the heart of this definition lies the assumption that national borders and policies may significantly influence mobility. Anyway, one may wonder whether - apart from political borders - other criteria that may be as relevant for mobility can be found to structure space. Looking at the heterogeneous structures within nations, it quickly becomes obvious that the distribution and relationships of mobile as well as immobile economic agents and their activities might be adequate starting-points to describe spatial structures. They might offer possibilities for deriving spatial structures endogenously on the basis of the rules governing mobility. Thus, spatial boundaries can be derived that are more flexible. As regards definitions we often use the terms of agglomeration, centres and peripheries or from a neutral point of view regions for spatial structures that are not politically predefined. Buzan (1998: 70-74) describes a region by at least three aspects that may be alternatives rather than complements:

- There are be shared characteristics (homogeneity) among the parts of the region (geographical, cultural). This is an assumption that is made by traditional approaches in international economics as countries are supposed to have homogenous technological conditions and preferences nationwide.

- There is a patterned interaction within the region, which means that the intensity of interaction is sufficient to mark it out as a distinctive subsystem. Buzan derives from this that the richness and complexity of international regions as we observe them today stem from the fact that there are many different forms of interaction that might define "regionness". Regions may thus differ by the type of interaction, certain attitudes that accompany it and the intensity of interaction. Buzan explains that a higher intensity of interaction may make it easier to derive clear boundaries of the region and will make an institutionalized support of the region – understood as a supranational entity - more probable. This point is interesting as it proposes that institutionalization follows economic rules or at least interacts with economic developments and not the other way round. Many times, in contrast institutional (political) boundaries are presumed as a given framework for economic analysis. Taking interaction as a basis to define regions we will have to deal with the flows resulting from this interaction. On a more local scale intensive interaction and flows of information may also be an important characteristic of a region, e. g. in the sense of industrial districts.

- Finally, Buzan states that there may be a shared perception of agents that a certain area constitutes a region. This perception will also influence their decisions about mobility.

The fact that regions do not seem to have a predefined size shows that the term region can in contrast to the nation state be filled with content in a number of ways (Meyer 1997: 27). "The definition of a region is a game which can be played with almost infinite variations." (Holland 1976: 4) Moreover, regions are not necessarily defined by political borders. Cultural, institutional, economic and geographical aspects are as relevant.

Buzan also counts geographical adjacency and contiguity to the characteristics describing a region. However, it may be challenging to question this. Do regions have to be constituted by a relatively continuous surface? If regions are defined by interaction that extends across space, we may wonder whether the region is only formed by the two points that are connected or also by the space covered by the interaction. This may lead us to the question if the locations of a multinational firm might from the firm's point of view be considered a special kind of region in the sense of an activity field. According to Perroux (1950: 96), space can be defined by a plan by private enterprises that is not necessarily geographically contiguous. It is an economic zone that defies cartography. Amin (1993: 288) underlines that "the meaning of place is becoming defined within the hyperspace of global corporate activity". In a world of global interaction it may therefore at first sight be doubtful whether regions can be identified by adjacent parts.

In contrast to the idea of a region the term location will be an important concept to be used in the following chapters. Locations generally have a point-like touch. They are rarely characterized by extensions, but rather as places. Nonetheless, small-scale interaction is an important matter at a location: interaction between economic and political decision-makers as well as among economic agents. Closely related to the idea of a location is the phenomenon of agglomerations. This term implies the characterization of locations as places with dense populations of firms and individuals.

Furthermore, accepting that different spatial horizons (locations, cities, regions, nations...) form the spatial framework for mobility, we have to analyze whether there are different determinants for the mobility of agents and dynamics on different spatial levels. Thus, Martin states that the laws governing spatial developments are "scale-dependent" (Martin 1999: 78). He complains that many theories dealing with spatial developments are based on the same mechanisms although the spatial horizons they aim at are different. We might suggest that different types of decisions might be made against the background of different spatial horizons (local, regional, national, international, global). In addition to this, political decision-makers on several levels will shape locational qualities in an interplay of decisions.

But how does space enter individual decision-making? Many theoretical models assume that space is from an economic point of view also dominated by geographical distance that causes costs. The developments described in chapter 2 may suggest a more complex point of view. This is why Nicol (1983) proposes a concept of locational connectivity with locations being described by their openness.[10] Space is a topography of connectivity levels that is determined by policies, cultures, institutions and technological developments. However, the relationship of information to distance is completely different from the one of physical goods. Moreover, if mobility has to be understood against the background of individual decision-making, agents' perceptions of space are of major importance for spatial developments. E. g. Kulke (1990: 4) proposes that the entrepreneurial spatial search horizon might be dependent on personal experiences. If we agree that spatial borders are influenced by geographical, political, institutional, cultural and economic aspects, we will have to analyze how these enter individual decision-making and how individual decision-making is transformed into macro-developments.

3.3   Mobility, agents and time – sources of change and decision-making in time

The second dimension mobility is integrated into is time. Analyzing mobility and spatial dynamics on the basis of individual actions and interactions, time is relevant in several respects:[11]

- Mobility is strongly connected to notions of change. Mobile agents are able to change their locations and/ or to make new decisions about their interaction in space. They possess a spatial scope of action. These possibilities are not given and constant, they can be created actively in time and they may also diminish. We therefore have to ask how agents are able to develop the competences for mobility (motility) and what drives them to do so. Once started, change will diffuse in an interactive economic system. We therefore should be interested in the direction and speed of these processes of diffusion and in the frequency of changes. Can temporal patterns of mobility be discerned?

- In addition to this, decisions about location may not be reversible instantaneously, if there are sunk costs of moving. As regards the many facets of mobility different time horizons may be relevant. Thinking about different degrees of mobility we may ask about the criteria for describing agents as more or less mobile? These criteria can be defined from a spatial point of view

---

[10] Nicol speaks of space as a topography of connectivity levels; see Nicol (1983).

[11] Because of the many facets of time that are relevant, chapter 13 will take another time the opportunity to summarize the temporal aspects of mobility after having presented the main new approaches in part C.

as well as from a temporal starting-point: We may suppose that agents who change their location within a broad spatial horizon are very mobile. We may also suggest that those agents who have the capabilities to change their locations and patterns of interaction more frequently are mobile.

- Furthermore, the notion of change has important implications for methodological approaches to be chosen in formal modelling. Depending on the frequency and speed of change, we cannot be sure whether equilibrium modelling is adequate for the analysis. Concepts of equilibrium may not be compatible with the aim of modelling change that is induced endogenously by individual decision-making within a framework of mobility.

- Present decisions, capabilities and attitudes to mobility may be dependent on the experiences agents have gained in the past. If there is a "migratory biography" of the individual agent, decisions of the past may have an impact on future behaviour. Processes of learning may imply that the success of present locational strategies and decisions about interaction influence the future.

3.4   Mobility in space and time – a comprehensive framework

This chapter is to put the three elements of mobility (agents), space and time together into one conceptual framework of mobility in space and time. Mobility is a concept that reflects flexibility and freedom of motion within a spatial framework. It is based on the characteristics and capabilities of mobile and immobile agents and on the possibilities and restrictions economic space offers. Therefore, we have to analyze agents' relationships towards each other and towards space, the development of agents' capabilities and experiences as well as the way these developments are transformed into spatial dynamics. The analysis has to be directed towards an evolutionary path of spatial development as a result of the development of capabilities and strategies related to mobility and the diffusion of changes based on respective decisions and interactions. We have to get an idea about which agents might take special roles in this process, e. g. as pioneers or first-movers as regards their spatial decisions. Finally, we should be able to derive spatial patterns endogenously from these processes. Therefore, it is assumed that mobility is not only a result of given spatial structures, but it also creates these structures.

Boschma and Lambooy distinguish different patterns of spatial dynamics. On the one hand, the development of locations often seems to have cumulative features: Once firms have begun to recognize a location as a favourable environment self-reinforcing processes become important. There are pull effects in that more firms follow and processes of localized learning may set in. This is a pattern of development where structures that have been created before are confirmed and reinforced. On the other hand, regional development frequently implies spill-over effects on adjacent regions. These are dependent on the way agents are linked to each other and on the barriers to diffusion that might exist. Thus, gradual change may be induced with formerly peripheral regions being pulled into a processes of growth that started elsewhere. However, according to Lambooy and Boschma regional trajectories are not that smooth in every case. Sometimes, developments seem to be unexpected or discontinuous. New centers are created, for old centers decline may start unexpectedly. New technological developments may open a "window of locational opportunity". These stylized trajectories are illustrated in table 3.1.

Table 3.1: Trajectories of spatial dynamics

	cumulative development of a region	diffusion among regions	window of locational opportunity
nature of change	cumulative	continuous and gradual diffusion	new trajectory, discontinuous and generic change
selection	specific local conditions	proximity and links	discontinuous creativity
predictability	high	high	low
change in spatial structures	small	gradual	potentially dramatic

Source: adapted from Boschma, Lambooy (1999: 426)

In addition to this, we have seen that the spatial economic system has to be understood as a hierarchy of spatial horizons. Whether mobility takes place within or between parts of the system depends on the focus of our analysis. Like a zoom objective we may take a closer look at small parts of the system (e. g. cities) or try to grasp the whole framework (global economic system) into which the smaller parts are integrated. In any way, it is a dynamic spatial system we observe. There may be different aspects of space as regards its cultural, economic, geographic and political dimension which do not necessarily overlap. These ideas are summarized in figure 3.1 As it also shown in this figure, interaction among agents is considered an important aspect.

Finally, an aim of the following chapters is to show that it is the interaction of economic, political, institutional, geographic and cultural elements that creates spatial structures across space. What these spatial structures look like and how we can describe them is still in many ways an open question. We are confronted with terms related to the density of economic activity in space like agglomerations, centers, peripheries as well as qualitative descriptions like technological hubs or transport hubs, maybe even political or organizational hubs.

Furthermore, we also have to deal with immobility. Does immobility have a value of its own? Or is it nothing but a disadvantage, a restriction? Fischer et al. (1997, see also Fischer et al. 1999) hint at the relationship between the value of locational immobility and space. From their point of view agents may be able to acquire location-specific capabilities in the course of time, if they choose immobility as their strategy. These capabilities cannot or only incompletely be transferred to other locations. A decision for locational mobility will thus infer sunk costs. Rising geographical or cultural distance may reduce the transferability of this knowledge. Path-dependent development is therefore territorially bound.

The relationship between knowledge accumulation, time and space is in a slightly different context also underlined by Pred (1967: 24f). He starts from the assumption that agents can be characterized by two dimensions: quantity of information available to them and capability to use them. He emphasizes that information is accumulated in time by processes of search and learning. Thus, better and innovative locational decisions (pioneering acts) can be promoted which are followed by imitation that may be incomplete. Furthermore, if information is not available equally everywhere in space, established centers of production may be nuclei of communication and interaction so that firms located there may have the highest probability of obtaining access to information.

Altogether, the relationships of agents to space, but also – as will be shown in part C – the relationships among agents in space will therefore be dynamic in time.

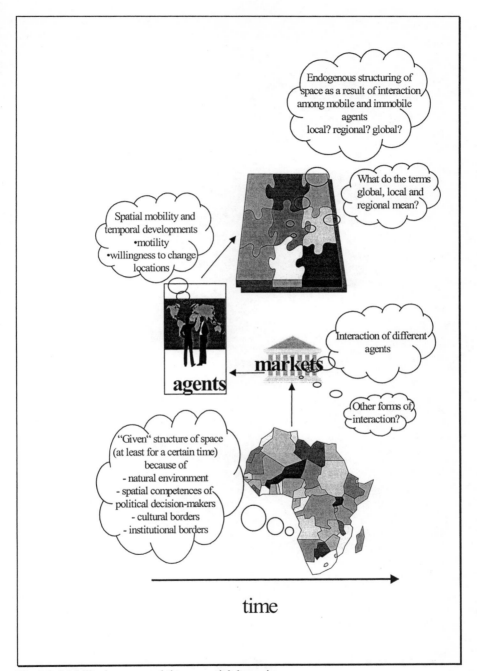

Fig. 3.1: Mobility in space and time – spatial dynamics

Part B **Mobility in the theory of international economics**

4 General possibilities and restrictions of theoretical modelling

"Real-world spatial interaction patterns and economic-geographic distributions are mercurial, kaleidoscopic, frequently tantalizing elusive things of the moment. These aggregate expressions of individual and firm decisions are as constant as the images of a dream. Static conditions are only fictions whereas motion is reality: for on any economic-geographic stage the cast of players is perpetually changing." (Pred 1967: 5)

In this chapter, general theoretical restrictions and opportunities in explaining patterns of mobility in space and time will be described against the background of the observations made in part A. Afterwards single theoretical approaches in international economic theory will be dealt with.

4.1 Mobility and agents in international economic theory - modelling the microlevel

Problems of modelling the microlevel in international economic theory are mainly reflected by a missing visibility or differentiation of heterogeneous agents and static views of maximizing behaviour. In the theory of international economics price mechanisms are considered as being of major importance for patterns of mobility. Thus, mobility of flows of goods and productive factors in models of perfect competition is e. g. frequently understood as being based on arbitrage with homogenous objects. The incentive to trade goods is signalled by price differences for goods produced by different countries.

In models with perfect competition locational mobility cannot be dealt with because of a lack of microeconomic foundations. Agents are invisible adapters, who react rationally and the system strives towards an equilibrium. The argumentation is mechanistic. The economic system functions like a "giant clockwork" following eternal laws (Allen 1990: 557). Explanations of mobility are restricted to the mobility of flows of goods and productive factors. Furthermore, the system lacks its motor that might drive changes. These can only be entered into the system as a reaction to exogenous stimuli. Mobility of flows is thus analyzed without having a look on those who decide about mobility.

Therefore, elements have to be introduced into market-models that help us to explain why certain actions are performed by a firm with a certain size. In market models agents can only be discerned explicitly if special assumptions about market structures are made. This is done by introducing economies of scale and imperfect competition, e. g. monopolistic competition. With monopolistic competition firms are assumed to represent certain discernable product varieties. However, in most models they are not different from a qualitative point of view as regards their production function or special qualities of their variety. We still deal with representative agents. Agents are thus only studied with respect to their quantitative features. The methodological problem of modelling the micro-level without increasing complexity too much has also been called the "no bridge controversy" between micro- and macrolevel by Marengo and Willinger (1997: 336). It is because of these problems that many theories seem to work with macro-models that are so similar to micro-mechanisms that the heterogeneity of agents does not inhibit the derivation of unique and deterministic macro-outcomes.

If it is still simple to make out the direction of mobile flows, this is more difficult in the case of locational mobility. This question has caught a lot of interest within the context of multinational firms. Decisions about locational mobility are in many models derived from profit calculations. In models of monopolistic competition the number of firms in a market is determined endogenously. Firms enter the market until profits are driven to zero. In combination with the assumption of representative agents this means that market entry and exit cannot be differentiated from changes of location.

The fact that firms are able to develop new capabilities of mobility is not dealt with in the models that have been developed in international economic theory. [12] Mobility is not understood as a decision with certain scopes of action behind it, but rather as a way of maximizing profits. [13] Economic agents are supposed to interact on the basis of prices.

---

[12] Few exceptions regarding product innovations should be mentioned, e. g. Grossman and Helpman (1992).

[13] For an extensive treatment of the role of the firm in international economic theory, see Pohl (1998).

4.2   Dealing with space and time in economic theory

"The separation of two items in space may be described by the distance between them and the separation of two items in time by the interval between....One of the most common relative space measures combines space with time, and distance with interval. Thus, in everyday life we consider the time it takes to get somewhere. This notion of distance and interval in combination is now frequently referred to as time-space metric. The geographer's space time is not a new physical structure, as is four dimensional space of Minkowski or Einstein; instead it is a technical convenience and a more realistic way of looking at the world." (Parkes and Thrift 1980: 4)

One of the major problems in economic geography is the question which aspects of space should enter theoretical thinking in which way. Clearly, a 1:1 modelling of space and time does not make sense from the point of view of economic theory. Most certainly, reductions of complexity have to be made and those features that make space interesting from an economic point of view have to be emphasized. From the point of view of international economic theory different approaches to model space and time can be found.

In mainstream economics space enters theoretical modelling in three ways

- because there are different given resource endowments across space (space = given amount of resources),

- because of distance that causes costs of transportation and is often regarded a nuisance that detracts from the elegance of the analysis,

- because the boundaries of political units are defined in space.

What is often neglected is e. g. that other aspects like culture are also defined in terms of space within units that are often smaller or at least different from nation-states. Furthermore, it is not recognized that there are loyalties and attachments of agents to space that may be a reason – besides transportation costs – why movement is costly and does not occur instantaneously.

"Point economies" and Newtonian Time

In traditional international economic theory, countries are the relevant spatial level of analysis. They are mostly distinguished by definition, but do not possess a spatial extension (point economies). The boundaries of these spatial points are defined by the assumption of immobility of certain factors of production or invisible agents. Sometimes distance inducing transportation costs are introduced as a spatial phenomenon between countries, but not within them. Spatial structures are given by comparative advantages of countries relying on given supplies of productive factors, consumers (preferences) and technological know-how. Thus, we deal with a special type of inside-outside perspective with the inside defined by the national-political. However, in a world where nearly everything seems to be mobile, taking given endowments as a starting-point of analysis may be misleading. The neoclassical and also some more recent approaches are the best example for the fact that the "social landscape" of the economic approach is like a "desert – far from the sociological concern with actual towns and cities" (Lie 1997: 344).

The idea of point economies as a theoretical simplification is illustrated in figure 4.1. Countries that have an extension in two-dimensional space are assumed as given and provided with given features like the distribution of immobile agents and resources among them. They are theoretically reduced to points.

Only recently have models tried to combine given comparative advantages with the idea of self-organization of mobile economic agents in space (within given boundaries, but also in endogenously defined spaces, see next paragraph). These models assume that the locations of agents are not given. Their decisions about their location are interdependent and guided by a number of external parameters.

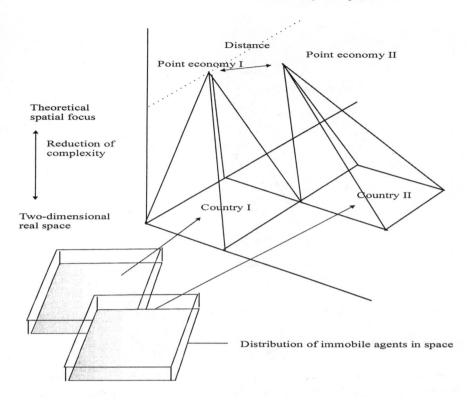

Fig. 4.1: Point economies as theoretical concepts of space

A similar way of simplification is frequently applied as regards time. O'Driscoll and Rizzo (1985: 53) call this Newtonian time. They draw the analogy that time is in many models "spatialized" from a methodological point of view. ("Time is analogized to space.") Points in time are supposed to be by definition homogenous. Time is characterized by change, but has no importance on its own. Points in time are considered isolated from each other. They are divided by processes of adaptation to exogenous stimuli that pass with infinite speed. Sequences of time are not recognized. We deal with comparative statics, which consider the relevant points in time are equilibria. We are thus not able to draw any conclusions about the duration of processes of adaptation between equilibria. Nor do we know about the period during which equilibria are stable. Finally, there is no notion of historical sequence integrated into the concept (fig. 4.2).

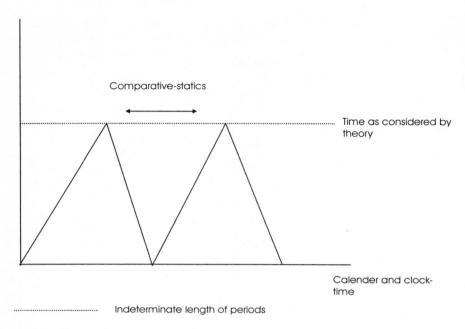

Fig. 4.2: Newtonian time and comparative statics

Thus, temporal and spatial concepts as the framework of mobility enter economic theory in an extremely simplified way by setting exogenous boundaries to both and ignoring important interdependencies.

Endogenous boundaries and event time

Recently, models have been developed under the headline of New Economic Geography which determine characteristics and boundaries of regions endogenously from processes of self-organization of mobile agents. Thus, spatial-economic boundaries are not defined ex ante. Starting from a homogenous spatial structure where immobile agents and resources are distributed with equal density, spatial structures are derived that are characterized above all by the density of mobile activities. Economic space itself is only characterized by distance and is structured by characteristics and decisions of mobile and immobile agents. Thus, we are able to deal with spatial structures that are relevant from an economic point of view, e. g. cities as agglomerations of economic activities. Space in general is in these models not dealt with by using "point-concepts", but as a one-dimensional continuum, where only cities are considered points of agglomeration whose location and size are endogenously derived and the hinterland is an extension of immobile agents and factors (fig. 4.3). Working with point-city concepts the size of spatial aggregations is measured by the number of agents and firms at a certain location.

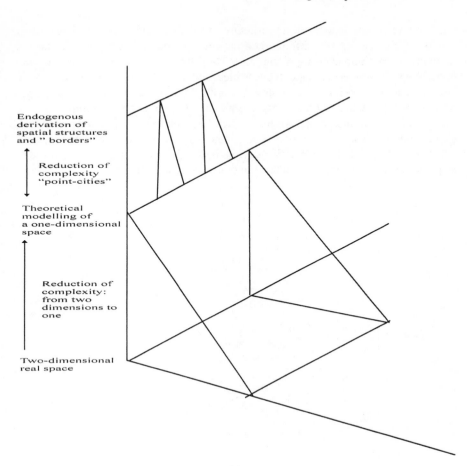

Endogenous
derivation of
spatial structures
and " borders"

↑

Reduction of
complexity
"point-cities"

↓

Theoretical
modelling of
a one-dimensional
space

↑

Reduction of
complexity:
from two
dimensions to
one

Two-dimensional
real space

Fig 4.3: Endogenous derivation of spatial borders

These models dealt with under the headline of New Economic Geography treat time within mathematical simulations of underlying parameters of the model. Change is still induced exogenously, but we do not use comparative-static methods. Dynamics are mostly non-linear because of externalities among individual decisions. Often certain critical values of parameters can be discerned that cause dramatic changes in the spatial economic system. Time interpreted as event time does not have to be a linear phenomenon, if changes of parameters and systemic changes do not go hand in hand. We are able to make out ranges of parameters where equilibria are stable and critical values where they become unstable. These ranges however do not necessarily go along with concepts of time measured in hours or months, if parameters do not change their values continuously in time. This is especially true if we consider non-linear dynamics that are often also characterized by the possibility of multiple equilibria. Anyway, this method makes it possible to structure event time endogenously because of economic changes and to differentiate between periods of stable equilibria and dramatic or continuous changes (fig. 4.4). Thus, the relationship between the way underlying parameters change their values and the response of the economic system becomes much more complex. We are able to make out effects that do not become obvious when working with comparative statics. A good example may be lock-in effects of the spatial system which are defined as situations in which system parameters are changing, but spatial structures are stable nonetheless. What is still neglected in this notion of time is that decisions of agents are made in sequence and may be logically related to one another in time.

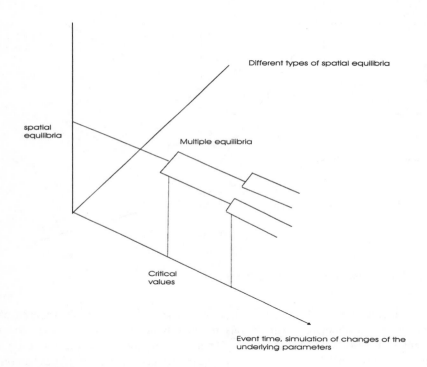

Fig. 4.4: Event time

Networks and "real time"

Approaches to model space up to now have assumed that space does not have an economic importance of its own, except that it restricts movement by distance and political barriers and that it is the location of immobile factors/ agents. Relationships among agents were purely assumed to be guided by price-interaction.

Especially, approaches that have a sociological basis consider space a lattice of agents and relationships with agents as nodes and their links as graphs (fig. 4.5). Spatial structures can thus be defined as a net of locations of more or less mobile agents and the interdependencies between them. This concept leaves the question about the type, directions, intensity and determinants of interactions between economic agents open. These will have to be defined more concretely in part C. Sometimes it is assumed that territory-specific assets may determine the relationships of networks to space. Moreover, the idea of networks may lead us to a new understanding of distance.

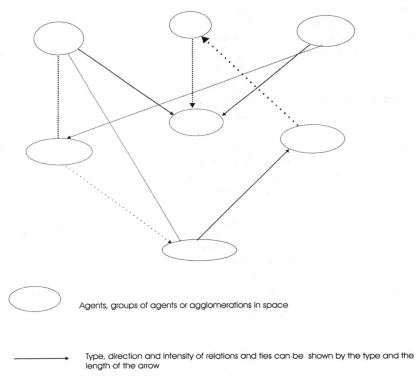

Agents, groups of agents or agglomerations in space

Type, direction and intensity of relations and ties can be shown by the type and the length of the arrow

Fig. 4.5: Spatial networks

Similar interdependencies might be true for the temporal dimension. O'Driscoll and Rizzo (1985: 60) start from the idea that time is a flow of changes. They call this "real time". "Flow is not in time, but constitutes time." The difference of their ideas to those described before is that the present is linked to other periods of time by individual perception. There are linkages not only in space, but also in time. Time is heterogeneous, if we recognize the importance of "memory" and "expectations". "Each phase of real time is novel precisely because it is linked to previous periods by memory." (O'Driscoll and Rizzo 1985: 61) Time is irreversible, which means that future and past cannot be treated symmetrically. This notion of time may be of special importance in models that recognize that time is related to processes of learning. Information about the past and the future is fundamentally asymmetric. The past is more or less certain, while the future can only be predicted with some degree of probability. Expectations are important for decisions related to the future. In addition to this, sequences of events that may be logically connected have to be considered.

It may be doubted whether phenomena of mobility that are nowadays characterized by permanent changes based on individual initiatives can be compatible with general equilibrium thinking. Such equilibria need exogenous stimuli to create dynamics. This cannot be combined with the idea that it is agents' capability and creativity that is changing the world. Most certainly equilibrium thinking makes things easier in that it creates "a mental laboratory in which various causes can be isolated from one another."(O'Driscoll and Rizzo 1985: 85) However we have to make certain whether this concept is adequate for dealing with a topic that is so strongly related to dynamics.

The purpose of the following chapters will be to provide a closer analysis of the problems that have been summarized here with reference to different classes of models in international economics. For the question of mobility in space and time it will be convenient to divide the relevant theories into two main groups:

- models that are commonly adopted by international economic theory (part B),

- other approaches that are interdisciplinary by nature or at least not positioned in the context of mainstream international economics, but that might be helpful to overcome the restrictions that may be true for the former class of models (part C).

5   International flows of goods and factors - traditional theory of international economics

"The difficulty lies not in the new ideas, but in escaping from the old ones, which ramify for those brought up as most of us have, into every corner of our minds." (Keynes 1936)

Traditional classical and neoclassical models of international economic theory (based on the theorems of Heckscher/Ohlin, Ricardo, Leontief) start from the assumption of perfect competition. Their aim is to analyze mobility in the sense of flows of goods and factors. Mobility follows, if there are price differences that are based on differences in country characteristics. Agents are not modelled explicitly in these models, they are atomistic, invisible and hidden within the institution "market". Based on the assumption that productive factors are immobile from an international point of view, production and consumption are also tied to certain countries. Locational choice is not possible. Therefore, the aim of these models is to derive ideas about the direction and intensity of flows from a given distribution of productive factors, technologies and preferences. Flows follow given locations.

Historically, it was Adam Smith (1961: 477) who stated that behind the mechanism of the invisible hand there is self-interest of economic agents. Neoclassical approaches reduced this view to models where deterministic mechanisms (prices) are intermediaries between the micro- and macrolevel. Therefore, we are only able to observe mechanistic, deterministic reactions in these models. Dichotomy between micro- and macro-levels is impossible because of the working of this invisible hand (Hinterberger 1994: 36). The system is inevitably striving for optimality and equilibrium. Innovative, creative pioneers cannot be found in these models because agents are representative (Erdmann 1993: 99). Firms are represented by a production function that is a given relationship between input and output (Dunn 1998: 42-52). Neoclassical models of international trade assume fully informed, although invisible agents. All the information necessary is submitted by the price system. Thus, entrepreneurs become passive maximizers and calculators of optimality. The construction of the models does not allow individual decision-making within a set of alternatives. What is analyzed in these models are pure maximizing mechanisms and not mobility based on decision-making including all the "imperfections" that render decision-making difficult and strongly influence the flows he observed in reality.

Dunn in this context argues that striving for profit does not mean maximizing profits. While the latter goes along with a given situation for decision-making, striving for profits means permanent search for new alternatives. This should also be the case for decisions about mobility. Profit in that case in principle does not have a fixed upper boundary. Thus, the concept of profit-maximization like the notion of equilibrium seem to be based more on methodological considerations than on real behaviour.

In addition to this, neoclassical models do not acknowledge adequately that mobility is a spatial phenomenon. Space in neoclassical theory is conceptualized by point economies interpreted as nations. As explained before countries do not have a spatial extension in these models. To reduce complexity the theory of international trade most of the time assumes that factors of production are immobile within these countries which implies an arbitrary distribution of these factors in a world of mobility. That means that international is contrasted to national or home to foreign. Countries are considered homogenous within their boundaries. Regional differences are not explained or entered as an input.[14] Chapter 2 already gave an idea of the decreasing importance of national borders that is often assumed with respect to mobility nowadays. Anyway, even if this were not true there is one more thing that is peculiar about the definition of countries. Countries may inhibit mobility because of political decisions. However in these models, political decision-makers do not enter the model explicitly. Certainly, the effects of political actions like tariffs or other protective measures as well as the effects of regional economic integration have been analyzed in detail. However, the political decision-makers behind these measures are invisible because they are introduced into models as exogenous stimuli. Thus, they are not part of the interplay of decisions that might be important for spatial dynamics.

---

[14]   Courant and Deardorff draw our attention towards the importance of inequality of regional (subnational) factor supplies for national trade structures; see Courant and Deardorff (1992).

6 New trade theory and multinational corporations

"The world has an uncomfortable way of not permitting to be fitted into clean classifications. " (J. G. March)

After the early models by Lösch, v. Thünen, Christaller et. al. new trade theory may offer new starting-points to model locational mobility in international economics, especially with consideration of multinational firms.[15] The foundations for this possibility were established by choosing monopolistic competition as the main market structure for these models. Thus, economists were able to define the boundaries of individual firms that produce special varieties of a good. Markusen and Venables (1995: 1) also call this strand of theorizing the "industrial organization approach to trade". Curiously enough, the argument of ownership advantages of firms goes along with the idea that production and cost functions were similar for all firms. Thus, firms are representative agents that are distinguished without being different from each other. One argument to explain the specifity of advantages and factors is that some factors, especially information, are more mobile within the firm than on the market. Thus, firms are explained using mobility as an argument whenever there is intrafirm exchange of goods, services and information. There is an intrafirm exchange of "headquarter services" as a collection of services that are produced at one location and used at several others (marketing, R+D, advertising) (Markusen 1984). Multinational firms are considered as special channels for mobility. It therefore becomes obvious that two different frameworks for mobility in international economic theory are set up: Markets belonging to different countries and the set of spatially dispersed functional units of multinational corporations. Thus, we are able to identify three facets of mobility in these models:

---

[15] Examples for models are: Markusen and Venables (1995); Brainard (1993); Markusen and Venables (1996); Helpman and Krugman (1986), ch. 12, 13.

1. locational choice of multinational firms in the sense of how many plants to establish where,

2. mobility of intrafirm flows of headquarter services and intermediates, whose direction depends on the location of the plants of the firm,

3. exchange of goods between firms and consumers at different locations.

In these models, flows and locational behaviour follow the assumptions about interaction that are contained in the market structure.

In addition to this, mobility of firms is treated in terms of a market entry of firms making decisions about the number and spatial dispersion of their functional units. Locational dynamics in the sense of moving from one location to another cannot be explained. In models of representative agents it is quantities that matter, not qualitative differences among agents.

The term of the multinational corporation is therefore strongly related to matters of mobility. Multinational corporations in these models are either horizontally or vertically integrated. Depending on the type of intra-firm integration multinationality may enhance international flows of goods or decrease them. That means that mobility can be understood not only as the flexiblity to choose one's location, but also as the possibility to disperse activities and to be active at several locations. The determinants of mobility in this context are distances and transport costs (or barriers related to national borders) as well as factor price considerations. Thus decisions about location are made on the basis of a maximizing approach. Space is introduced into decision-making as part of the cost function. Additional plants imply fixed costs and multinational firms act as mobile demanders on factor markets and suppliers on consumer and intermediate markets. Most of the time, locational changes do not have any impact on the technologies firms apply (technology interpreted in the broadest sense). Only in few cases, reflections are made about the fact that technologies might be more or less adequate when operating at different locations.[16]

Altogether, the decision whether a firm is mobile or not does in no way depend on its capabilities in these models. It is purely based on price and cost considerations. As regards their capabilities, all firms are mobile by principle. What is uncertain is whether the economic parameters are such that firms come to the result that mobility in the sense of a duplication or dispersion of activities is an optimal strategy. That means that the question is whether mobility is used, but the idea that potentials for mobility may be different is not recognized.

---

[16] These models operate under different assumptions as to whether the level of costs is dependent on the country of operation or the country of origin of the multinational corporation; e. g. Markusen and Venables (1995).

Therefore, mobility is not related to individual diversity. There is always a number of agents who act in the same way. This is also why multinational and national firms can only coexist in special parameter constellations of the models. Even in this case, the existence of different firms is in no way related to ideas of heterogeneity. As agents are representative, it does not matter which firm becomes a multinational and which does not. Numbers matter because they are necessary to fulfill equilibrium conditions. Heterogeneity of agents in contrast is not taken into account and might even be destructive for equilibrium-based modelling (Kirman 1992). The explanatory potential of these models therefore lies in their ability to derive the production regime of an economy endogenously (number of multinational firms and national firms as well as flows between different location) on the basis of patterns of interaction that are predetermined by market structures.

However, as Kogut (1985: 38) states the models only deal with the initial decision to become multinational. They neglect the fact that new potentials might arise within the multinational as a "globally maximizing network". He explains that the primary advantage of multinationals lies in their flexibility to transfer resources. Thus, multinationals create new channels for mobility of flows and we have to consider flows as well as stocks to evaluate the advantages multinationals' mobility may offer.

7 Non-linear dynamics and self-organization - New Economic Geography

"Was ist die Zeit? Ein Geheimnis – wesenlos und allmächtig. Eine Bedingung der Erscheinungswelt, eine Bewegung verkoppelt und vermengt mit dem Dasein der Körper im Raum und ihrer Bewegung. Wäre aber keine Zeit, wenn keine Bewegung wäre? Keine Bewegung, wenn keine Zeit? Frage nur! Ist die Zeit nur eine Funktion des Raumes? Oder umgekehrt? Oder sind beide identisch? Nurzu gefragt!" (Thomas Mann, Der Zauberberg)

7.1 The type of the models

Models dealing with economic geography have only had a resurgence since the beginning of the 90's. These models – often subsumed under the title of New Economic Geography - emphasize that economic space is structured by the distribution of mobile and immobile economic agents and their activities. Still all approaches rest on the assumption that agents' maximization of profits or utilities is the basis for their locational decisions. Agents are assumed to be completely informed about all relevant market parameters and their decisions are reversible, so that there are marginal possibilities of locational adaptation. There is an optimal spatial distribution for any agent which depends on the values of certain parameters like e. g. transport costs. As the approaches are based on market structures of monopolistic competition, assumptions about structures of interaction are relatively rigid and purely based on market mechanisms.

The idea of spatial-economic centers versus peripheries on the one hand and of agglomeration on the other hand, is one of the central terms of models of New Economic Geography. In addition to this, assumptions about the mobility of the relevant agents are crucial. It will be shown that firms' locational decisions depend on the price of inputs and intermediates and the distribution of consumers and customer firms. This is why the mobility of private households in their role as consumers and owners of productive factors is of importance. It is decisive for the level of wages at different locations and for the importance of costs of transportation. These considerations in turn enter the cost functions of firms and thus their locational decisions.

The phenomenon of agglomeration has already been subject of Alfred Marshall's (1922: 225) analysis in the beginning of the 20's:

> "When an industry has thus chosen a location for itself, it is likely to stay there long: so great are the advantages which people following the same skilled trade get from near neighbourhood to one another.... while men seeking employment naturally go to places where there are many employers who need such skills as theirs and where therefore it is likely to find a good market."

In the models to be presented tendencies of agglomeration are based on linkages among agents and circular causation (Fujita 1996 or Venables 1995). Several kinds of linkages between different agents can be discerned. On the one hand demand   (backward) linkages: This means that a locational change of agents influences expenditures for goods. For example, a greater number of consumers attracts more firms. On the other hand cost (forward) linkages: They imply that a locational change of industries changes costs of production and prices. For example, a greater variety of goods (firms) in a city increases the real income of workers. Linkages can exist between consumers/workers and firms or among vertically linked firms. These linkages are not due to direct ties among agents, but rather to price interdependencies. Linkages between agents lead to locational patterns where it is advantageous for agents to choose locations near to each other. If positive linkages are strong enough, agglomeration will result from processes of self-organization of mobile agents.

Meanwhile, the existence of costs of transportation leads to tendencies of dispersion. This is true whenever some of the agents are tied to their location. Especially if costs of transportation are high, producers have to locate near to their markets, while with low transportation costs, factor costs will be more important.

Models of New Economic Geography derive spatial structures from centrifugal and centripetal forces. The models of New Economic Geography follow the older tradition of spatial economic theory. Earlier models above all dealt with questions of urbanization and central places. After v. Thünen it was Weber who combined transportation and labour cost calculations with agglomeration and dispersion forces into a concept of optimal location. Later many others have also used concepts of isolines (= lines in space designating points with similar characteristics) to make reflections about optimal spatial locations (e. g. Schilling, Jonasson, Palander...).[17] Thus, the ideas applied here are not basically new. It is

---

[17] See Ponsard (1983) for a historical overview.

the aim of formal modelling of spatial developments and interaction that makes the models of the New Economic Geography distinct from older approaches.

Modelling linkage effects and circular causation in these models makes non-linear equations necessary. Change is derived from simulations with varying values for relevant exogenous parameters like e. g. transportation costs. This way temporal trajectories of spatial patterns measured by the distribution of agents across space can be derived. Non-linearity arising from linkages has the effect that changes of parameters and changes in spatial structures do not go hand in hand. There may be long periods where parameter changes are not at all reflected in spatial structures (lock-in-effects) and there may be radical changes in spatial patterns, although the underlying parameters did not change fundamentally, but just reached critical values. Equilibria are characterized by the distribution of agents in space. In addition to this, multiple equilibria are possible whose realization depends on the path the system took in the past and whose selection is often attributed to historical hazard. This path-dependence reflects the fact that time in these models is in some sense irreversible. Where the system gets to depends on where it has come from. Temporary fluctuations may thus have a strong impact on system dynamics. The system does not get back to previous structures, even if parameters reach their former level after a fluctuation. Those points in time where the system can "decide" between two or more equilibria are called bifurcations. Some of the equilibria may be stable, others become unstable when parameters reach certain values. It is therefore necessary to analyze carefully which parameters determine the dynamics of the system and when these parameters reach critical values.

Martin (1999: 76) criticizes that this dependence on past developments and the dynamics of the model are nothing more than a simulatory sequence that is only determined by exogenous variations of one parameter. Real complex and locally embedded evolutionary processes are not explained.

In addition to this, the combination of principles of self-organization and homogenous space often brings about indeterminism. The choice between different equilibria is explained by historical hazard. Fujita and Thisse (1996: 372) call this "putty clay geography", which means that a priori uncertainty about which equilibrium will be reached is high. But once established spatial structures are often very persistent in time. One reason of this indetermination is that most models assume that space itself is homogenous and combine this with agents that are representative. Thus, any possibility to analyze spatial ties of economic activities is fundamentally missing. Space only matters in the sense of transport costs caused by geographical distance.

Models of New Economic Geography have taken up the idea of a decreasing importance of nations:

- Some models work with given regions instead of nations (core-periphery models chapter 7.2). As to their relative importance these regions are structured by processes of self-organization between mobile and immobile agents. That means that their role is derived endogenously. Anyway, this idea of given regions is not sufficient because we still have to explain how the borders of a region are defined and why a certain region is our relevant level of analysis.

• At least as interesting are those models that derive structures of economic space endogenously (city structures). These models introduce space as an infinite, but one-dimensional continuum of locations that are in the beginning homogenous.[18] Fujita et al. (1999: 308) describe this as a seamless world where national boundaries are ignored and economic regions are observed rather than defined ex ante. However, it would be interesting to analyze the influence of these agglomerations on cross-border flows.

7.2   Core-periphery models and spatial dynamics

This chapter will deal with the class of models dealing with the distribution of acitivities between regions. In these "core-periphery" models mobility is based on interdependent decisions of different agents. As consumers/ workers are assumed to be immobile within the boundaries of their regions, linkages between mobile firms and their suppliers of intermediate goods are the basis for tendencies of agglomeration. We thus make a difference between upstream-firms (suppliers of intermediates) and downstream-firms (suppliers for final consumers). Both sectors are integrated into markets with monopolistic competition and every firm produces a specific variety. All varieties of intermediates enter demand of all downstream firms and all final products are consumed by every consumer in space with quantities and prices depending on costs of transportation and other barriers to trade. The number of firms in a market is determined endogenously.[19]

Locational decisions of individual firms depend on the number of firms in both sectors that are active at a certain location. It is assumed that firms are completely informed and make their decisions instantaneously. Interdependence of locational decisions of different agents can be explained in the following way: The parameters that are relevant for locational decisions are the size of the market at different locations and the costs of factors and intermediates. Downstream producers demand intermediates from upstream producers. If downstream is mobile, the market size for upstream is an endogenous variable. Because of costs of transportation there is a tendency to locate in huge markets. At the same time costs for downstream are determined by the location of upstream. (This is decisive

---

[18] The following chapters are examples taken from a number of possible constellations of linkages and space. However, they can be considered typical and adequate to illustrate the main features of the approach.

[19] A good example for these models can be found in Venables (1993).

for the transport costs that enter intermediate's prices.) With monopolistic competition every firm has to cover a certain level of fixed costs and thus reach a certain output. The output that can be sold depends on prices and on expenditures of consumers. Prices are determined as a mark-up on marginal costs. The price level of a location is thus dependent on input (factors and intermediates) costs. Because of costs of transportation and barriers to trade the proportion of intermediates that have to be imported from other regions and those that are produced in a region is important. For intermediates that are imported these barriers to trade have to be taken into consideration. However, it does not become clear why there should be transport costs only between regions and not within regions. This concept therefore only catches traditional border related barriers like tariffs, but not transportation costs that vary continuously in space. The relevant relationships are depicted in figure 7.1.

These relationships provide an explanation why locational decisions of different sectors may be interdependent and why patterns of agglomeration or dispersion may be derived. Economies of scale that are internal to the firm are transformed into external economies of scale by using prices as signals for agents' locational decisions. However, if workers are immobile, this means that the supply of work at a location is fix. Prices (wages) will adjust to demand. Agglomeration of producers may lead to rising wages. On the other hand, wages are income at the same time and income generates demand. Therefore, immobility of private agents has ambivalent effects on locational decisions. High factor costs may under certain constellations counteract agglomeration.

Simulating decreasing costs of transportation the following u-shaped spatial pattern can be observed: With high transport costs firms have to be close to their markets. If space is homogenous with respect to the density of immobile consumers/ workers, that means that the symmetric (symmetric distribution of firms among regions) equilibrium is stable. Decreasing costs of transportation foster agglomeration in one of the two locations. However, if agglomeration is too strong, factor costs serve as a force of dispersion. Spatial equality is increased.

The linkages described may underline the idea of an industrial basis: There are some key industries (downstream here) that are important as attractors for other sectors. In order to identify these industries, linkages, economies of scale and price elasticities may be important parameters to be taken into account.

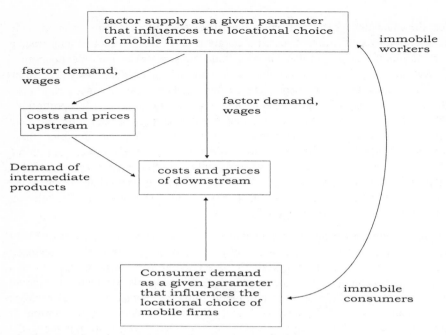

Fig. 7.1: Agglomeration, circular causation and vertical linkages

Variations of the basic model:

- A number of models deal with the fact that the parameter we called transport costs may also represent barriers to trade related to borders, if we define the relevant spatial unit as a nation. Simulations of these barriers are simulations about the effects of regional integration. However, in reality these processes take very different forms and have to be analyzed in multi-country frameworks. This leads to a more differentiated view on barriers to trade as space-structuring elements. [20]

- Krugman and Venables (1995) also have a look at the effects of multiregional modelling. This allows the derivation of more types of equilibria besides complete agglomeration or spatial equality between two regions. Multiple agglomerations can be derived. Furthermore, some authors have tried to operate with more complex versions of space. Krugman (1996) e. g. arranges the different locations on a ring in order to avoid differences arising between locations at the end and in the center, if space is considered a one-dimensional continuum as will be done in chapter 7.3. Venables (1999) even chooses a set of locations lying on a two dimensional disc with a centre and an edge. He

---

[20] As examples see e.g. Puga and Venables (1998) or Puga and Venables (1995).

structures this disc with given locations by putting a square grid on it where the points outside the disc are deleted. Using this structure he is able to derive concentric circles of specialization and complex belt structures. For example we get "ripples of activity", that means industrial belts with industries occupying alternating concentric circles. He distinguishes between high frequency agglomerations describing situations where neighbouring locations (rings) have different specializations and low frequency agglomerations meaning large areas of specialization.

• Martin and Ottaviano (1996) deal with the relationship between agglomeration and growth. They use the same basic model, but assume that intermediate products enter an R&D intensive sector that is responsible for locational growth.

• The structure of the model makes it obvious that special attention has to be paid to aspects like factor intensity of production, the specifics of the relevant market, sector- specific costs of trade and the strength of linkages. The spatial patterns to be derived, if industries differ in this respect, are analyzed by Puga and Venables (1996, see also Krugman and Venables 1996).

• Peculiarly, there are only few models that take into account the possibility of multinational firms. This is true although these might be able to render the influences that are important in the model described above partially irrelevant.[21]

We may resume that the strength of the models lies in deriving spatial structures within given boundaries from processes of self-organization. This reflects the notion that the locational decisions of mobile agents are interdependent. In this type of models interdependence is reflected by price mechanisms. The broad range of models shows that much attention has been paid to the relationship between space and economic activities.

---

[21] See Ekholm and Forslid (1997) as an exception.

7.3   Cities and endogenous spatial structures

The models to be presented in this chapter deal with the endogenous derivation of spatial structures.[22] This means that both, the size and the location of spatial agglomerations are taken as an outcome rather than an input of the model. Relevant agents are divided into private households with the economic functions of workers and landlords on the one hand and firms on the other hand. Landlords are immobile and derive their income from ownership of land. Workers are sectorally and spatially mobile. In addition to this, there are firms as relevant agents. They are free to choose their location. Two goods are produced: A (agricultural) and M (manufactured). While A is homogenous and produced under perfect competition, M is differentiated and produced in a market characterized by monopolistic competition. The production of A uses labour and land as inputs. That is why it is tied to immobile land. M uses only labour and is thus mobile. Spatial structures are described in terms of cities as point-agglomerations of M production and a hinterland. The M good is consumed within these cities as well as in the hinterland around the city. Cities import A goods from their hinterland. The size of the hinterland is determined by the demand for A, that is by the size of the population. Distance is introduced as transportation costs.

Thus any equilibrium can be described by the distribution of consumers and M producers in space as well as by the level of wages and prices of goods (including a mark-up for transportation costs).

First, we will have a look at the aspect that influence spatial structures. A and M goods enter demand in given proportions. In addition to this, the subutility functions for M varieties imply a preference of consumers for variety. This parameter is related to the elasticities of substitution of demand, which determines how demanded quantities change when some producers locate farther away from consumers and transportation costs are included in prices. With transportation costs producers tend to locate in big markets. Finally, workers choose their locations according to real wages. These include a nominal wage and a price component. On the other hand wages are also costs of production and thus determine prices. These relationships are the basis for linkages among workers and firms. The relevant interdependencies are depicted in figure 7.2.

---

[22] For a basic model see Fujita and Krugman (1995).

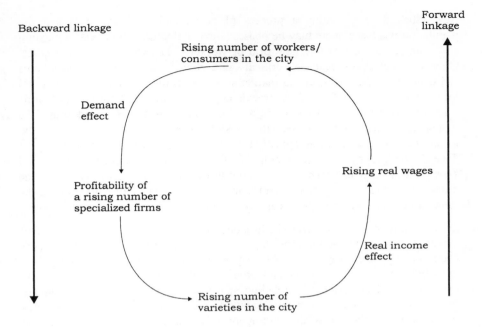

Fig. 7.2: City agglomeration, source: Fujita, M. (1996: 42)

Both, the A and M good are transported with costs. Let us first assume a monocentric equilibrium. What about the incentives to locate in a new city? The consumers/ workers in the rural market as well as the transportation costs that are relevant for the agricultural goods create an incentive to disperse manufacturing production. If transport costs of A are high, there will be a tendency of spatial dispersion. M producers and workers locate near to A producers. If these costs are low and M goods are strongly differentiated, tendencies of agglomeration will be high, especially if the population is small. Choosing another location would in that case imply higher wages for the respective firm and only small additional demand. Only if the goods are close substitutes and the population is large (which implies a large hinterland as well), there will be an incentive to choose a location different from the central one.

A simulation of increasing population can in this framework allow the derivation of an evolving multi-city pattern with cities that are of equal size, have the same functions and are located at equal distance to each other. The reason for this is that the size of the population determines the size of the relevant hinterland. If the hinterland grows, agricultural products will have to be imported to the old city from far away and M goods will have to be delivered to landlords at distant locations.

New cities develop within a process of catastrophic bifurcation. When the population increases, there may be phases when agglomeration effects of existing cities are so strong that any new firm or worker is absorbed by existing cities. Only when population reaches a critical value, new cities can develop. New cities can develop because of growing market size, new firms entering the market and locational changes by firms from preexisting cities. However both types of firms (those entering the market and those moving) cannot be differentiated within the model as we deal with representative agents. The incentive to choose a new location is reflected methodologically by defining a market potential function that depends on the size of the population, transport costs, price elasticities and expenditures. It gives us knowledge about those locations where wages/ average profits are higher. The spatial system is in equilibrium when all workers have the same utility, there are zero profits and no incentives for firms to change locations.

Space is in these models introduced as a one dimensional infinite continuum. This makes it possible to model transport costs as rising continuously with distance. Cities are agglomerations of mobile agents surrounded by a hinterland where immobile agents as consumers and producers of A are located. However, this methodological approach to modelling space is still in some way inadequate. Firms that are located within the continuum face competition from both sides, firms located at the end of the continuum only face competition from one side. This is why Krugman (1996) also presents a model where locations are arranged on a ring.

Altogether, this class of models has the advantage that the set of relevant locations and their size are derived endogenously within the model. As space is assumed to be homogenous (equal density of immobile agents), spatial structures are derived from the distribution of mobile agents in space and the distances between agglomerations (critical distances). It is assumed that existing cities create an urban shadow within which no new city can develop.

Spatial structures are explained as self-organizing mechanisms. They are based on locational advantages of second nature (proximity). Fujita and Mori (1996) combine these with traditional advantages of first nature, that is certain features of heterogeneity in space, like ports or other nodes of transportation. Their model shows that transportation nodes are places where cities are likely to emerge, unless they lie in the urban shadow of a preexisting city. However, this does not take into account that transportation nodes that are not given, but "manmade". It seems unreasonable to assume that transportation nodes are created independently from existing city structures. Nodes will probably not be a prerequisite for city development, but they will rather co-evolve with cities.

Extensions of the basic model:

- Assuming that the goods of different industries have different transportation costs and face different elasticities of substitution by consumers, we can derive that their "locational sensitivity" and the strengh of lock-in effects of agglomerations will be different (Fuijita 1996). The more willing consumers are to substitute goods and the higher the transportation costs, the "earlier" will firms have incentives to locate in a new city when population grows. Fujita describes these industries that change their location easier as being of lower order. The assumption that sectors change their locations or enter the market at a new city at different parameter constellations makes it possible to explain hierarchical city systems. As the earlier changes of lower order sectors influence market potentials for other sectors, they have a locomotion function. Higher order cities develop from lower order ones.

- Mori (1997) develops a model where cities merge into a "megalopolis" consisting of core cities linked by an industrial belt. The megalopolis thus is a continuum of point cities.

- With respect to time, Krugman (1991) shows that expectations shape locational choice whenever mobility is costly. Thus, mobility has to be treated as an investment. With agents' decisions being interdependent, self-fulfilling prophecies may become true. The relative importance of history and expectations for locational developments depends on the importance agents ascribe to future developments when choosing their location, the strength of interdependencies among agents and the speed of processes of adaptation. Revisions of expectations can create fluctuations of spatial structures. The fact that expectations play a role in locational decisions means for political agents that they have to make an effort to create optimism about future developments of their territories among mobile agents.

- Several authors have included different types of congestion effects into their models. These may find their expression in traffic jams and transportation bottlenecks, excessive pollution or crime in cities.[23] Especially in their relationship to transportation congestion effects may contribute interesting insights as they show that transportation costs are not a given input into the model, but they are rather dependent on the interaction among agents which is an endogenous variable.

7.4   A critical point of view

The developments within New Economic Geography can today be considered as state of the art in mainstream international economic theory. However, the models still leave many questions open regarding the microfoundations of mobility, patterns of interaction among agents and the way space and time are dealt with.

---

[23] For a survey see Junius (1999: 32-40).

Microfoundations of mobility:

It becomes obvious that models working with the assumption of representative agents and exogenous stimuli will not be able to offer adequate microfoundations of mobility. The idea that novelty and change are based on agents' characteristics and diversity is not part of these models. The models are striving for equilibria.[24] Thus, they do not help us to explain how it matters that spatial change might be driven by those agents that are more mobile than others. This is also due to the fact that agents are assumed to be completely informed about spatial characteristics. Töpfer (1969: 59) argues that the task to calculate information about costs and profits at all locations will be impossible, especially if conditions are changing rapidly. In reality, the way agents perceive spatial opportunities and the willingness to take risks will be of major importance. Finally, interdependence of decisions in models of New Economic Geography is price interdependence in space. But what about the idea that imitation and learning from others' decisions are important, that effects of chain migration are relevant where first-movers increase ·information for others and facilitate decision-making for potential followers and that immaterial informational ties relate agents to each other? These aspects can only be modelled by taking sequences of decisions into account and by modelling interaction in a more flexible way.

We therefore have to ask about the determinants of the spatial perception and the availability of information for different agents. These questions will probably be related to informational and communicative structures in space.

In addition to this, the models of New Economic Geography do work with the idea that different industries will behave differently as regards their locational choice. What they do not show is that industries are not static constructs. This idea is taken up by Storper and Walker (1989: 75) who explain that we may have to interpret locational dynamics within a lifecycle concept. Young industries are relatively free in their locational decisions. They are able to create the conditions necessary at their locations. There is a "window of locational opportunity" in this phase of the lifecycle. Later in the product lifecycle, spatial clustering occurs followed by growth and spread of the industry to peripheral locations. Only these latter two phases can be explained within the models described above. Finally, at the end of the lifecycle, there may be radical changes in products and the "window of locational opportunity" may open again.

---

[24] Fujita et al. state that explicit modelling of firms and households making intertemporal decisions based on rational expectations would greatly complicate an already difficult subject; see Fujita et al. (1999: 7).

Patterns of interaction:

Patterns of interaction in the models discussed are predetermined by relatively rigid market structures. E. g. by principle all consumers demand all varieties with quantities depending on the price and thus on transportation costs. This means that global price coordination determines the outcome of the model. Firms do not have the freedom to influence their patterns of interactions and non-price interaction is not taken into account. Reality however shows that agents often interact in small subsets of the economy that are not predetermined.[25] This means that the global economy consists of a set of multiple networks that influence the level of information, the capabilities and the locational decisions of agents. It is doubtful whether models of New Economic Geography really deal with interaction in the strict sense because agents are never influenced directly by other agents, but by macro-parameters like prices.

Models of New Economic Geography are often described as part of a class of theories of self-organization. Self-organization describes the property of a system "where collective macroscopic features of multicomponent systems emerge from and are sustained by the interactions between units of the system at the microscopic level" (Witt 1985: 571). The patterns that are created are determined by the specific characteristics of the system's components and their interaction. However, different phenomena seem to be subsumed under the headline of self-organization (Göbel 1998: 130). Some authors define self-organization as spontaneous order of a system. Others underline that self-organization is self-determined, which means that agents within the system can shape the order. Although models of New Economic Geography can be integrated into the former class, they do not correspond to the latter definition. Thus, creativity, learning and intelligent development of agents are excluded from these models.

Space:

Martin (1999: 75, 81) explains that the mathematical approach of New Economic Geography is extremely restrictive. "Messy social, cultural and institutional factors are neglected because they do not lend themselves easily to mathematical formulation". This refers to non-market interaction among economic agents as well as certain territorial conditions shaped by political decision-makers. These factors however may be key factors in spatial development. According to Martin, mathematical feasibility dominates visible variety in the economic landscape in the models of New Economic Geography.

---

[25] The irrealistic characteristics of the assumptions going along with monopolistic competition modelling have also been acknowledged by Fujita et al., whose argument is that monopolistic competition offers so many methodological advantages that it will serve as a good starting-point nonetheless, see Fujita et al. (1999: 6f).

This also implies that distance is either geographical or related to national political borders. Linguistic, cultural and institutional distance is neglected, although it might influence mobility.

Time:

Time is simulation time. Evolutionary systemic developments are not modelled. Still the driving forces of change have to be superimposed onto agents - be it by exogenous discrete stimuli or continuous simulation.

These are issues that should be on the agenda for future research in the field of mobility and spatial dynamics.[26] They are however not inadequacies of existing theories as all of these are centered around certain given targets, have been developed in a certain point in time and have had to cope with a number of – above all methodological – restrictions.

7.5   Agglomeration, cities and the service sector – some basic considerations

In some sense it seems peculiar that up to now the industrial sector has been taken as a basis to derive city structures, although we can empirically observe that cities are nowadays above all service centers.[27] This is e.g. very obvious in the case of the financial sector that is from a spatial point of view nowadays dominated by very few centers around the world: London, New York and Tokyo. While capital is most of the time considered footloose, the activities of these sectors take place in agglomerations that have been more or less stable in the last decade. Although many authors have acknowledged that the financial system may have to be considered an evolving system, the formal treatment of aspects of the rise and decline of financial centers is up to now rudimentary. At first sight we might be induced to take similar models like the ones presented in the last three chapters as a starting-point to explain this agglomeration (Reszat 2000). However, at second sight this may be misleading. This is first of all true because financial flows and the activities related to them have a relationship to space and distance that is

---

[26] Although Fujita et al. also make some remarks about future research projects they do not include these aspects in their agenda; see Fujita et al. (1999), ch. 19.

[27] E. g. in their agenda "Industry 21" decision-makers in Singapore have formulated the aim of becoming a hub for "ideas, talent, resources, capital and markets, while developing its own world-class capabilities and global reach"; Singapore Economic Development Board (2000).

completely different from the transportation of industrial goods across space. Although there may be border related barriers to transferring capital internationally, continuous "transport costs" in space will hardly be relevant in this sector. Although several authors suppose that agglomeration economies of financial or producer services are important, it is frequently underlined that this agglomeration is due to the necessity to exchange non-routine information. Non-routine information is a major in- and output in the sector of producer services (Drennan 1996: 362). However, information has not been a relevant production factor in models of the New Economic Geography and it has a number of features that will require special approaches also from a theoretical point of view. The role of a special local atmosphere and information will be emphasized another time in chapter 9.3 when dealing with industrial districts.

Other authors underline that the existence of financial centers is due to an informational spatial bias. In a more general context Pred (1976: 42-46) states that there are place-to-place variations in the availability and accessibility or costs of information. Cities and service centers may be considered centers of access to information.

Thus, we may conclude that the relationship between the footloose global flows of capital and the determinants of agglomeration in the financial sector are fundamentally different from the phenomena we have dealt with in the industrial sector. Sassen (1999a) describes that national and global markets as well as forms of global integration are coexisting with central places where globalization is realized. Worldwide networks go along with central functions of coordination. This centrality is provided by cities.

Thus, we may suppose that although we observe results that are very similar to those that have been derived in the previous chapters in some aspects, the determinants of agglomeration in this sector as well as the relationship between flows and local activities will be fundamentally different. This will pose new requirements for theoretical approaches. It seems reasonable to assume that the special characteristics of different branches in the service sector will have to be deeply analyzed in order to understand their dynamics. This topic is very much related to the idea of hubs that may have global, regional and / or local functions and that are places exerting pull effects and creating linkages to the outside world at the same time.

Part C   **Future agenda – towards a theory of mobility in space and time**

8   Between old and new concepts

"What forces determine the spatial pattern of industrial specialization? Near the top of an economist's list of answers...would probably come differences in technology and endowments. A good deal further we might find geography." (Venables 1999)

This chapter is intended to create a bridge between the traditional and newer models presented and the agenda for the following chapters and future research. All the preceding chapters have shown that *space* is an important – although complex - dimension into which mobility is embedded. The recognition of the importance of the spatial dimension is certainly rising in international economics: "It should not ... be hard to convince economists that economic geography ... is both an interesting and an important subject." (Fujita et al. 1999: 1) Moreover, we have also seen that the phenomenon of mobility is even more complex as it is guided by different causalities and channels. (Im-)mobility may be related to activities on markets, but other institutional frameworks e. g. multinational firms as well.

Furthermore, chapter 3 has outlined that mobility is inseparable from individual decisions and individual development. The theory of international economics however strongly works on the basis of the assumption of the homo oeconomicus, representative and sometimes even invisible agent. Firms and individual agents are regarded as rational, completely informed and able to adapt to changes immediately. They are on this basis able to maximize their profits and utility. However, the way firms are modelled gives an idea of a reacting object rather than an acting entrepreneur. In addition to this, the range of relevant decision-makers is relatively restricted in many theories. There are firms and individuals and there is certainly the state as a political decision-maker, but none that is integrated into the model as a decision-maker or only a reacting entity. Although space has traditionally been delineated in terms of political boundaries, *political agents* only enter the models as exogenous stimuli. This is true despite the fact that they do play an important role in shaping the conditions within countries, regions and at locations and therefore in guiding mobility and spatial dynamics.

Moreover, mobility does not only involve the individual agent or firm, but it has to be interpreted within a framework of *relationships* and *interaction* among agents and between agents and space. The models presented up to now only take this into account by modelling price interaction. In order to understand the phenomenon of mobility better we will therefore have to analyze the relationship between locational choice and interaction across space more closely. Our interest will have to be devoted to the patterns of interaction and location in space as well as to the sources of change and the dynamics of these patterns.

All this means that we have to endow our agents with characteristics and capabilities that are decisive for their spatial behaviour. We will have to fill the "black box" agent with characteristics that show that mobility is not a given feature, but a variable that takes different values according to the characteristics and strategies of agents and their relationships towards each other.

On the one hand, our point of view will therefore have to be agent-oriented. We will have to ask why agents differ in their decisions about mobility and what effects this heterogeneity of agents has on the dynamics of the whole system. This will be strongly related to the temporal structure of change as we will have to analyze the interplay of mobile first-movers or followers for example. Moreover, the neoclassical assumption of completely informed agents is unrealistic and gives us ideas about spatial dynamics that are misleading. This is especially true when spatial and temporal considerations are taken into account (Barnes 1988: 481). Spatial distance may restrict the availability of information. Temporal distance between the present and the future in addition to this means uncertainty. Even if this may be rendered less important by new technologies, uncertainty and risk (-taking) will vary in space and among agents because of the different availability of these technologies and because of the different willingness of agents to tolerate uncertainty. Besides heterogeneity, novelty will be a key term as dynamics will be determined by the speed and frequency with which agents change their decisions about locations and the exchange of goods and factors. Novelty as well is strongly related to the existence of incomplete information. It is due to the fact that there is no intertemporally constant upper level of maximization.

On the other hand, we will have to realize that patterns of interaction and relationships among agents may have a diversity that exceeds pure price interaction by far and that is frequently related to "local" rather than "global information". Altogether, the notion that agents are heterogeneous and tied to each other by a number of relationships may also help us to understand their relationships to space and to modify the simple image of completely footloose global players (completely informed, acting on markets, maximizing) into a more complex version of mobile agents and spatial structures.

It is obvious that these suggestions can only be realized by models that are at the edge between macromodelling and an understanding of microeconomic behaviour, interdependencies and diversity of agents. Certainly, a microeconomic foundation of a theory of mobility – if we do not want to enter the field of case studies – will have to presuppose the existence of certain patterns of mobility, of strategies that are more or less stable and of core capabilities for mobility. We will have to get better ideas about what is the right aggregate to start from (firms, individuals, networks, business groups) and which patterns of behaviour we can take as given.

Finally, we will have to put emphasis on the meaning of space. Is space more than just a "dead surface"? How can we structure the relevant spatial entities? We have already seen that space in the sense of location is mostly understood as point space, while space as distance implies spatial extensions. Moreover, space has been structured by borders or boundaries that have up to now been mostly political borders. Nonetheless, one hypothesis of the following part will be that there are a number of other criteria that give space its structure and mobility its direction. These are related to cultural, historical and institutional differences in space.

Therefore, a theory of mobility in space and time may pose questions that cannot be answered by traditional approaches of international economics. Of course, from a methodological point of view, the assumption of rationally acting agents being connected by given market structures helps us to get determinate results. Clearly, whenever we discard one of these assumptions, results will be much more indeterminate. In some cases, problems of analytical feasibility will appear. Interpreted positively however, we may also say that more realistic models will be more open. They leave space for several outcomes. This may be considered negative by economists who emphasize clear results as a criterion of the quality of a theoretical model. However, it may also be a step towards reality.

The keywords representing the agenda to be dealt with in the following part are illustrated in figure 8.1, emphasizing the aspects of agents, their interaction in space and time in their relationship to mobility in its different facets.

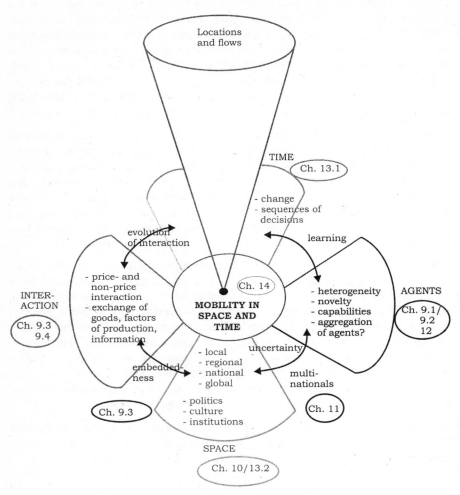

Fig. 8.1: Agenda for part C

There are several approaches that may be promising for solving these questions. Some of them may deal with fundamental ideas, others with methodological questions.

The capability of economic agents to develop and the corresponding effects on the economic system will be discussed under the headline of Evolutionary Economics (ch. 9.1). These theories aim at an analysis of the development of novelty and processes of learning under incomplete information. There may be two aspects that might be solved within this framework: the creation of new ideas and capabilities in the sense of innovative spatial behaviour as well as the diffusion of information and change in the economy. However, this approach only gives us a formal concept containing the main questions. It is not specifically related to the idea of mobility. Moreover, the relevant characteristics of agents may be much better understood after having had a look on the many facets of mobility. We will therefore go back to the question of capabilities in chapter 12 after having presented the relevant theoretical concepts.

Having discussed the general concept of Evolutionary Economics, chapter 9.2 is going to discuss approaches lying at the fringe of international economic theory and dealing with heterogeneity of economic agents as well as the role of political agents, sequences of decision-making and migratory biographies. Chapter 9.3 will give us more ideas about patterns of interaction in space. From a more methodological point of view chapter 9.4 will evaluate whether there are other disciplines that might offer useful methodological approaches for modelling interaction in a more flexible way. One of these approaches is the field of sociodynamics that borrows methods from physical science.

Chapter 10 will deal with concepts of distance and their effects on mobility. Besides traditional borders other concepts of distance and borders that might shape interaction in space and locational choice are discussed. These are cultural, institutional and historical aspects. Chapter 11 will deal with the special role of multinational firms. In chapter 13.1 the special importance of temporal aspects of mobility will be resumed. Similarly, chapter 13.2 aims at summarizing the results of the previous chapters to get a new understanding of the relationship between mobility and space.

Chapter 14 will try to formalize those spatial aspects that are relevant for decisions about mobility in a graphical way.

Finally, the possibilities for creating a more integrated concept of a theory of mobility in space and time will have to be evaluated in chapter 15. Integrated in this context will mean two things:

- integrating approaches from different disciplines and

- integrating international economics in its traditional form into a wider approach.

Altogether, besides the ideas related to the determinants and patterns of mobility, we will have to deal with the methodological restrictions and opportunities to model patters of mobility in a more open and flexible way and with the relationship between the various potential determinants of mobility.

9 Economic agents, capabilities and relationships in space and time

"Evolutionary Economics is what evolutionary economists do." (Wagner 1992: 279)

9.1 Evolutionary Economics and the sources of spatial dynamics

The aim of the following chapter is to give an outlook on the possibilities and difficulties to analyze the sources and effects of novelty or changes in agents' capabilities and behaviour within formal economic models. A set of approaches that is centred around this question has become known under the title of Evolutionary Economics.

Evolutionary Economics comprises a building of thought that was developed from a critical position towards neoclassical equilibrium theory. The main criticism is that equilibrium theory deals with individuals who only react to exogenous parameter changes and that it assumes that individual actions are mutually compatible. The economic system seems to be relatively frictionless, but also lacks its "motor" to create change. Evolution is defined as the transformation of a system in time by endogenously created change (Marengo and Willinger 1997: 333). If the economic system is considered an evolutionary system, we may characterize it as open-ended. That means that we have to deal with a system that has features of a never ending emergence of novelty. As Fagioli (1998: 79) states novelty can involve any component of the system. This cannot be analyzed within an equilibrium framework, but has to be based on an understanding of the economic system as a permanently changing, evolving structure. Time therefore is an important element. Key questions of Evolutionary Economics deal with innovation and variation among agents as a source of change, adaptation to this change, selection and diffusion of change. Marengo and Willinger (1997: 332) give the following description: "In evolutionary modelling dynamic properties are the outcome of the interaction among heterogeneous units with an endless introduction of novelty."

One main aim of these approaches is to analyze the sources of novelty and to find the methods to model it. It is underlined that agents are heterogeneous. There is microdiversity as a central feature of the economic system. Processes are analyzed within a framework of co-evolution of agents and the system itself. One of the main ideas is inherent in the term of "evolutionary drive" (Allen 1998: 61). If agents as microcomponents of the economic system have internal dynamics, this will shape the evolutionary pattern of the whole system. Elements of entrepreneurship are underlined. Steiner (1990: 296f) therefore makes a difference between two functions of the market: the allocative and the creative. While the first one can be analyzed within a static framework, the second one is dynamic by nature. The main idea Evolutionary Economics tries to establish is that macroeconomic systems cannot be analyzed without having adequate ideas about the dynamics of the underlying microeconomic components. This framework of thought follows the tradition of the old Austrian School. It is Schumpeter's (1991) merit to have emphasized the permanent tendency of the economic system to develop. He devoted himself to analyzing endogenous change by underlining the role of entrepreneur firms as dynamic pioneers. Heuß (1965: 10) pursued this idea by distinguishing four types of firms: creative and spontaneously imitating entrepreneurs as initiative entrepreneurs and those only reacting under pressure or not reacting at all (conservative entrepreneurs). Hayek (1937/52: 64ff) in addition to this underlined the importance of individual access to and processing of information. He doubted whether the variation and flexibility of prices will lead to equilibrium. Kirzner (1973/78) followed the concept of an *homo agens* permanently searching for new possibilities of action - an idea that had before already been established by v. Mises (1949). Recently, Nelson and Winter (1982) have underlined the importance of bounded rationality, routines and rules of thumb.

From a theoretical point of view, we may distinguish different types of theories according to the way they deal with novelty:

- theories that suppress novelty (e. g. neoclassical economics);

- theories that insist that novelty is prevalent and so radical that it ruins regularity; in that case it is no concept that is open to theoretical modelling;

- theoretical approaches that try to make out patterns of the creation and effects of novelty.

It is only the latter class Evolutionary Economics is aiming at.

The explanation of novelty brings requirements with it that are opposed to basic principles of modelling in traditional economic theory. These are related to the way agents are aggregated and also to the importance equilibria play from a methodological point of view. Equilibrium modelling may have to be abandoned as novelty will not result from equilibrium. Novelty destroys equilibrium. The main problem of the approach of Evolutionary Economics lies of course in finding bridges between basic microeconomic ideas and macroeconomic modelling. One of the main sources for novelty is heterogeneity of agents. To find approaches to deal with change we have to analyze the structure of individual decision-making. We may suppose that agents base their decisions

- on the scope of action they are able to choose from,

- on the rules of decision-making they apply and

- on the pay-offs they get or expect to get from a decision.

Some authors therefore approach this problem by proposing to model a possibility space of behaviours, thus predefining the set of possible choices (Allen and Phang 1993: 15). But how can we be able to identify behaviours that will be new in the future? Novelty refers to things we do not know yet. It is therefore doubtful whether we are in the present able to delineate the borders of a playing field for the future. Allen (1990:558) describes that there is a trade-off between aggregation and reduction of complexity and the loss of information when reducing microdiversity to representative agents. Fagioli (1998: 79) has two other proposals to model change:

1. to introduce time-dependent algorithms of choice for agents. In that case change is not necessarily related to individual unpredictable development;

2. to model variable pay-off structures for agents' decisions. A model where this might be applied is the one by Schmutzler described in the next chapter.

Dalle (1998: 135) adds that a stochastic parameter might be introduced into agents' decision-making that reflects that with a certain probability (error) agents do not follow the behavioural rules of the past. Apart from the problem of modelling the sources of change, there may also be a need to give agents learning devices to face novelty created by others.

A basic question when dealing with change is whether we derive change from evolution, that means gradual and possibly time-dependent change or from novelty in its purest sense of unexpected and unpredictable change. While the former already poses a number of new challenges to theory, theoretical handling of the latter – as has been explained – is considered an unsolvable problem by many economists. This is why Nelson and Winter in their pioneering approach deal with routines as predictable behavioural patterns that may have stochastic elements.

Gradual change will be due to learning processes. In order to deal with them time-dependent algorithms of decision-making and changing characteristics of agents will have to be assumed. This is alright, if we suppose that learning is in some way a predictable process. In the field of mobility learning may also be related to intercultural/ locational aspects. Whenever we accept that locational choice is shaped by incomplete information about different locations, there will be gradual learning and collection of experiences about locations that are more or less distant from a geographical, cultural and institutional point of view. Bergman (1998: 92) even states that seeking for experiences is a motive for choosing a location ("intertemporal cross subsidizing effects"). Thus, experiences can be collected that are only used later. He considers intercultural competences as major organizational capabilities.

Novelty in its pure sense however seems to have features of a random process. This may lead us to stochastic theoretical approaches which only makes sense if we know about the probability distribution. We will have to deal with the question whether there are any predictable patterns how novelty emerges.

The questions posed by Evolutionary Economics imply the problem in how far it is adequate to model sources of change as exogenous stimuli in theoretical modelling and in how far they have to be endogenously explained. Finally, there is nothing that is truly exogenous. Exogeneity is a methodological tool to reduce complexity. This is why we will be forced to choose carefully between those aspects that may without loss of information be taken as exogenous stimuli and those that have to be analyzed more deeply. In the context of mobility one main question will therefore be: Is mobility simply a reaction to exogenous stimuli or is it a potential within a given, but also an extendable scope of action?

Allen (1990: 557) describes that evolution corresponds "to the appearance of new cogs, wheels and linkages over time". This is an allegory that fits our idea of spatial dynamics very well. The wheels that drive movements in space are heterogeneous agents that have internal dynamics. Linkages are relationships, ties and interaction of diverse contents between these agents. Cogs are bridges that translate micro- and meso-dynamics into macro-results. The following questions will have to be dealt with in the next chapters:

- In which way (that is relevant for their spatial behaviour) are agents heterogeneous?

- Which scope is there for them to develop new capabilities and patterns of behaviour?

- What types of relationships between agents do have to be taken into account?

- What can be said about the macro patterns of spatial dynamics resulting from this?

Most of the time, we will have to acknowledge not only that the empirical basis to answer these questions is still weak, but also that the most challenging task will lie in overcoming methodological problems. Allen (1990: 560) concludes that "the motor which drives evolution must be contained in what has been taken out from complex reality in order to reduce it to the model."

Altogether, we may expect that an evolutionary view of mobility may deliver new insights on the question why and when firms change their locations, on the patterns of spatial evolution and on the political implications of this. However, even if Evolutionary Economics is nowadays considered an approach of its own, it seems to integrate ideas and conceptions rather than a common methodology to deal with these problems. Despite the methodological problems of modelling novelty, there are approaches in the field of game theory (ch. 9.2), but also in sociodynamics (ch. 9.4) that might open new possibilities.

9.2   Interacting agents in a mobile society

Market models of imperfect competition have assumed that agents' decisions about their location are interdependent in that they respond to a price that functions as a signal on the macro-level. Moreover, distance and proximity as expressed in transport costs matter and create a relationship between mobility and space. This has been shown on the basis of price interaction in combination with special assumptions about patterns of interaction for example dealing with the exchange of goods. If we therefore recognize that it is important for locational decisions and mobility with whom agents interact how, there will be good reasons to seek for deeper insights about the special characteristics of agents, the way they interact and also the flexibility of interaction as regards its temporal and spatial structure. This will be done in chapter 9.2 and 9.3. While chapter 9.2 puts more emphasis on questions of heterogeneity of agents and the structures of interaction emerging in time, chapter 9.3 focuses on different types of interaction and their relationships.

9.2.1   Heterogeneity of agents and externalities

One of the main points not recognized by models of New Economic Geography, but underlined by Evolutionary Economics, is that agents are heterogeneous. The idea of the representative agent neglects the fact that firms' locational needs, their willingness to move and their mobility may differ because of reasons beyond the general conditions of an industrial sector or a market. However, as Dalle (1998) states, few special actions can have a dominant influence on collective dynamics, which is why heterogeneity matters.

Schmutzler (1995 and 1998) has developed a model which works with heterogeneous agents and localization externalities. In the following paragraphs this model will be presented in a more detailed way in order to illustrate the potentials similar approaches may offer to deal with mobility. Schmutzler starts from an approach of dynamic games. There is a continuum of players differing according to their preferences for one of the two locations. In addition to this, locational choice is subject to externalities depending on the number of agents in the two locations. There are positive externalities among agents which means that a location is more attractive the greater the number of agents that have chosen it. There are several periods in the game in each of which every player (firm) decides about his location. Schmutzler analyzes the dynamics arising in response to an exogenous shock that affects the relative attractivity of the regions. Thus, locational decision-making is regarded as a huge game with many players that do not necessarily act according to the same calculus.

He emphasizes the effects of the level of externalities among agents and their heterogeneity on the robustness of locations and patterns of spatial dynamics. The two main parameters, heterogeneity and externalities, influence the system's dynamics in two phases: the initial decision of first-movers to change their location and the sequence of imitators following them. Thus, the willingness to move or the degree of mobility of an agent depend on the constellation of his locational preferences and externalities as well as the relative attractiveness of the regions. Whenever externalities are strong, the alternative region is unattractive and heterogeneity is low, an initial agglomeration in one location will be robust to shocks. An increase in externalities will lead to stronger lock-in-effects of agents in their initial location. However, once started, spatial dynamics (= locational change from one region to the other) will be the stronger the stronger externalities are because the number of follower firms is increased. On the other hand, an increase of heterogeneity among firms may - under certain conditions - increase the number of first-movers and decrease the number of induced movers.

In addition to this, Schmutzler shows that the long-run equilibrium may depend on the initial spatial distribution of agents: The more even the initial distribution, the smaller is the initial agglomeration advantage of one location, the smaller is the initial push necessary to induce spatial dynamics and the less important is the first-mover effect. This effect appears somewhat strange because it proposes that equal or balanced distributions might be more unstable. Of course, it is only due to the fact that the models' dynamics are strongly related to the number of agents at a location and many more complex relationships are neglected.

What about the advantages this approach may offer? On the one hand, it recognizes that heterogeneity of agents as regards their locational preferences is important for spatial dynamics. This idea is related to the fact that agents may have different roles in shaping spatial dynamics: first-movers and followers. Thus, in some sense, the model is much more concrete as to the sequence of steps of locational change. The starting-point for spatial dynamics can be found either in a shock on relative attractivity of regions (regional policies) or in increased heterogeneity of agents. The latter may refer to any change within firms that make locational changes and higher mobility possible. Pioneers are those firms that have strong preferences for a location with rising attractivity and who are not tied to their former location by strong externalities. Heterogeneity of firms implies several aspects: Methodologically firms are assembled on a continuum between 0 and 1. In order to calculate the pay-off of firms changing their location the "position" of a firm is multiplied with a constant. The higher the value of this constant, the stronger is the heterogeneity of firms. Schmutzler models rising heterogeneity by increasing the constant. This has an impact on all firms simultaneously. However, another approach might be to change the distribution of agents within the continuum. Thus, although the shocks modelled are still exogenous, they are clearly related to the internal characteristics of the firms and they are open to include many events on the micro-level that might serve as a source of spatial dynamics. In this context, it should be interesting to find a way to model internal dynamics of the preferences of firms following a certain internal logic, e. g patterns of learning. In addition to this, the model is formulated in such an open and abstract way that externalities between firms may take different shapes and are not restricted to price interaction.

The model:

- 2 locations: 0, 1
- infinite number of discrete periods   t= 1,2...
- continuum of players i=(0,1) spread uniformly according to their preferences

    Each player chooses an action a^i in each period. Action is based on the decision either to stay at one's location or to move to the other location. This reflects that immobility is understood as an action. What results is a sequence of actions for each player.

    n_t is the fraction of players choosing location 1.

    The decision between the two locations is based on a comparison between the pay-offs related to this choice. The pay-off of choosing one region depends on the fraction of agents present in this region in the period before:

    pay-off region 0: $f^{0i}(1\text{-}n_{t\text{-}1})$

    pay-off region 1: $f^{1i}(n_{t\text{-}1})$

    The pay-off of each player i in t therefore can be defined as:

    (1) $\pi_t^i = (a_t^i, n_{t-1}) = (1 - a_t^i) \times f^{0i}(1 - n_{t-1}) + a_t^i \times f^{1i}(n_{t-1})$

    As the decision is based on the relative attractivity of the region, we define the difference: (2)$P^i(n_{t-1)}) = f^{1i}(n_{t-1}) - f^{0i}(1 - n_{t-1})$. Combined with (1) we get (3)$\pi_t^i(a_t^i, n_{t-1}) = f^{0i}(1 - n_{t-1}) + a_t^i \times P^i(n_{t-1})$

The pay-off function contains - as explained above - an externality term $\hat{Q}$ that depends on the number of players in a location and in addition to this an attractivity term R that is different for each player and independent from the number of agents in one location:

$$(4) f^0(n) = \hat{Q}(n), f^{1i}(n) = \hat{Q}(n) + R(i)$$

$$(5) R(i) = a - b \times i$$

$$(6) \int R(i)di = \int_0^1 (a - b \times i)di = \left(a \times i - \frac{b \times i^2}{2}\right)\Big|_0^1 = a - \frac{b}{2} = c$$

The attractiveness term is related to an agents' position on the continuum. The higher the position on the continuum, the less does an agent prefer location 1. c describes the attractiveness of the locations across all players. b measures heterogeneity of agents. The larger b, the stronger heterogeneity among agents. Schmutzler assumes that the externality function is linear in n, but he also tests his model under different assumptions about externalities.

Flexibility of the model/ additional assumptions to be made:

- Heterogeneity: Schmutzler has chosen a way of modelling heterogeneity of agents and simultaneously avoiding many of the problems that go along with the disaggregation necessary for this. The "trick" he applies is that he uses agents' position on the continuum as an input in their pay-off function. Heterogeneity as modelled in Schmutzlers approach implies that those agents with "high" positions on the continuum are those that react last when there is a positive shock on location 1 and who react first when the shock is negative. Thus, even if they do not create novelty, agents can be assumed to react with different speed. Some agents will act as first-movers, others will only change their location when externalities created by early-movers are strong enough. However heterogeneity in this context simultaneously means biasedness towards a location.

How can such a bias be justified? It may be argued that each player has some kind of natural ties towards a location that are due to cultural, institutional and legal affinities or his migratory biography (ch. 9.2.3). Biases may also develop in the course of time because immobility means territorial learning at the same time (ch. 9.2.3). This would imply that we might have to introduce a factor into the pay-off function that is proportional to the number of periods an agent has been staying at a certain location. This term should diminish the pay-off of moving to another location.

Introducing a time-dependent term of immobility in combination with externalities might however have serious effects on the dynamics of the whole system. The opportunity of a location to gain players depends on the dynamics of the system and thus on individual mobility. If this immobility is purely self-reinforcing, this might have a paralysing effect on the system. However, we might assume that there may be changes in the environment that prevent knowledge accumulation as a reason for locational biases from being a purely positive linear process in time.

Locational bias may also be due to the fact that mobility is more probable within a short-distance horizon. Information about locational characteristics decreases with distance and thus the willingness to change a location may depend on the distance between the present location and potential locations. This will however only be relevant whenever there are more than two locations. We therefore might imagine locations also distributed along a continuum. From a methodological point of view a term measuring the distance between home and host locations might have to be introduced.

- Moreover, a sequence of decisions is created by putting agents into order on a continuum. Movements of the first agents are based on pure attractiveness effects. Thus, this might reflect the idea that mobility within a "linked" economy is triggered by few critical agents or pioneers. Afterwards in every period there is a number of imitators or followers, whose decision to change locations is purely due to externalities. The behaviour of these agents is dependent on the behaviour of agents that are principally more willing to move and would therefore take this decision earlier, if they do not decide to stay permanently. Whenever there is a period when no agent moves, the model's dynamics come to an end.

Therefore, the spacing of agents on the continuum might be decisive for the dynamics of the model. This concerns the density of agents in a point of the continuum as well as the distances between agents. Interesting effects on the number of agents moving in a period may be due to the density of agents. The number of agents following a group of agents in the next period might be a reflection of the density of ties. On the other hand, breaks or long empty spaces on the continuum might inhibit dynamics.

The sequence of agents moving in this model might also be interpreted as processes of diffusion rather than clock-time periods. It becomes obvious that there are indirect ties between first movers in t and agents that might be willing to move in t+1+x.

- However, what is not included in the model is some kind of unbiased mobility term expressing that some players have better capabilities for mobility than others independent from the direction of mobility. This mobility term should therefore be included in the payoffs of all locations. It becomes obvious that the pay-off function is a concept that is very flexible. It does not only express pure pay-offs from moving, but it is also able to integrate propensities to move.

Moreover, we will have to consider that dynamics may have different sources. Apart from an exogenous shock on locational attractiveness (based on political decisions and the qualities of agents that are immobile by principle), cases may be important where agents develop new competences, get new information or see new opportunities. The source of dynamics might therefore be modelled varying the mobility term of an agent. Permanent dynamics of the model might result without any exogenous shocks, if certain patterns of individual mobility could be discerned.

- If we define players as firms, there may be firms that choose more than one location. Multinational firms may altogether exhibit another type of mobility being characterized by the choice of multiple locations. We may have to introduce ideas about the reasons why firms decide to act as multinationals.

  This kind of choice cannot be modelled by relying on the difference between the pay-offs of the two locations. An adequate model should recognize that there are intrafirm interdependencies between the functional units of a firm.

- In addition to this, the assumptions about externalities have to be chosen carefully. We have to think about which agent interacts with whom and what type of externalities might arise from that. If players are heterogeneous, there will be a time sequence of decisions having an internal logic. This may be due to special relations between agents as well as to the history of their relations (path-dependence of externalities). It should matter in which sequence agents take their decisions.

  Externalities like learning about locational characteristics in addition to this have a time dimension. We therefore have to think about the time lags introduced into the model.

- What is not shown by this approach is that first-movers should be interested in whether other agents will follow. Otherwise they will not take into account that pay-offs might rise in later periods. We therefore have to wonder in how far agents are able to predict the behaviour of others or whether agents coordinate their behaviour. If this is not possible, incomplete information might lead to suboptimal decision-making.

- The dynamics the model creates give us a hint on the task of territorial decision-makers to trigger locational changes in their direction by influencing decisions of first-movers and to bridge critical gaps and weak ties among agents within the process of diffusion by setting special incentives (ch. 9.2.4).

The importance of sequences of spatial decision-making when agents are heterogeneous and linked by externalities is also underlined by Arthur (1989). Modelling market entry within a spatial context, he assumes that locational choice orders of heterogeneous firms are random for the observer: Agents differ with respect to their locational preferences and the sequence of types making a decision is unknown. History is thus understood as a sequence of decisions. Arthur shows that heterogeneity and sequence of choice are important parameters for patterns of spatial dynamics and the choice of dominant locations. Thus, he is able to explain what is often called historical accident. Historical accident in Arthur's terms is randomness of decision-making in time. This does not necessarily mean that economic decisions are in fact random. But it reflects the observation that in many cases we are not able to grasp what is behind decisions of individual firms. Randomness might be considered a possibility to circumvent the problems related to modelling dynamics explicitly. Whether it is adequate to model this by a random approach may be discussed. In contrast to the models described above, Arthur assumes that agents make their decisions about locations only once because there are transaction costs of moving. Arthur's model clearly reflects the importance of patterns of interaction in time in the sense of sequences of decision-making. He admits that in reality, we may find an internal logic within this sequence relying on complementarities or differentiation patterns of products or technological paths.

9.2.2 Mobility and the option value of waiting

The preceding chapter has underlined that sequences of decision-making will be important, if agents are heterogeneous and linked to each other. However, the question of a sequence of decisions does not only concern the individual decision whether to move or not, but also who moves when. This has also been underlined by Arthur's approach of random sequences. Interest has been paid to the fact that agents might decide to stay, even if other locations offer advantages in the present. Adaptation to new constellations is not instantaneous. This will be true if migration implies fixed costs and uncertainty about future gains. In that case, deferring the decision for mobility may be rational, as it may allow the migrant or firm to profit from a more favourable turn of events in the future. New information may be acquired by waiting. This shows that the decision about mobility is not only a dichotomic decision between moving or not, but the possibility to move is postponable in time. It creates an option that is valuable, if the future can evolve differently from the present (Burda 1995). With fixed costs taking the decision to move also means killing this option right. Thus, the decision to move today is only rational, if the expected future benefits exceed the fixed costs of moving and the value of the option of waiting.[28]

Therefore, several questions have to be answered:

- Can we make out situations when uncertainty is a dominating feature of the decision about mobility?

- Is there a logic behind waiting that secures that uncertainty is lower in the future?

- In how far is the problem related to sequences of decision making?

Thimann and Thum (1998) suppose that uncertainty is higher in newly opened economies (terrae incognitae). This is due to the fact that there are no experiences that might help moving (investing) firms to evaluate the advantages and disadvantages of the location. Thus, experiences of early movers are considered as sources of information, so that it is rational for agents to wait until the success of first movers can be observed. Depending on the type of linkages, pioneers cannot only provide information to followers, they are also able to give support that reduces the costs of migration. Thus, there are positive informational externalities among investors and there may be too little investment in initial stages, if these external effects are not internalized.

The idea of an option value of waiting may be of different importance for different regions. This is due to the fact that information is not available equally everywhere in space, but also because informational distance and affinities between regions differ. Such an approach might be able to explain why investors of a certain nationality may be more likely to invest in some regions than in others. Relationships between regions will have to be described by a distance parameter different from geographical distance. Business literature has argued that companies begin their internationalization in countries that are psychically close because this reduces the level of uncertainty and makes learning easier (Johansson and Vahlne 1992). Nordström and Vahlne (1992) define psychic distance as "factors preventing or disturbing the flow of information between potential or actual suppliers and customers" or "actors preventing or disturbing firms learning about and understanding of foreign environment". The following indicators have been used for operationalization of psychic distance (Vahlne and Wiedersheim 1977):

- level of economic development,

- level of education,

---

[28] Mathematical models of option pricing have traditionally been developed in investment theories.

- differences in business language,

- differences in culture (moral, attitudes, personal ties, customs, habits) and language,

- existence of historical connections or animosities, common membership of a preferential trading area.

How can we distinguish pioneer firms from others? Thimann and Thum propose that there may be some firms that have lower requirements for public inputs so that they are more likely to be successful even in a weakly developed environment. These firms may be inclined to act as early movers.[29] For them the investment has an experimental character. Again heterogeneity of agents is emphasized.

In a sequential decision model individuals observe the history of previous decision-makers' actions to update their own behaviour. This is why the decision to move may have "herd behaviour" characteristics.

As will be discussed later, the "sequencing" and "management" of these market-failures may be an important field for territorial (political) decision-makers to foster regional development. Waves of optimism may thus be created, if they succeed in attracting early-movers and in providing a favourable environment for their activities. In later periods the success of these early-movers may have self-reinforcing effects and create a locational reputation of offering a favourable environment.

9.2.3   Heterogeneity of agents, space and time: migratory biographies

The preceding chapters have shown that migratory dynamics may be shaped by the sequence of decisions of heterogeneous agents. Thus, elements of path-dependence are important. However, this may be true on the meso-level among different agents as well as on the micro-level as regards the individual sequence of decisions of an agent or firm. Therefore, we will have to analyze the determinants that shape the "individual migratory biography" and the structures in space and time resulting from that. If there is an inner logic of decision-making and development of capabilities, this might be related to the idea of learning. For example, Pred (1967) characterizes agents by the quantities of information available to them and their capabilities to use them. Differences in the information level may be due to the search strategies of agents as well as locational information policies. Together the two elements shape the way they perceive restrictions and opportunities in space. The position of firms can be improved by

---

[29] Like Schmutzler, Thimann and Thum arrange agents on a continuum (0,1) according to their requirements for public inputs.

processes of learning that need time. Fischer et al. (1997) relate the idea that learning and information are important to specific locational features. They describe that an insider approach might be applied to questions of mobility: Agents who decide to stay at a location for some time may be able to accumulate insider advantages. Therefore, insiders are characterized by a certain behaviour in space as well as in time. Insider advantages comprise location-specific assets and abilities. This may be an argument why immobility has a value of its own. It may be an optimal or utility maximizing strategy, if mobility induces a loss of non-transferable abilities and assets and requires new entry investments. Thus, the duration dependence of locational learning creates a bridge between space, time and different degrees of mobility. Insider advantages may be partly recovered and updated when agents return to previous locations. Thus, the opportunity costs of staying away as well as the value of moving depend on the speed with which old knowledge looses its value and the ability to acquire new insider advantages. Agents may be heterogeneous regarding the ability and speed to accumulate location-specific knowledge. Thus, the capability to render immobility an optimal strategy may be different among individuals or cultures. In contrast to the positive evaluation of agents that are more mobile than others, there may be agents who are able to learn rapidly and who can therefore use immobility as well as mobility as a tool. On the other hand, successful mobile agents are those who are able to adapt their skills rapidly to new locations. For example, mobile ethnic networks, the advantage of having compatriots at the new location, may decrease the losses or costs resulting from mobility. This is why it is important that areas of origin and destination of mobility are not only markedly different (in order to make relocation attractive) in some characteristics, but also have important similarities (in order to avoid making movements to costly). Moreover, the informational networks within multinational firms may contribute to reduce uncertainty.

Individuals are thus able to influence the utility that can be realized at a location and the value of mobility or immobility will depend on their specific skills. We are not able to evaluate without ambiguity whether mobility or immobility is more advantageous. The continuity of processes of learning however is not linear. It may be disrupted by acute changes in the environment or the technologies that are available. That implies that the value of location-specific assets is not stable in time and the utility we get from immobility does not rise linearly. If there are frequent and strong structural changes, the value of existing knowledge may deteriorate rapidly. Therefore, optimal strategies require searching for an optimal duration of immobility. Immobility cannot be equalized with linear learning in time. It can easily be imagined that there may be locations where the acquisition of location-specific knowledge may be more important than at others (depending for example on the transparency and accessibility of the administrative-political system and the importance of personal contacts as well as on the stability of the system). Moreover, chapter 9.3 will show that learning may not only be location-specific, but also specific to relationships.

Equivalently, we might suggest that agents may differ as regards their ability to transfer their assets and to adapt to new conditions. Processes of learning about how to cope with mobility might be important. The transferability of assets might in addition to this strongly depend on the conditions at past locations and future locations and the differences between them.

Finally, if insider advantages depend on the behaviour of others, internationaly (-culturally) different mobility patterns may be discerned. In nations/ regions where basic mobility is high, it will be difficult to acquire location-specific knowledge because it is agents' collective behaviour that makes up the dynamic environment of the individual. On the other hand, mobile cultures may induce pull effects because ethnic networks may make integration of newcomers easier.

Finally, patterns of learning may strongly depend on the sequence of agents entering a location or leaving it. Moreover, with multinational firms locations are not mutually exclusive which makes our picture more complex.

9.2.4   Territorial decision-makers in international economics

Up to now, we have mostly dealt with heterogeneous private economic decision-makers. The actions and decisions of political decision-makers have only appeared by introducing exogenous stimuli to the system. They are hidden behind interventions at national borders like the introduction of tariffs. This is due to the fact that it is difficult to integrate them in a framework of market-mechanisms. Decision-making of political agents obeys different laws than pure maximization of profits. However, the attractiveness of locations will be strongly influenced by them and it is the interaction of economic and political decision-makers that will determine the structure of the spatial economic system and its dynamics.

Explaining mobility within a framework of interaction of different agents however, we cannot leave out such territorial decision-makers as an important part of this network. This is why it will not be sufficient to model political decision-making by simulating different values of the relevant parameters. Political decision-making and bargaining processes have frequently been analyzed by Public Choice Theory. However, within this approach agents are mostly integrated into a broad range of more or less powerful interest groups. Formal approaches to understand political decisions are also often game theoretic. Clearly, models integrating political-decision making as well as the interplay of heterogeneous economic agents will be difficult to manage because different "mechanisms" of decision-making would have to be considered. In addition to this, political decision-making comprises a hierarchy of institutions and persons. For the topic analyzed here, all those agents and institutions will be relevant who shape the attractivity and rules of regions, locations and nations. The easiest way to introduce territorial decision-makers into models would be to assume that their actions follow common rules of economic maximization. Territorial decision-makers might be interpreted as sellers of economic territory, not only in a quantitative sense, but above all with respect to its quality. Thus, local political decision-makers might take the role of a coordinator of activities that are related to certain territories. They have the task to give economic space a value of its own.

Most certainly, a number of models have been developed that deal with locational competition mostly among nation states which have the aim to attract internationally mobile factors and to raise the incomes of the complementary immobile factors confined within the borders of the nation.[30] Curiously enough however, these models (that mostly deal with factor or capital mobility rather than agents' or firms' mobility) have not entered mainstream thinking in international economics. None of the models described in the preceding chapters deals with the scope of action available for the state or similar decision-makers and on the other hand models of locational competition do not take into account the complexity of the mechanisms underlying mobility.

Similar ideas of modelling territorial decision-makers as agents within an economic framework are comprised in a model developed by Rauch (1993). He assumes that an institution called "developer" has an incentive to capitalize the complementarities among firms. Complementarities among firms at a certain location arise from learning by doing. With progressing industrial settlements at a location knowledge about how to operate efficiently there spreads. Every new firm contributes to the knowledge basis although possibly to a different degree. The complementarities described here are different from those described in the models of New Economic Geography because they are intertemporal by nature, it is complementary accumulation of knowledge in time that is analyzed. This also means that any additional firm may increase knowledge, but knowledge is not decreased if firms leave. In economic terms: We deal with dynamic external economies of scale. Therefore, this approach fits well into the idea of a relationship between immobility and location-specific learning, but is extended by the idea of complementarities among firms. It recognizes that the phenomenon of complete information is illusionary. Firms differ to the extent that they contribute to learning and they differ in their willingness or ability to change their location. Because of the intertemporal point of view, profits at a location are discounted in time. Therefore, the temporal preferences and the speed of learning of firms are important. Rauch also deals with the problem of "wait and see behaviour" of firms. Under certain circumstances, it will be preferable for firms to stay at their old location and move only when a new location has been established by the efforts of early movers. There is a strategic side of locational decision-making.

If a "developer" buys the land necessary for production, he is able to sell it to firms by applying a price policy of intertemporal discrimination. Firms entering

---

[30] For a survey see e. g. Siebert (1994).

the location early pay less, while latecomers benefit from the learning processes and have to pay more. Thus, lock-in-effects because of preexisting agglomerations may be overcome. If there is competition between locations, the "developer" has to be capable to differentiate his product "location" from others.

First the developer will sell his land to "seed tenants" that create a good reputation of the location and are decisive for the character of the industrial district and the mix of firms at a location. If there are linkages among firms, more firms will be attracted. The locational decisions of the first firms also decrease the uncertainties for firms entering the market later. The developer may be able to internalize the advantages of agglomeration by his pricing policy. Another interpretation might be that developers compensate firms entering the location early for existing uncertainties. Thus, economic space becomes a network good that the state as a developer or other territorial decision-makers offer.

As described in chapter 9.2.2 externalities may not only be related to the gains that can be achieved at a certain location, but at also to the information available about the attractivity of a location. Therefore, another task of planners is to internalize these informational externalities and to overcome the problem of suboptimal movement towards newly opening locations. However, to succeed the planner has to make sure that a type of firms is attracted that fits his territory because like the information on successful firms, information on failures will spread as well.

If the learning process for the first firms is fast, the developer might have an incentive to sell only few units of land in the first period and sell the rest later when the value of the location has risen. Thus, the speed and sequence of dynamics of learning and spatial dynamics are interrelated.

This approach is in many ways similar to the one chosen by Schmutzler (ch. 9.2.1). It is based on the idea that agents are heterogeneous and linked by externalities. However, it focuses on another side of the problem and that is how attractivity of regions might be related to policy-making. The model shows that it is interaction of heterogeneous agents and the developer that *creates* externalities. Externalities are not given, but evolve in time. Integrating the idea of a developer into Schmutzler's model of heterogeneous agents should be possible: The pricing behaviour of the developer would in that case influence firms' pay-offs. The question whether there are early movers and when would in that case not only depend on heterogeneous characteristics of economic agents, but also on the incentives set by the developer.

Park and Markusen (1995) describe that the state (or state agents on different levels) has had an important role for the establishment of industrial activities especially in developing economies. State agents have been active as developers and locators of business activities by creating incentive packages within the confines of their territory.

The idea that political agents might behave economically may seem to be far-fetched as arguments of bureaucratic rent-seeking have been manifold. However, we should not totally neglect this idea. In the case of China, e. g. Oi (1995) argues that incentives were designed such that local state agents were promoters of economic growth. In addition to this, there may be other decision-makers boosting the creation of industrial districts beside state agents.

Rauch's approach leads us to the question whether ties among agents can be used as vehicles for regional policies. This may be relevant as regards the creation of technology parks as well as the promotion of endogenously created development and growth (Goldstein 1991). Can regions be produced? Is region-building a tool for governments? Can "designer regions" be created (Blotevogel 1996: 63)? It seems reasonable to assume that regional development must be boosted by the interaction of both economic and political pioneers/ leaders.

However, as Iwer and Rehberg (1999: 335) underline, we may have to distinguish between the potentials to pull firms into a region and the possibility to shape existing locations, to promote and stabilize them. Apparently, a number of geographical and historical conditions are inherent in spatial development. It is regional specifics that distinguish one region from the other - specifics that are to a great deal not based on political decision-making at a point in time.

Studies about the special economic zones in China have shown that overcoming informational barriers and „marketing" locations to potential investors is one – "coordinative" – task of local political decision-makers. Fostering an innovative and flexible environment however is the creative task of these decision-makers that is at least as important (Heiduk and Pohl 2001).

To summarize: The preceding chapters have tried to introduce the relevant agents that may either be more or less mobile like in the case of economic agents or have decisive competences to give mobility its direction. It has been shown that the heterogeneity of these agents is of major importance for changes in spatial structures. Not only can we distinguish first-movers from followers, but the existence of uncertainty about locational features will lead to complex temporal patterns of development. Thus, it is mainly locational decision-making we have dealt with in these chapters. However, whenever we agree that the interaction among these decision-makers is important, we cannot deny that there will be mobility of flows at least in the sense of an exchange of information. This will be analyzed more concretely in the following chapters.

"Change does not follow automatically from the balancing of the underlying factors. Nor is it striving towards a future balanced state. The winds of change will rage. It has no beginning nor end and it comes from nowhere and blows everywhere and it changes the world." (Hakanson and Lundgren 1997: 122)

9.3   Patterns of interaction: networks, industrial districts and milieus

The following chapter is to deal with questions of agents' interaction in space. Models dealt with previously underlined that it is distance expressed for example in transport costs and prices as well as aspects of competition that makes it favourable for agents to locate near to or farther away from each other. In addition to this, a first look on economic reality today seems to suggest that it is globalization that renders distance and space in many ways neutral. These propositions will be critically reviewed in the next chapters while laying emphasis on the fact that many aspects of interaction in space can neither be captured by models of price interaction nor in models conceiving space as given country structures.

9.3.1   The evolution of patterns of interaction in time: the network approach

The analysis of the models of New Economic Geography has shown that many of the results can only be derived after having made certain assumptions about patterns of interaction that were governed by market structures. These assumptions are important determinants for the locational decisions of agents and they may shape evolutionary patterns in space. In many cases however, it will be necessary to distinguish global interaction (any agent interacting with any other) from local interaction (agents only interacting with their "neighbours"). Alfred Marshall (1920: 182) wrote: "Everyone buys and nearly everyone sells... in a 'general' market.... But nearly everyone has also some 'particular' markets; that is some people or groups of people with whom he is in somewhat close touch: mutual knowledge and trust lead him to approach them ... in preference to strangers." To some extent, the approaches of New Economic Geography also dealt with local interaction, but in these cases interaction was only restricted and structured by price and transport cost aspects. It was price interaction and no direct interaction that was analyzed. In many cases, local interaction patterns will be due to a much more complex set of determinants. Local – as defined above - first of all has an interpersonal dimension: Who interacts with whom across which distance?[31] It implies interaction with a limited number of agents. Local interaction makes the introduction of a spatial dimension into the economy necessary. Agents are physically distributed in a spatial environment and distance that is not restricted to geographical distance may be one important determinant for the set of agents interacting and its limits (Fagiolo 1998: 54f). As Fagiolo states a locally interactive economy is strongly decentralized. He describes the relevant models as Spatial Interaction Models in Decentralized Economies (SIDDE). In these models interaction structures synthesize relevant information about space, locations of agents and neighbourhood sets. There is imperfect information in a spatial or interpersonal sense. The idea of neighbouring relationships with "significant others" is of importance. And finally - if the different neighbourhood sets are not disjoint - space becomes a dense network of interactions. Above all, dealing with local interaction in a context of mobility makes it necessary to get ideas about whether non-price interaction is neutral or not for questions of mobility. Furthermore, as regards time local interaction will have strong effects on the speed of the diffusion of change. With global interaction change diffuses instantaneously within the whole system. If interaction is local in contrast, the consequences of agents behaviour will take time to reach agents that are not directly linked to them or will never diffuse completely. The spatial direction and temporal patterns of mobility may be supposed to become much more differentiated. We can therefore assume that the localization of patterns of interaction can deliver a number of new insights on patterns of mobility in space and time.

Therefore, a new strand of theorizing has come up that deals with the shape and evolution of patterns of interaction in time. In these approaches the price is only one of the determinants of interaction. Non-market relationships are important as well.

Approaches dealing with this question are manifold and differ strongly as regards the methods applied. Thus, Fujita and Smith develop (1990) a model relying on static optimizing behaviour where agents take into consideration utility and costs of interaction (in the sense of communication). That means that agents are supposed to be able to measure their utility from interaction with others, which makes it possible to calculate optimal behaviour. In addition to this, Fujita recognizes that there are several types of interaction. This is why a contact activity vector may have to be applied. Although this approach reflects a certain awareness of the problem, it is static by nature and neglects questions of learning, development and incomplete information as well as problems of quantifying the value of communication and interaction.

---

[31] As will be seen in the following chapters, distance is not merely a matter of geographical measures, but a multidimensional concept.

Much emphasis is also put on game-theoretic approaches under different assumptions.[32] Some approaches are in this context able to model sequences of decisions and time-paths of interaction. Many models start from the assumption that the choice of a strategy (interaction with a certain partner) depends on the relative profits to be gained by choosing that strategy. Some models recognize that experiences of the players are important, others work with stochastic elements and are therefore able to include questions of uncertainty. Very few models make the introduction of completely new strategies within the course of the game possible.

A final category of models deals with the way relationships between individuals evolve in time according to their experiences. The central idea of these approaches is that economic agents are organized in networks. Networks are "a regular set of contacts or similar social connections among individuals or groups" (Swedberg and Granovetter 1992: 9). Transactions between agents are neither purely of the market nor of the hierarchy type. It was Granovetter (1985) who stressed that all economic action is embedded in social relations. The term embeddedness not only expresses the idea of ties very well, according to Coleman (1988: S97) it also is

> "a structure that springs into place to fulfil an economic function, but as a structure with history and continuity that give it an independent effect on the functioning of economic systems."

Hakansson (1995) explains that firms are complex combinations of activities, agents and resources. Within networks activities are tied, agents are set into a certain relationship and resources are bound. Multi-layered relationships result which are to some degree stable in time. Networks can therefore be considered a net of agents, activities and resource constellations. Within these networks firm behaviour is not determined by an anonymous market, but by more complex, differentiated and intensive relationships. "A business network consists of several firms that have ongoing communication and interaction, and might have a certain level of interdependence, but that need not operate in related industries or be geographically concentrated in space." (The Competitiveness Institute 2000)

Firms in networks act as linking units whose strategic attributes are determined by the way they create and use relationships to other agents (Hakansson 1995: 21). In some cases, the network idea is also applied within the multinational firm and its different plants as well as among different firms (intra- and interfirm networks).

Why are relationships important? According to Hodgson rules and institutions are important for decision-making and formation of expectations in a world of uncertainty. Without these rigidities, social routines and institutional frameworks a world of uncertainty would "present a chaos of sense data in which it would be impossible for the agent to make sensible decisions and to act" (Hodgson 1988: 20). Networks fit well into this idea because it may be assumed that the

---

[32] For an overview of approaches see Kirman (1999) or Kirman (1995).

availability of information within networks is better than on the anonymous market. Search costs are thus reduced. Similar to the arguments economists found to define the boundaries of the firm, networks are often explained by network-specific assets. International economic theory frequently works on the assumption that there are ownership advantages and that some assets may be easier to transfer within the firm than on the market. This mechanism may also be true within networks and thus networks may be able to develop insider-knowledge. Specific competences are embedded in networks of social and economic relationships and new ones are acquired in circular processes of knowledge transformation. Networks offer some kind of social capital, that is characteristics that make coordination and cooperation easier. The idea of social capital was first introduced by Coleman (1988). He argued that the concept of social capital can be used to combine the principle of rational action with aspects of social organization. Coleman sees social capital as a resource that is available to agents, but that inheres in the structure of relations. He gives obligations and expectations, informations channels as well as norms and sanctions as examples for social capital. Especially the idea of social capital providing information is an interesting aspect as the circulation of information is one of the most complex expressions of mobility of flows. Baker explains that firms use networks in order to mobilize social capital (1990: 589). This aspect is interesting as it introduces the idea that there may be assets that are created by processes of exchange, interaction and mobility of flows e. g. of information. Social capital is thus derived from social structures. Social capital can be considered a prerequisite for the accumulation and mobilization of human, financial and political capital. This might mean that immobility within a network (building up stable relationships) is worthwhile because agents loose valuable access to knowledge when leaving a network. This hypothesis can be considered an analogy of Fischer's insider theory which was explained before. As already stated before, insider positions can be created by spatially and temporally positioning agents. Thus, the economic links within networks have the durability features of physical capital. They are devices which facilitate interaction and investments in interaction capabilities reducing transaction and interaction costs. The capital invested can only be used by the firms involved (Johansson and Westin 1994: 247). Colletis and Pecquer (1994: 12) call this "Beziehungsrenditen" (relational rents). This shows that patterns of interaction are not given by nature. They require active decision-making and investment to create special channels for exchange. Andersson (1986: 11) summarizes that in networks a combination of competence, culture, communication and creativity is present. As Baker (1992: 397f) states the network organization may moreover evade organizational inertia. Networks adapt by the interaction of problems, people and resources. He calls this self-adaptability or feature of self-designing organization and compares it to a market mechanism allocating people and resources to problems and projects in a decentralized manner. Rauch (1996a: 4) makes the assumption that the underlying search processes to establish ties and develop them are promoted by a common language and already existing ties, as well as personal contacts. Similarly Fischer and Gensior (1998: 38) underline that trust which relies on culturally and socially common orientations and experiences is important in networks. However Rauch (1996b) adds that relationships will also be characterized by permanent search processes e. g. because of changing market conditions like finite product cycles. Relationships between agents are not data, but variables that can have different values and characteristics in time and space.

Furthermore, immobility within a network does not necessarily go along with spatial immobility. If agents within a network are mobile in space, they may nonetheless be integrated into more or less long-term network structures. A good example for this might be the supplier - manufacturer linkages in the automobile industry.

According to Uzzi (1996: 676, 681) a network bears a certain logic of exchange that shapes agents motives and expectations and promotes coordinated adaptation. Agents may thus not search for globally optimal solutions, but rather act in a more "local" (within a restricted set of agents) context. Social networks may be able to shape agents identities as well as their rules of action. In general the network approach proposes that mobility of flows of information e. g. goes hand in hand with temporal immobility of agents within a network. Thus, this special combination of different types and degrees of mobility creates special advantages. Mobility is not a one-dimensional decision, but rather a strategy consisting of a set of decisions. The distribution of industries and the direction of international flows in space may among other things be related to the availability of social capital (Herrmann-Pillath 2000).

Networks imply the existence of certain affinities of interaction. Casella and Rauch (1997) emphasize the special importance of networks and group ties in an international context. They assume that group ties can take the role of a matching technology between home and foreign agents and therefore develop models where agents can choose between actions on the anonymous market and within group ties (ch. 10.3.2). This way, they are able to show that there may be processes of self-selection: Firms with certain characteristics will have stronger tendencies to choose market transactions or network interaction. Rauch and Casella (1998) add that the fact that group ties are relevant for decision-making and that networks are not equally distributed in space, may be important for questions of information distribution.[33] While the anonymous price system gives information to all agents, but information may not be complete, networks offer better informational access, but not to everybody. This is an assumption that is contrasted to the market models presented in the chapters before, and which assumed perfect information

---

[33] Belussi (1999: 5) calls this the asymmetric distribution of physical and cognitive resources in economic space.

of agents. Markets are anonymous intermediaries that treat all agents similarly, while networks imply direct linkages with a restricted set of agents (fig. 9.1).

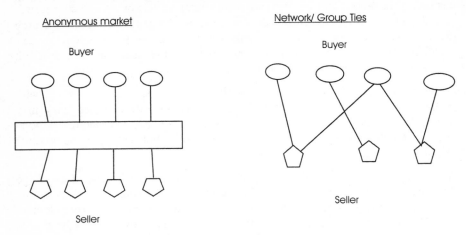

Fig. 9.1: Anonymous markets and networks, source: Rauch (1996b)

Thus, path-dependence is inherent in networks, path-dependence with respect to patterns of interaction and creation of social capital. There is an internal logic of transactions and relationships in the course of time that is different from the spot transactions based on the market-price mechanism. Interaction patterns and their use are not imposed on agents, but created by their decisions (Hakansson 1995: 19). What about the relationship between the organizational modes of firms, networks and markets? Following the tradition of transaction cost economics and institutional economics Loasby (1999) explains the existence of networks by opposing transaction costs to production costs within networks. Assuming that productive knowledge depends on organization and that incentives for opportunism are especially low in networks because of intimate connections, he concludes that network structures bear many advantages. From his point of view a transaction cost related argumentation leads to the result that networks have to define a balance between internal coherence and external linkages. Similarly, Bergman et al. (1991b: 286) explain that networks are "hybrids that reduce the administrative burdens and the loss of innovation arising out of hierarchical control, yet help to reduce the uncertainty and stability of pure market transactions." They arise "to minimize and control expensive transaction costs." Johansson (1991: 23) states that the firm may be the ultimate form of an interaction network where the links have been internalized. It is a "logistical device" for the continuous coordination of resource flows". This may especially be true for multinational firms. However, this also shows that there is no agreement as to the concrete definition of networks.

As Baker explains, the concept of the network organization "suffers from semantic ambiguity, multiple interpretations and imprecise definitions." Generally, all organizations are networks defined as certain patterns of roles and relationships. Whether or not they fit into the network organization image presented here depends on their organizational type, that is on particular patterns and characteristics of the network. A network organization is often characterized by a high degree of integration across formal boundaries of multiple types of socially important relations. Baker (1992: 400f) calls this "thick" network organizations. Integration describes the degree of interaction among the organizational units. Networks can be vertically, horizontally and spatially differentiated with differentiation meaning the division of the organization. However, similar to the establishment of firms, the links that make up networks have to be considered capital objects which are sunk costs (Johansson 1991).

Maillat et al. (1994: 34) define four dimensions of networks:

- the economic dimension (agents aiming at realizing their aims better when being integrated into networks),

- the historical dimension related to the process of building long-term relationships,

- the cognitive dimension based on the fact that the knowledge of the whole network (creation of social capital) is bigger than that of the network parts and

- the normative dimension consisting of particular rules.

Most certainly the task of integrating ties and networks into formal models still is a difficult one. This is due to the fact that most of the elements underlined can hardly be quantified. As Swedberg and Granovetter (1992: 1) explain, economic theory often makes simplifying assumptions that on the one hand allow formalization with the help of mathematics. But on the other hand, it leads us to a "radically non-social approach". According to them social influences are mainly considered as something that basically disturbed economic action. In order to explain interaction structures in formal models we will first of all have to acknowledge that interaction (with whom, how, when) is decision-making. We therefore have to realize that there is a more or less measurable value of interaction. Furthermore, in order to explain the evolution of interaction structures, we will have to apply a historical context to interaction. Interaction in the past in some way will have to influence present decisions. Thus, we will have to formulate some kind of algorithm of decision-making about interaction. Such an algorithm also will have to include information about the knowledge agents use to decide. This knowledge may vary from own experiences in the past or the experiences of others up to expectations about future strategies of others. These inputs will strongly shape the dynamics of such a model. Finally, we will have to impose an initial structure of interaction on the model that may also be a determinant for the outcome of the model's dynamics. For "quantification" transaction cost approaches have been considered appropriate. E. g. Johansson (1995) uses such a transaction-cost framework and integrates the idea of trade affinities as measurable variables. They enter a "preference value" that influences the decision of firms with whom to transact. This underlines that interaction and the use of ties are object to decision-making. They cannot be considered given parameters of the model. Affinities make changes in partners of interaction less probable. They are influenced by cultural, language and communication distance, the interaction costs associated with close contacts, the existence of established networks and the barriers vis-à-vis other nodes. In addition to this, the ties to partners of interaction in the past are strengthened by fixed costs invested into a relationship that become sunk costs whenever ties are broken. These elements make up the difference between "established" firms and newcomers on the market. A model that recognizes that interaction structures are not only influenced by sunk costs, but also by constant evolution because of new experiences is built by Weisbuch et al. (1996) They assume that future interaction is influenced by experiences made in the past as well as a tendency to search the market.

A visual approach to illustrate network structures is the graph approach. This approach starts from the assumption that the economy can be visualized as a graph structure with agents as nodes (ch. 4.2). Every agent is influenced by a restricted number of (neighbouring) agents. Thus the economic system looks like a lattice filled with structures of interaction. A point to be debated however still is how to define the notions of proximity, spatial ties and the rules that are necessary to model evolutionary patterns of interaction. Geographical criteria might in this context be as useful as closeness of characteristics or criteria based on the profits that can be gained by interaction.

How can we describe the relationship between networks and markets? Are there more alternative types of economic organization and exchange? From a transaction cost oriented point of view networks have frequently been considered an intermediate mode between markets and hierarchies. Taking transaction cost approaches as a starting-point to explain possible logics of organization also fits well with the idea that information matters. For example Boisot (1995: 234ff) stresses that the use of information will support transactions independently from whether it is central or peripheral to the exchange. He distinguishes transactions as regards three dimensions: abstraction or concreteness of knowledge, degree of diffusion of knowledge and degree of codification (fig. 9.2). Markets are supported by well-codified, abstract information which is available to everybody. This information is above all related quantities and prices. It can be transmitted independent of the identity of the other party of the transaction. The three other forms Boisot distinguishes are bureaucracies, clans and fiefs. Compared to markets, knowledge in bureaucracies is restricted to a limited number of individuals. There are artificial barriers to diffusion and the distribution of knowledge is built upon roles and therefore impersonalized positions. In clans, communication constraints are imposed because knowledge is uncodified and concrete. Clans depend on a relatively small number of face-to-face contacts and exchange of information with insiders. They are held together by interpersonal trust and shared values as well as a common background. Their structure is non-hierarchical. The idea of clans is somehow near to the phenomenon of networks presented here, although the non-hierarchical structure of clans imposes some restrictions on the type of the networks.

Finally, Boisot points to the importance of fiefs. Historically, this term was related to territories and inhabitants over which a vassal was empowered to rule. In Boisot's terms fiefs are based on the exchange of uncodified knowledge which is hard to transmit. Their structure is highly personalized and hierarchical. The social acceptance of exercise of personal power is of major importance. Thus, fiefs are related to another type of network structures and they are more vertical and hierarchical by nature.

Traditionally, the idea of clans and fiefs has started from an anthropological point of view. However, many authors – especially those dealing with Asian economic structures – have pointed to the importance of social organization for economics. Although Boisot does not distinguish them as a category, multinational firms may also be introduced into his scheme. As their structure however is by no means given, their position is not predetermined.

These transaction modes are concepts that have two implications: On the one hand, they may help us to conceive meaningful aggregations of agents like in clans or fiefs. On the other hand, they give us information about the way exchange is done within these aggregates, e. g. exchange of information, and also in how far modes of transactions may differ. If we accept that societies may differ as regards their preferences for certain modes of transactions, the latter aspect may be interesting concerning its implications for the possibilities of interaction among members of different societies. Different forms of organization may also create distance between the members of different groups.

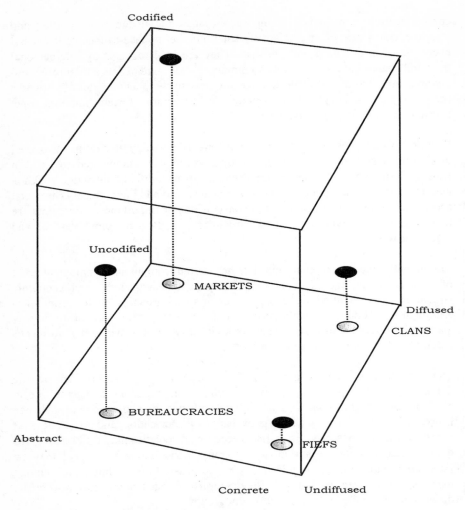

Fig 9.2: Information space, source: Boisot (1995: 237)

Biggart and Delbridge distinguish two other dimensions to characterize patterns of exchange (table 9.1). These are

- whether rationality is instrumental (based on a calculation of means to ends) or substantive (oriented towards values); common market models in international economics assume instrumental rationality and maximizing behaviour;

- whether it is universalistic (all exchange partners are the same) or particularistic (aspects of social capital matter shared with insiders).

Table 9.1: Patterns of exchange

	UNIVERSALISTIC	PARTICULARISTIC
INSTRUMENTAL RATIONALITY	exchange based on prices	exchange based on association
SUBSTANTIVE RATIONALITY	exchange based on moral	communal exchange

Source: Biggart and Delbridge (1999: 12f)

Spot prices are typical mechanisms working on markets. Agents' motive on markets is striving for individual gain. Agents are assumed to be autonomous, rational and individualistic. Markets form impersonal frameworks that are assumed to be self-regulating. Meanwhile exchange in associations is based on an interest in mutual gain. Networks may be typical examples for this. They rely on social ties and reciprocity. Moral frameworks of exchange are based on principles and values. Finally, communal exchange is relational. Agents have to be understood in their role as group members. It is the community of familiars or a collegial order that matters. Exchange relies on subordination to shared group norms.

What can be seen is that we have to distinguish different types of economic actors, different motives of agents for action and different relationships between agents. It matters with whom exchange is done and on which norms and principles exchange relies. Later we will see that a number of phenomena are nowadays subsumed under the headline of networks. While some of these belong to the category of associative exchange, others may be better described as communal exchange because they rely on a much stricter distinction between insiders and outsiders of their group which is often ethnically defined as in the case of Chinese networks.

Network-analytical measures used frequently in sociology are (Jansen 1998: 50)

- the density of networks,
- their cohesion,
- their multiplicity and overlapping in different aspects
- and the homogeneity of their members.

Granovetter (1973) has pointed to the strength of weak ties. Strong ties generally rely on homogeneity among agents. They imply the risk of sluggishness and closeness to the outside. Burt (1992) explains that weak ties may be a bridge between different clusters of agents. Agents having such an intermediate function have better access to non-redundant information. Meanwhile maintaining several strong ties is costly and only links agents that are already linked naturally be homogeneous characteristics. Weak ties may thus be important for mobility, processes of modernization, innovation and diffusion. Burt explains that intermediate agents with weak ties may bridge structural holes in the economy.

A point to be further analyzed within the context of mobility is how networks can be interpreted as spatial phenomena. Certainly, networks are mirrors of interdependence among agents, but what results can be derived as regards their spatial ties and flexibility? Do strong ties necessarily go along with spatial proximity? Do stable ties lead to immobility? These questions will be approached in the next two chapters.

9.3.2   Spatial ties of interaction: industrial districts and innovative milieus

The idea of networks structuring the economic system does not automatically answer the question about the spatial effects these patterns of interaction might have. However, the concept of industrial districts is in many ways very near to the network phenomenon and industrial districts are defined within a spatial context. This is why Loasby (1999: 5) states that industrial districts are "localized networks". They are reflexive with respect to space and time (Windler 1991: 26). Similarly Bergman et al. (1991b: 289) explain that the concept of the industrial district is a spatial variant of the network idea. Territory is not only a defined space of resources, it generates conditions of communication-language and collective learning. It creates technological and organizational rationalities. It is a process of simultaneous generation of dynamics and constitution of the networks that can be observed. Organizational dynamics are correlative to the dynamics of the local milieu. Industrial districts are sizeable and spatially delimited areas of economic activity. This idea may serve as a linkage between industrial and spatial economics (Belussi 1999: 13). Of course, in a world that is characterized by ongoing progress in the field of information and communication media, there is at first sight no reason why locations and proximity should be important for the generation of network specific assets. As regards the importance of proximity Audretsch and Weigand (1999: 134) explain that new technologies may be useful for the transmission of codified knowledge. The marginal costs of transmitting this knowledge across space are near to zero. Tacit (uncodified) knowledge on the other hand is context dependent. The costs of transmitting this knowledge rise with increasing distance. With respect to spatial ties of networks, the concept of the innovative milieu may deliver new insights. Nelson and Winter explain that the core of processes of innovation, learning, discovery and diffusion is the selection environment. This environment is the context that determines how the use of technologies changes. It comprises market- and non-market components, conventions, socio-cultural factors and institutional structures (Nelson and Winters 1977: 61 and also de la Mothe and Paquet 1998a: 6). This gives us a new understanding of the meaning of space for mobility and development. Innovative milieus give us an idea why space is more than a passive framework for mobile agents or a stage for political decision-makers. Space is not a simple relationship of economic functions defining activities' location and structure as well as the hierarchy of economic regions as a consequence of their internal logic (development from above). Garofoli (1991: 122) describes territory as "a sedimentation of specific and interrelated historical, social and cultural factors in local areas". This description has various implications:

- a definitional one: Interpreting space in this sense of "territory" may lead us to a much richer picture of regional development with territory as an active element rather than a passive container of mobile and immobile agents.

- The description underlines that history may create heterogeneity of territories.

- It assumes that local culture and other non-transferable local features are sedimented in space in order to give it its territorial face.

- As Bergman et al. (1991: 294) underline, processes of regional development are a result of many actors and protagonists belonging to networks of quite different dimensions (economic, cultural, technological, institutional and political exchange). It may be this interpretation of space that helps us to explain the many facets and patterns of regional development because the joint appearance of these features distinguishes one milieu from another. This is also why firms' locations may be considered strategic factors of development.

Many terms have however been used to describe geographic agglomerations of firms in an industry or related industries.[34]

- "An industrial cluster is a set of industries related through buyer-supplier and supplier-buyer relationships, or by common technologies, common buyers or distribution channels, or common labour pools." In this context clustering seems to denote close relationships rather than any statement about the geographical scale of this phenomenon.

- "A regional cluster is an industrial cluster in which member firms are in close geographic proximity to each other."

- "Industrial districts are concentrations of firms involved in the same industry or industry segment, that are embedded in the local community ...." Thus, we would have to distinguish between clusters in single industries (industrial district) or those clusters that involve a range of related industries (regional cluster).

- The idea of an innovative milieu underlines not only the idea of intensive linkages, but also that these are places of knowledge creation. Other terms like learning regions, regional systems of innovation or knowledge-based industrial

---

[34] For a survey of definitions see The Competitiveness Institute (2000).

clustering have been used in a similar context.[35] The term of industrial districts underlines the production aspect stronger, while innovative milieus emphasize innovation. However, the success of all these regions seems to be knowledge-based.

The different terms will in the following parts be used with a similar meaning. This is not to neglect the differences existing, but it is justified by the observation that they are used to describe "aspects of the same broad phenomenon" (The Competitiveness Institute 2000). This is in the literature reflected by a reliance on externalities and localized information flows as main explanations for the persistence of the different agglomerations.

In general, these clusters are characterized by a combination of

- a special set of relations among agents,

- which is enforced by a spatially immobile institutional/ political framework

- within a limited geographical space.

The following figure 9.3 summarizes the main elements of industrial districts.

Many authors have dealt with processes of knowledge creation within industrial districts and innovative milieus. Belussi (1999: 1) e. g. states that industrial districts can be characterized by an accumulation of locally sticky tacit knowledge. Industrial districts are understood as producers of contextual knowledge that is territorially specific. This is a process that is not only due to the network-specific advantages described above, but may also be fostered by political decision-makers. As de Vet (1993: 118) states international competition forces regions to mobilize their assets. Bergman et al. (1991b: 294) similarly underline that network participation enables regions to mobilize resources and gives access to vital information and knowledge. Innovative and informational processes within networks are from this point of view guided by their territorial base and the system of productive relations. The spatial milieu is therefore characterized by competences and skills not existing in other contexts. It is this stickiness of knowledge that creates spatial ties of networks. The knowledge-based interpretation of industrial districts implicitly contains the idea of economic space as a set of places where inputs are "consciously organized and enriched in a cognitive content" (Belussi 1999: 5). Ayadalot and Keeble (1998: 1) even state "that it is often the local environment which is ... the entrepreneur and innovator rather than the firm."

---

[35] See the different contributions in de la Mothe, J./ Paquet, G. (1998b) as an example.

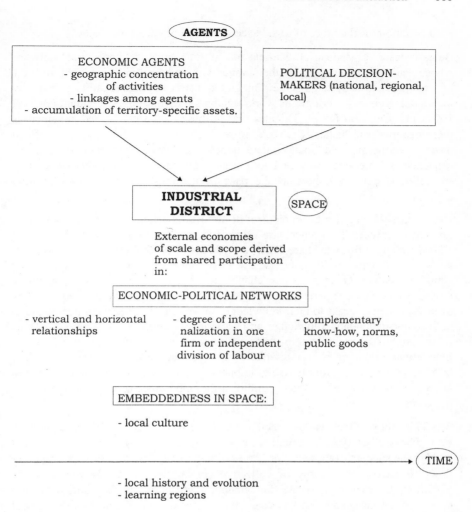

Fig. 9.3: Characteristics of industrial districts

Boschma and Lambooy (1999: 415) enumerate the following features of industrial districts:

- mobility of human capital as the carrier of tacit knowledge,
- transfer and feedback of information via dense networks of local actors,

- a common local culture of trust based on shared practices and rules.[36]

Belussi describes industrial districts as an inter-organizational hyper-network whose density is determined by the number and kinds of links. The point of view of local production systems is their integrated matrix of firms and this is also why locational decisions of single network members may not be independent (Belussi 1999: 11). Camagni (1999: 7) states that in these networks "space, assumed as mere geographical distance, is replaced by territory (or relational space) defined through economic and social interaction; time, usually understood as mere sequence of intervals on which to measure quantitative variations of smooth variables, is conceived here as the pace of learning and innovation/ creation processes."

Human capital seems to be an element of utmost importance for the creation of an innovative milieu. Thus, there are nowadays new trends in places like Silicon Valley for small firms to share expert knowledge (Streitfeld 2000: K9). This gives such firms - who would otherwise not have any possibility to get experienced Chief Executive Officers – a chance to survive in a highly competitive environment. Thus, experts are employed by several firms simultaneously. They offer these firms access to their knowledge and are on the other hand positioned to collect non-redundant knowledge and experiences from several sources. Thus, there may be important links to connect the various players in a spatial network or innovative milieu even if individual firms do not necessarily exchange their knowledge directly. With the rising impact of the internet rising, we may have to analyze in how far this is able to diminish the importance of space in innovative networks.

The Third Italy as well as other regions like Baden-Württemberg in Germany have been discussed as typical examples for a new industrial district (Piore and Sabel 1984). The success of these regions is according to Voelzkow (1999) among other things based on the supply of collective competitive goods. However, as he explains, the two regions are fundamentally different in that horizontal co-operation among small firms is characteristic for the Third Italy, while vertical integration of big companies is dominant in Baden-Württemberg. Those collective goods that are externally provided in Italy are produced within the companies in Germany. While in Italy, local governance is of major importance, the "Bundesland" is the main actor in Baden-Württemberg. We may suspect that the latter constellation is less flexible than the first.

To summarize: What is it that gives the industrial district its local character? As Amin and Thrift (1992: 587) point out, it is no longer industrial production. While traditional (Marshallian) industrial districts were self-contained territories,

---

[36] See Boschma and Lambooy (1999: 415); personal interviews in Silicon Valley have confirmed the importance especially of the local and interfirm mobility of human capital and the exchange of ideas.

nowadays physical backward and forward linkages have more and more become global. Thus, industrial districts are increasingly integrated into an international production chain. Nonetheless, many of the old districts have not lost their profile of expertise centers that has been historically developed. What holds them together are knowledge, creativity and innovative atmosphere. For their future it will be decisive "whether, without the hand, the head will loose its might or successfully engineer a transition into other industrial ventures."

The idea of networks and industrial districts is presently used in many contexts and we will have to take care not to define every clustering of firms as an industrial district per se. Park and Markusen (1995) have pointed out that there are several types of similar regions whose local embeddedness may be more or less strong. Furthermore, empirical investigation has shown that clustering may also be due to infrastructural aspects with firms' embeddedness in international and national rather than local networks within their parent firms. Schmutzler underlined that clustering can also be due to homogeneity of agents' locational preferences. This is why we may suggest that in industrial districts locational proximity has to be supplemented by a critical degree of intensity of interaction that is localized and an innovative atmosphere.

While transaction cost theory has frequently been used to deal with networks, this may not be appropriate for industrial districts. Of course, transaction costs are apt to handle the specificity of resources and uncertainty, but they are not able to deal with the phenomenon of embeddedness of agents in a local milieu (Colletis and Pecquer 1994: 15).

We may conclude that mobility is important in two ways in innovative milieus: On the one hand, local mobility of persons, ideas and information that is the source of an innovative atmosphere. On the other hand, flows in a much wider international context within which the innovative milieu is competing.

9.3.3   Networks, mobility and change

What is the relationship between networks and locational mobility? Up to now we have considered networks as stabilizing elements of the economy. Networks create relatively stable ties to agents and space. They are based on routines and may thus create rigidities. Whenever these ties are sensitive to distance, locational decisions among agents will be interdependent. We have to deal with interdependencies that are not exclusively related to prices. Networks and ties seem to be related to immobility. However, this is a very restricted point of view because of several reasons:

- Networks may be mobile in space, if they are able to relocate or cross large distances.

- Networks may offer opportunities for individuals and firms to integrate in new territories rather than restrictions for mobility (ethnic networks).

- Agents are integrated in a multiple set of networks that may offer them a number of alternatives.

How can agents tied to each other in different ways react to change? Let us e. g. first assume the simple case that change is created exogenously by a shock on locational attractivity and leave - for simplification - the question of individual evolution aside. The reaction to a shock on locational attractivity (triggered by changes in locational environment or attitudes and capabilities of agents) will be dependent on the following aspects:

- the attractiveness a new location offers (strength of the shock),

- the ties agents have developed to their old location (e. g. migratory biography, cultural ties, embeddedness),

- the strength of ties among agents,

- the possibility and willingness of agents tied to first-movers to follow them (advantages of network participation and possibility to build up new ties),

- the degree with which ties are sensitive to distance (geographical, cultural, legal, political distance; strength of agglomeration economies), the degree with which exchange can take place despite relatively large distances between agents.

Faist (1997a: 194) explains that spatial movement may strain, rupture, change or reinforce previous ties. Possible reactions to a shock may thus be:

- A breakdown of existing ties and a relocation of first-mover firms: This will be the case if the attractiveness of a new location is high, ties are distance-sensitive and embeddedness into relationships makes movement unfavourable. In that case, the losses from breaking up ties may not be that high that the advantages of a locational change are compensated. The firm acts like a global player permanently looking for new opportunities. Network ties are weak or non-existent.

- Network movement: This is probable, if the agents that are tied to the first-mover are willing and able to follow him. This depends on their capability to move, the strength of the ties and the distance-sensitivity of ties. If all these factors are strong enough, there may be relocation of (parts) of the network.

- Extension of ties in space and relocation of the first-mover: This will be true if ties are not too sensitive to distance. Leaving a location may not necessarily go along with cutting ties. Networks may have local or global extensions.

Finally, there may be ties that are rather strong and bound to space. These may be cultural ties or ties created by learning e. g. that might influence the willingness and ability of agents of different cultures to interact and to choose locations embedded into a different cultural background. These ties may render it advantageous to be immobile and to act within a framework whose rules are known.

Of course, setting the sources of change as exogenous to the system, simplifies the problem a great deal. Modelling dynamics in a setting of endogenous change will make it necessary to model relationships more detailed, e. g. as regards their direction and the possibility of some agents to exert power

- because they are mobile "pioneers" who determine the dynamics of the system,

- because they are dominant in that they may prevent partners from terminating a relationship or duplicating it with others and they may exclude newcomers from entering a network,

- because they may alter the organizational setup of a network,

- because they may dictate network responses to outside dangers and opportunities (Kamann 1991: 51).

Patterns of interaction among economic agents can therefore be characterized by three features: the strength of ties among agents and to a territory as well as the spatial extension of the network (distance sensitivity). Two of these dimensions are combined in table 9.2.

Table 9.2: The strength of ties and spatial extensions

SPATIAL EXTENSION STRENGTH OF TIES	AGGLOMERATED	SPATIALLY EXTENDED
WEAK	loose agglomeration	global market transactions
STRONG	local network	global network

As Tödtling (1999: 156) remarks embeddedness of firms into regional and national networks may be as important as embeddedness into national or even wider international networks. Thus, we will have to get better insights into the relationship among different spatial levels. Fuchs and Wolff (1999: 197f) explain that ties may also be relevant on a global scale. They may be useful to prevent the inertia that may be created in regional economies because stimulation for innovative behaviour from outside is more probable. Economic bridges to national and international markets are necessary. Nonetheless, globalization does not describe floating within an abstract space. As Amin and Thrift (1994: 259) describe local embeddedness also highlights

> "the importance of a set of local institutions and attributes in capturing global opportunities with significant positive effects on the local economy, so as to avoid notions of bounded and internally integrated territories."

One may thus argue that local and global ties are not alternatives. Any region is part of a larger, possibly global context. Whenever we analyze the localization of ties, we have to be aware of the wider national or even supranational horizon they are simultaneously embedded in. The global does not exist without the local and the other way round. The same is true for the relationship between international economics and intranational economics.

Even if there is globalization of interaction by flows, local groundedness of activities with locational mobility as a periodic and relatively longterm development may be important. Those types of interaction that serve as a basis for a good performance may be localized (e.g. information), while a firm may at the same time compete on global markets. Therefore, localization is different from putting up borders. If it is to be a successful strategy, penetration by stimuli from outside still has to be possible. The slogan therefore has to be "Act on a global scale from a local basis by letting stimulating impulses in." We thus get a very complex relationship between the mobility of locations and different types of interaction. This has been realized by business economics for a long time, which is reflected in the term "Think globally, act locally." The following matrix takes into account these global and local ties regions may have (table 9.3).

Table 9.3: Global and regional ties

local/regional ties global ties	LOCATION weak regional ties	LOCATION strong regional ties
TRANSACTIONS **weak global ties**	I fragmented/ isolated regions	II isolated industrial district
TRANSACTIONS **strong global ties**	III cathedrals in the desert	IV global regions

Source: Fuchs and Wolff (1999: 200), with permission from Metropolis Verlag

According to Fuchs and Wolff the different stylized constellations pointed out in table 9.3 tend to have the following strengths and disadvantages:

I. weaknesses above all in creating and adapting to novelty; such a constellation may also be the result of basic reversals in the environment destroying previous linkages;

II. high specialization; bad capability to adapt to changed environment, growth borders of a small market;

III. global ties above all by headquarters of big companies; no endogenous firm establishment in region; access to external know how and markets;[37]

IV. good potentials for global leadership; a good example for such a region might be Silicon Valley whose firms are leaders in global markets and at the same time share the advantages of their location.

These global and regional links of local economies are not only relevant from an economic point of view, but also as regards local politics that have to be updated

---

[37] This raises the question whether embeddedness into large companies can substitute local embeddedness.

according to the development of other locations in the region as well as global technological developments for example.[38]

Therefore, economic space is influenced by local and global aspects simultaneously. Individual decision-making is integrated into a spatial context of place and distance.

Are there further possibilities to characterize relationships and regions?

Hayter (1997: 341ff) distinguishes the dimensions

- degree of ownership integration and

- degree of coordination

to characterize industrial districts as one type of regions.

The degree of ownership integration describes the extent to which production is distributed among an interdependent social division of labour or concentrated within an internal division of labour. Coordination among firms refers to complementary behaviour in the sense of providing collective goods, adhering to common norms, being embedded in a community, trusting each other. Inherent in this is the assumption that localization is not a phenomenon that is limited to small firms, although industrial districts have mostly been analyzed within a context of small firms and even though multinationals are nowadays frequently considered footloose global players. It may as well apply to the local relationship of multinational's subsidiaries. "Regional clusters ... include industrial districts of small and medium sized craft firms, concentrations of high technology firms related through the development and use of common technologies, and production systems that contain large hub firms and their local suppliers and spinoffs." (The Competitiveness Institute 2000)

According to Hayter, this may be an approach to characterize the institutional basis of industrial districts. However, the degree of ownership integration can be considered a more or less legal concept and not an economic one. More interesting from a general spatial perspective might be a three-dimensional distinction of regions and relationships into

- horizontal or vertical relationships,

- strength of ties,

- importance of spatial proximity.

Figure 9.4 is intended to illustrate this. The axes of the ellipses delineate the strength of ties among or within firms and their orientation towards horizontal or vertical relationships. While the ellipsis in the upper part of the figure shows us

---

[38] This is also the result of a study by Heiduk and Pohl (2000) that was done in Chinese open zones.

examples without spatial agglomeration, the lower ellipsis has a look at similar cases where proximity among agents is important or at least observable. The third ellipsis at the left is to remind us that from an economic point of view all of these constellations evolve in a process of interaction among different agents. Nonetheless, there are a number of cases where political decision-making tried to foster developments similar to industrial districts and growth centers (technopoles). Finally, the local and global relations of the resulting regions are depicted at the bottom.

Horizontal is to describe relationships that are not necessarily based on competitive firms in one industry. Localized information flows may be important for a wide range of industries with common basic technologies. Thus, horizontal relationships denote a much broader scale of constellations in contrast to the buyer-supplier-relationships in vertically related industries.

Traditionally, the idea of industrial districts and embeddedness has been related to small firm agglomerations. However, the ideas described above also deal with large multinational firms as players. This is of course also due to their rising importance in the global economy. At first sight we may wonder whether there is any relationship between transnational corporations and local places. However, we have to remember that local may be understood in a sense of located and not in a sense of local isolation. Thus, subsidiaries of transnational corporations may be embedded locally, while at the same time being embedded into the corporate network. Mobility is a matter of relationships between firms, within firms and towards space.

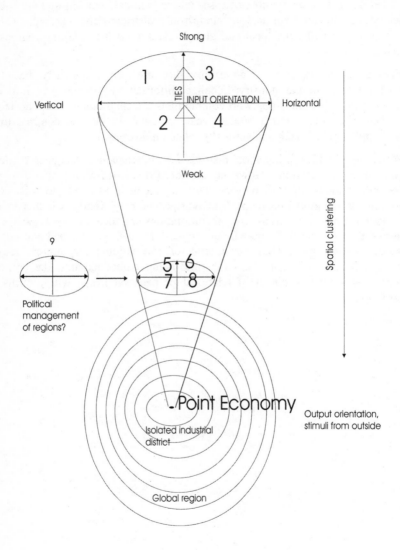

Fig. 9.4: Types of industrial districts

The resulting constellations might be characterized as follows:

1   strong vertical ties internalized in one firm or in a production chain (VERTICALLY INTEGRATED FIRM or PRODUCTION CHAIN) not necessarily combined with spatial proximity

2   weak vertical relations, SPOT-MARKET TRANSACTIONS WITH VERTICAL LINKAGES

3   strong horizontal ties by internalization in one corporation (HORIZONTAL INTEGRATION) or networking between independent firms

4   HORIZONTAL SPOT-MARKET COMPETITION

5   LOCAL PRODUCTION COMPLEX

6   INDUSTRIAL DISTRICT/ INNOVATIVE MILIEU...

7   This constellation seems to be a relatively rare one as there is no reason why agglomeration should occur, if ties are weak.

8   LOOSE AGGLOMERATION

9   political decision-makers trying to create TECHNOPOLES without historical evolution, but with an optimized plan in mind

As Dicken et al. (1994: 30,36) state the dilemma of today's firms is that they have to be globally efficient, multinationally flexible and capable of capturing the benefits of worldwide learning at the same time. Thus, we have to deal with complex global firms whose complexity is also reflected in their relationship to space. The degree of local embeddedness of transnational corporations subsidiaries may differ between companies and within them depending on the functions and activities in question. Within one company a highly globalized activity with important relationships outside the local area may be combined with another activity having predominant short distance business relationships. The same activity may in one company be localized and in the other globalized. Therefore, Bartlett and Goshal (1989) distinguish two key dimensions that lead us to four types of transnational subsidiaries (table 9.4):

Table 9.4: Transnational corporations and embeddedness

		STRATEGIC IMPORTANCE OF LOCAL ENVIRONMENT	
		low	high
LEVEL OF LOCAL RESOURCES AND CAPABILITIES OF THE SUBSIDIARY	**low**	implementers	black holes
	high	contributors	strategic leaders

Source: Bartlett and Goshal (1998), p. 122, reprinted by permission of Randomhouse Group Ltd. and Harvard Business School Press

Oinas (1995) enriches the idea of a local dependence of firms by localities depending on enterprises. These enterprises are called agents – in contrast to patients – because they have the power to initiate local change. Oinas adds further elements to explain why some firms (subsidiaries) are stronger embedded into the local environment than others.[39] These include

- fulfilling contact-intensive functions which make face-to-face interaction with mobile or immobile agents necessary. They are also called integrative functions. Moreover, the frequency and standardization of contacts will play an important role;

- ownership: Family-owned firms (which is for multinationals rarely the case today) pay more attention to their local image and have stronger relationships to local actors;

- age of the enterprise: an aspect which may be of ambiguous importance for embeddedness because in older enterprises there may be historical ties, but also more experiences with global action;

- factors related to the location.

The preceding chapters have given us an impression about the complexity of relationships among different agents. From a theoretical point of view, however, many questions still remain open: We still have to get more concrete ideas about network patterns and network evolution to assess their effect on spatial structures.

---

[39] Dependence on raw materials, fixed assets and proximity to customers of services will not be discussed here.

The relationship between markets, networks and firms have to be further analyzed. Moreover, the spatial dimension of networks deserves further interest. How is the local network system connected to global economic space? What roles may individual agents play in a network context? Which aspects determine the evolutionary pattern of networks? Network theories might give us an idea how non-price relationships might qualify our understanding of markets. These thoughts underline another time that mobility is a phenomenon that is much more complex than traditional theories might make us believe. Obviously, we have to recognize that multiple levels may be important in our analysis (mobility within the firm that may be integrated into networks, mobility of flows within networks, mobility of networks and spatial mobility on the basis of market mechanisms) and that interaction may to different degrees be tied to and influenced by territory.

As regards the relationship between innovative milieus and the organizational setting of the firm, many authors acknowledge that milieus may be more important for relationships among small firms. Therefore, Bergman et al. (1991b: 290) state that the function of space as a milieu might depend on the scale of firms. Other points of view have been presented above. This also underlines that firms, networks and markets are not purely alternative concepts. As regards individual transactions, there may be a choice whether to implement them inside the firm, within a network or on the market. But from a systemic point of view, firms and other agents are embedded into networks which are guided by price- and non-price interaction.

Altogether, the ideas presented in the last chapters have given us an understanding of mobility and space that goes far beyond traditional ideas about globalization and local phenomena. Traditionally, globalization has frequently been considered a phenomenon that renders space and time meaningless. Meanwhile, spatial or local aspects have been contrasted to this. The new understanding suggested here proposes that the global and the local have to be considered simultaneously, if we start our analysis from the idea of social relations stretched out in space. As Dirlik (1999: 40,44) describes the definition of global and local has to be understood in a more relative view of inside and outside. Place consciousness may imply a certain groundedness from below, but it does not necessarily go along with boundaries. Starting from an interaction-oriented point of view boundaries are porous and flexible. Networks can be defined without closing out the extra-local.

Thus, we may reach an idea of networks that are by nature neither exclusively local nor global, but more or less extended in space and more or less connected. This is also why on the other hand, the importance of the international/ global component is never fading when having a look at small-scale spatial phenomena.

9.3.4   Networks – an ethnic phenomenon?

The concept of networks being created by intensive, long-term interaction is strongly influenced by Western style thinking about network patterns. From a theoretical point of view, much interest has been paid to the networks versus markets discussion. Within this framework, networks cannot be analyzed in isolation from continuous interaction. Arguments for mobility within networks seem to be strongest when there is volatility of environmental conditions that renders embeddedness in networks more advantageous. Due to the missing clear-cut definition of networks another aspect of network mobility is frequently discussed.

The concept of networks however has also been prominent in the analysis of organizational structures in Asian economies.[40] Many authors have dealt with the influence of Chinese networks, but also with Korean chaebol and Japanese keiretsu as examples of business groups. E. g. wherever Chinese people live and work, the social networks they create seem to be similar in structure and mode of operation (Hamilton 1996a: 9). This shows that significant features of the Chinese way of doing business involve also a great degree of mobility. Chinese business is often explained by the strength of ties. However, it is a different kind of strength that is meant in this context than the one described before. Strength does not mean permanence of bonding, but rather strategic adaptability, flexibility and breadth of choice (Redding 1996: 27). Chinese networks are based on basic principles of organization of the Chinese society (religious values, family socialization, hierarchical principles...). These networks exist whether or not individuals interact (Hamilton 1996b). Fei (1992: 62) therefore describes that the Chinese society resembles concentric rings that are formed when a stone is thrown into a pond. Everyone stands at the center of the circles produced by his own social influence. Everyone's circles are interrelated. One touches different circles in different times and places. This is why linkage mechanisms are characterized by a capacity to realign relations and to cope with environmental turbulence (Redding 1996: 37,39). Chinese networks create multiple local assets that are located in the countries of origin and destination. They enhance mobility rather than restrict it. The description Faist (1997a: 193) gives of migrant networks may fit the differentiated phenomenon very well: Networks are "sets of interpersonal ties that connect movers, former movers and non-movers in countries of origin and destination".

The distinction between different types of networks shows that embeddedness does not necessarily have to be a local phenomenon, that it may be due to very different reasons and have different implications for mobility. Networks among overseas Chinese do not at all depend on spatial proximity. In contrast, the spread of a Chinese diaspora all over Asia may be one of the advantages these networks

---

[40] Questions of ethnic ties and their effects will also be dealt with in chapter 10.1.

offer. It is ethnic embeddedness in a group spread across space rather than spatial embeddedness we observe. The result is therefore not spatial agglomeration, but a global mosaic of relationships. It is not the "where" that counts, but the "who". Chinese networks offer a number of functions that support mobility. They are based on clans or regional identities, personal obligations and features of Chineseness. They help to control uncertainty by supporting the gathering of information, serving as stabilizing sources of supply and markets and cementing key relationships, but also in starting up a company (Redding 1990: 112).

Different societies may therefore be characterized by different types of network structures and logics as well as a differing importance of networks. Underlying this difference in the institutional character is a fundamental sociological difference (Hamilton 1996b: 284ff, 294). Chinese networks may allow higher dynamics in that they reflect rather than restrict the integration in local, regional and global environments. In addition to this, their reliance on general values of the Chinese society makes them suitable as institutionalized media in a number of fields (political, social, economic). Yeung (1998: 133) explains that intra-firm Chinese networks are tied by family and entrepreneurship, inter-firm networks are held together by friendship and partnership and extrafirm-networks between economic and political agents rely on intermediaries and political connections. Chinese networks seem to enhance mobility and international flows among Chinese people therefore may be more significant than between Chinese and other cultures. Indeed, this is confirmed by the existence of international Chinese associations based on kinship, locality, dialects or craft. These help in settling down at a new location, act as banks or trade information. Several authors report that a significant proportion of investment flows via ethnic Chinese connections and networks. Friends send funds to friends and relatives in host countries who invest on their behalf, so that those sums appear statistically as domestic investments. Moreover, there is a dominance of ethnic Chinese investments in mainland China. This is of course due to historical and cultural links as well as linguistic advantages, although it is not sure whether this is a specific Chinese phenomenon or a general principle. In a network context it can also be argued that special connections to local officials may be important (East Asia Analytical Unit 1995: 45f).

Rauch and Trinidade (1999) have tried to measure the effects of ethnic Chinese on countries' bilateral trade volume. Using a gravity equation they operationalized the existence of ethnic Chinese networks by the product of ethnic Chinese population shares in the respective countries considered. Their analysis confirmed that in Southeast Asia with its large Chinese communities and numerous direct connections between Chinese, ethnic networks above all help to match international buyers and sellers in an environment of uncertainty. In Southeast Asia a wide range of business niches is occupied by Overseas Chinese. This effect of enlarging the volume of trade is largest for differentiated products and much less discernable for homogenous products with reference prices on organized exchanges or those in trade publications. On the other hand, outside Southeast Asia, the influence of Overseas Chinese is quantitatively smaller. They constitute small fractions of the population, but nonetheless share close-knit networks. It can be assumed that these networks have the effect that community sanctions that deter opportunistic behaviour can be enforced. Members of the networks share their information thoroughly. However, the type of good considered does not seem to play an important role for the effect of these networks on trade flows. Thus, Rauch and Trinidade are able to make out geographical spaces where ethnic networks are of more or less importance and have different effects.

However, a certain type of organization does not necessarily have to be equally successful in any environment. Chinese controlled firms investing in the West for example often face business environments that are unfamiliar to them (East Asia Analytical Unit 1995: 250). Although the Chinese capability to transplant some of their cultural strengths and to interact with new environments is strong, their comparative advantages become most obvious in areas where rules and institutions are underdeveloped. The existence of Chinese networks lowers transaction and information costs. Chinese are thus apt to find niches. They create their own information networks. However, in Western societies, it is argued that market information seems to be distributed much more evenly. There are fewer niches that might be discovered by connections and networks. Therefore, Chinese comparative advantages may be little and sometimes there may even be hindrances for Chinese concepts of organization. Thus, although networks may be stabilizing or mobility enhancing by nature, there may be boundaries to the "transplantation" of cultural and organizational specialities to new localities.

9.4   Sociodynamics and stochastic approaches

"Zeit und Raum sind relativ." (Albert Einstein)

9.4.1 Modelling locational decision-making

The preceding chapters have argued that the possibilities to model non-price interaction in international economics are above all restricted by methodological aspects. One alternative methodological approach to deal with mobility as a phenomenon in space and time has been presented in the form of game-theoretic models. By making appropriate assumptions about the structure of pay-offs, we have been able to deal with interdependencies in locational choice. This chapter is to deal with another methodological approach that is adequate to cope with questions of interaction. This approach has become known as "sociodynamics" or "synergetics". Apart from its stochastic qualities, it is able to derive interesting dynamic patterns of spatial configurations.

Weidlich (1992: 39) defines synergetics as the science "of the macroscopic space-time structures of multicomponent systems with co-operative interaction between their units". Space is in this respect defined not in a geographical sense, but as regards to certain "states" the components of the system may take. Originally launched by Haken (1977), synergetics were applied to social systems by Weidlich who called this framework sociodynamics. The respective approaches are a combination of relevant mathematical methods, which are mostly stochastic and non-linear differential equations, and concepts of social sciences.

Because the approach is not at all common to economists, it will be necessary to explain a number of definitional terms and methodological aspects. These will first be enumerated and then be explained in more detail:

- general concepts for stochastic multicomponent systems:

  - stochastic transition rates,

  - Master Equation,

  - mean average equations;

- specific concepts to apply synergetics to social systems:

  - behavioural vector,

  - socio-configuration,

  - dynamic utility function.

The approach aims at modelling the relationship between the micro-level of individual decision-making and the dynamics of the macro-level by use of the Master Equation. It is accepted that individuals are able to choose from a number of alternatives so that it will not be possible to work with deterministic equations of motion within a sociodynamic context. This is a difference to the models of international economics presented above that assumed that it is possible to derive such equations by starting from the assumption of rational and completely informed agents striving for maximization. Methodologically, sociodynamics therefore works with stochastic approaches. In addition to this, the models are cyclical and non-linear because interaction between micro- and macrolevels is assumed.

The explanation of the approach will proceed along an example: Let us assume a system of C regions. The decisions of individuals or firms refer to the choice of one of the regions as their location. First, the relevant variables of the system will be presented:

a) collective material variables: m

Extensive variables, whose value is proportional to the size of the system, are distinguished from intensive variables. An extensive variable is e. g. the difference between the number of firms staying in each of the locations. Intensive variables in contrast describe densities e.g.

b) extensive personal variables: n

We assume that firms make decisions about different topics. One of these is the choice of their location. Only this choice is explained in the restricted model used here. More complex versions however may be feasible. For any of these aspects of economic life, agents are able to choose among a number of alternatives, in our case locations, $i=1,2...C$. Firms that are homogenous with respect to certain criteria are grouped into *subpopulations* P^a. The attitudinal index i and the background index a are not related to the size of the system. We are able to state that n_i^a firms of subpopulation a have the "attitude" i. We get a vector of n across all subpopulations and attitudes.

c) intensive personal variables: υ

They describe the internal characteristics of firms depending on the attitudes considered and the subpopulation.

d) trend and control parameters: κ

These are coefficients that are relatively constant in time and which describe background variables of the subpopulations as well as control parameters to represent certain boundary conditions. These are e. g. the agglomeration and dispersion parameters among and within the subpopulations that will be introduced later.

The configuration of the system thus has the form (m,n,υ,κ). If these values are constant, we have a stable macro-equilibrium. However, we are interested in analyzing the dynamics of the system within several steps:

1. Characterization of the system

First, the *behavioural vectors* of the system are defined. These consist of a multidimensional space that represents the types of decisions the firms have to make. The number of dimensions of this space will be proportional to the complexity of the system. There are i alternatives within any behavioural aspect. The points within the space reflect the choice-set individuals face. Therefore, this approach elucidates the fact that there is a set of alternatives behind every visible action that were rejected by the decision-maker. Economic agents have the possibility of choice. In our special case the decision to be made is the choice of a location. As described, agents are aggregated into relatively homogenous subpopulations. The *socio-configuration* of the system which gives us information about the number of firms in each of the subpopulations choosing location C thus can be described by the following notation: $n = \left\{ n_1^1,...,n_C^1,n_1^a...n_C^a,n_1^P...n_C^P \right\}$

Afterwards, a *utility function* of the subpopulation with respect to the behavioural vector is defined $-\infty < u_i^a(n,\kappa) < \infty$. This describes the utility of an agent from choosing a certain location. Within this utility function it is possible to integrate preferences for locations or agglomeration parameters for example. κ is - as described above - a set of trend parameters including certain relatively constant features of the members of a subpopulation (biographic, cultural or certain restrictions for behaviour e. g.) They are represented as constant parameters within the utility function. The utility function is an important element guiding the decision-making of economic agents. However, it is much more flexible than the price mechanisms used by traditional models in international economics. Reiner et al. (1988: 181) propose to introduce the following elements into the utility function:

- an agglomeration term which catches all the influences on the attractivity of a region that are proportional to its size or the number of agents within the region,

- a saturation term that describes negative effects of growth of a region, [41]

- a preference term for all those factors that are independent from the size of the region. This may be related to characteristics of economic space as well as of the agents making their choice within this space,

- variables that are external to the region, e. g. distances between regions.

The utility function is thus able to catch the interaction within as well as between subpopulations, e. g. in form of tendencies of agglomeration or dispersion (Weidlich 2000:233). The definition of the choice-set, the coefficients in the utility function and the definition of subpopulations are therefore important determinants of the dynamics of the system (Reiner et al. 1988: 179). The formulation of the utility function requires detailed empirical research and prudent choice of the relevant parameters. The utility function is an open concept in so far as it is able to catch material as well as immaterial aspects, rational and irrational behaviour and dynamic developments of utility as a source of evolution or motivation potential. This may be an advantage compared to traditional concepts

---

[41] Distinguishing different subpopulations, we can work with internal and external agglomeration parameters within the subpopulations or among them and with a negative or positive sign.

in international economics. Weidlich also states that time lags can be introduced easily.

2. Dynamics

Change is in these models represented by *probabilistic transition rates* of the relevant variables per unit of time. We deal with Markov-processes. That means that it is possible to derive the probability distribution of a set of variables for the future, if the distribution in the present is known. Probabilistic modelling leads to the fact that members of an ensemble of identical structure can develop in different states. The best information available is the probability that the system reaches a certain state.

Changes on the microlevel can occur, if agents change from behaviour i to j (location i to j). Methodologically, individual transition rates are defined that are dependent on the utility functions of the agents. Agents compare the utility derived from possible locations and make their choice according to the highest utility. Transition rates describe the change in the probability that a firm changes its location from i to j per unit of time. Transition rates per unit of time may e.g. have the form $p_{ji}^a = v \times e^{(u_j^a(n_{ji}^a,\kappa)-u_i^a(n,\kappa))}$. As the transition rates in our case are dependent on macrovariables (the distribution of agents in space), we get a relationship between macro- and microlevel. Individual transition rates are a function of a mobility factor v and the push-pull factors of the region. While the latter can be found in the exponent, the migration factor is in the basis of the term. Big differences in the attractiveness of locations lead to high transition rates. The mobility factor comprises those effects that make migration between locations easier independent from its direction. The mobility factor thus introduces a degree of mobility. This may include costs of mobility like transportation or information costs. The push-pull factor in contrast describes the specific use of migrating from i to j and the relative preferences between the two alternatives. This factor has an asymmetric impact on the choice of different regions and depends on the direction of movements.

Transition rates thus have the following characteristics:

- They are stochastic by nature.
- They describe individual choice in dependence from macrovariables of the system.

The macrovariables in turn change in dependence from the aggregated microeconomic changes. Together with individual decision-making, the socio-configuration of the system changes:

a)   There may be a change of locations from i to j:

$$n_{ji}^a = \left\{ n_1^1, ..., n_j^a + 1, ..., n_i^a - 1, ... n_C^P \right\} \quad \text{or}$$

b) there may be market (entries or exits) into i: $n_{i+/-}^a = \left\{ n_1^1, ..., n_i^a + 1, ..., n_C^P \right\}$

In the following we will only deal with the former alternative. If n firms change their locations with the same transition rate, the *configurative transition rate* is

$$w_{ji}^a = p_{ji}^a \times n_i^a .$$

3. Equation of motion for sociodynamics

The *Master Equation* is the equation of motion for sociodynamics. It includes the evolutionary equations for the probability distribution of the macrovariables of the system P(m,n,υ,t).

If stochastic fluctuations are recognized, P (n,t)[42] is the probability to find socio-configuration n in time t. The Master Equation is formulated in dependence of time:

$$\frac{dP(n,t)}{dt} = \sum_{i,j,a} \left(w_{ij}^a (n_{ji}^a) \times P(n_{ji}^a, t) - w_{ji}^a (n) \times P(n,t) \right)$$

The equation includes the probabilities of inflows from neighbouring configurations as well as outflows to neighbouring configurations.

Thus, we are able to describe an average development of the spatial economic system in the configuration space and the development of the probability of derivations from the average behaviour (depending on the peaks of the resulting probability distribution of spatial states).

The Master Equation reflects the change in the probability of all possible distributions. It contains macro-effects of individual behaviour modelled stochastically. If the subpopulations under examination are sufficiently big, the effects of changes on the microlevel are small. The only exception are those cases in which the unpredictable behaviour of individuals leads to strong effects and which are called social phase transition. In that case the most probable path of

---

[42] Here, we do not take changes of υ into account.

development gets instable and there is a bifurcation in a multimodal distribution because variables take critical values.

Neglecting fluctuations we are able to work with expectation values and quasi-deterministic models. We therefore use quasi-averages. They are derived by looking at the bundle of trajectories at a point in time (locally concentrated clusters of stochastically evolving systems). Then the average future development of these trajectories is derived. Thus, we get a weighed distribution of possible equilibria and we get a transition rate as a function of the quasi-meanvalue within a system of non-linear equations. The reason why we are not able to work with common averages is that this is not possible when distributions have several peaks. In that case common averages, which are uniquely defined values, would lead to an improbable value in-between the peaks. Quasi meanvalues describe the mean path of stochastic trajectories at each point of the configuration space. The stochastic trajectory of the system performs a "stochastic hopping" from a given point in the configuration space to neighbouring points. The different directions have different probabilities determined by the transition rates. The weighted mean over these "hopping processes" from a given point is the equation of the preferential mean direction and mean velocity by which the trajectory bundle proceeds (Weidlich 2000: 77). However, whenever there is a phase transition averaging will not be helpful at all. In addition to this, averaging by definition eliminates all those behaviours that are different from the average. This is why an additional look at the range and variance of the distribution may be helpful.

Weidlich uses this method to describe for the example of two subpopulations their choice between two regions.[43] By simulating different values of the parameters described above, he models the development of quasi-meanvalues and the stationary probability distribution. It is thus a 2x2-model with two subpopulations and two regions he uses. For different parameter constellations he is able to derive distributions with one as well as two peaks. In addition to this there may be constellations with never ending migration. This result is in contrast to the equilibrium orientation of international economic theory. He shows that there may be phase transitions in the system, if agglomeration and dispersion parameters are allowed to change slowly.

The most important parameter is $\kappa^{\mu\nu}(\kappa^{\nu\nu}/\kappa^{\mu\mu})$ as the expression of agglomeration trends/ tendencies of dispersion within subpopulations μ and ν and among them.

---

[43] A similar method has been applied by Bertuglia et. al. in order to model the interdependent choice processes of the adoption of new technologies, modes of transportation and location; see Bertuglia et al. (1995); the figures and the calculations on which these are based are also taken from Weidlich (2000) with permission from Gordon and Breach Publishers.

The results and dynamics of the models are illustrated in flux diagrams as well as probability distributions. The axes show the differences in the distribution of the two subpopulations in the two regions with the center reflecting a symmetrical distribution and the edges asymmetrical distributions of each of the subpopulations being in one of the regions (B,C) or both in the same. Different scenarios can be imagined depending on the values of the key parameters:[44]

Scenario 1:

If there is weak, but symmetric interaction among the subpopulations that leads to dispersion among them in combination with weak tendencies of agglomeration within each of the subpopulations, a symmetrical structure of both regions will be probable (fig. 9.5a,b). Other distributions are possible, but with a much lower probability.

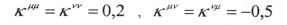

$$\kappa^{\mu\mu} = \kappa^{vv} = 0,2 \quad , \quad \kappa^{\mu v} = \kappa^{v\mu} = -0,5$$

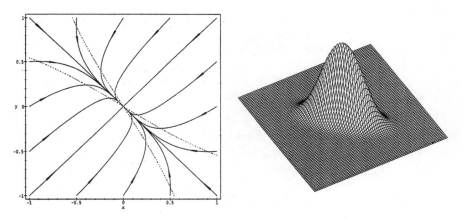

Fig. 9.5a,b: Sociodynamic simulations – case I, source: Weidlich (2000: 90), with permission from Gordon and Breach Publishers

Scenario 2:

If there is strong dispersion among the subpopulations and strong agglomeration within them, the distribution will be asymmetrical with a majority of each of the

---

[44] The following examples do not explain the parameters in detail. They are meant as an illustration of the method and the resulting dynamics.

subpopulations staying in one of the regions and separation among the subpopulations (fig. 9.6a,b). The symmetrical distribution has a lower probability.

$$\kappa^{\mu\mu} = \kappa^{\nu\nu} = 0,5 \qquad \kappa^{\mu\nu} = \kappa^{\nu\mu} = -1,0$$

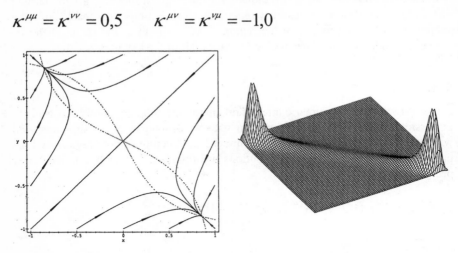

Fig. 9.6a,b: Sociodynamic simulations – case II, source: Weidlich (2000: 92), with permission from Gordon and Breach Publishers

Scenario 3:

If interaction among subpopulations is asymmetrical in the sense that one group wants to be near the other, but the other tries to avoid this and if these effects are only weak, there will be a symmetrical distribution with spiralling dynamics (fig. 9.7a,b).

$$\kappa^{\mu\mu} = \kappa^{\nu\nu} = 0,5 \qquad \kappa^{\mu\nu} = -\kappa^{\nu\mu} = 1,0$$

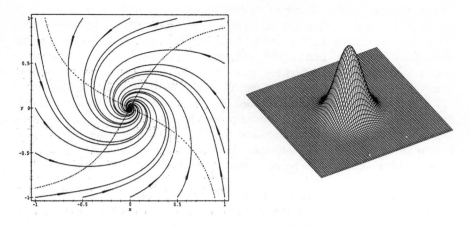

Fig. 9.7a,b: Sociodynamic simulations – case III, source: Weidlich (2000: 93), with permission from Gordon and Breach Publishers

Scenario 4:

If the effects of scenario 3 are strong, there will be no stable equilibrium, but only metastable states with a longer lifetime than other transient states (fig. 9.8a,b).

$$\kappa^{\mu\mu} = \kappa^{vv} = 1,2 \qquad \kappa^{\mu\mu} = -\kappa^{vv} = 1,0$$

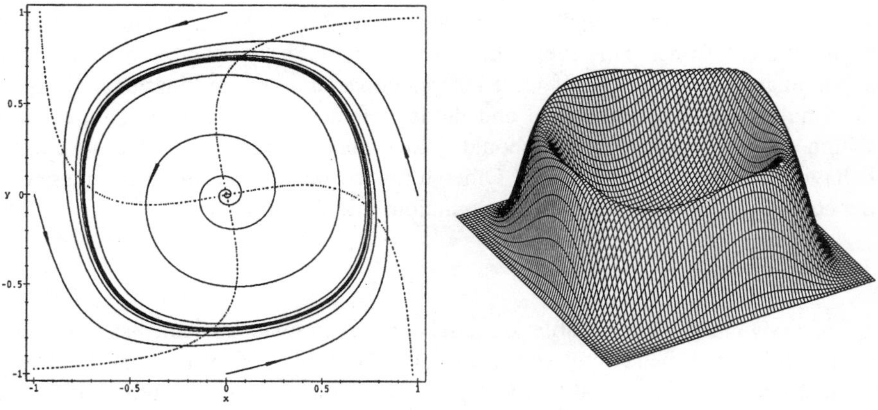

Fig. 9.8a,b: Sociodynamic simulations – case IV, source: Weidlich (2000: 94), with permission from Gordon and Breach Publishers

These examples give us a new understanding of the importance of equilibria in spatial dynamics modelling The advantages of this approach can be found in the empirical foundations of the utility function. The models have been tested empirically under a number of different conditions.[45] What we observe empirically with huge numbers are the meanvalues of the system. The way from empirical observation to theory is the following: First we start from an empty utility function which is afterwards filled up with parameters and variables that fit the empirical observation. This can be proved by correlation analysis. Regional utilities are determined from empirical migration data. These are correlated to certain key determinants of migration. However what remains open is whether these correlations are able to reflect logically causal relations.

As the choice between different locations in these models is a discrete choice, regions have to be predefined although a very fine structuring of regions should be compatible with computer simulations that are not too complex. The image of different locations within an attitude space in addition to this reflects very well the importance of individual agents' spatial perceptions. The multidimensional attitude space shows that individuals are positioned on the basis of a number of decisions that may be interdependent.

However, the state of the art in this field still leaves many questions as regards its application to economics, but also possibilities open that are of special interest for international economics. These problems may be less due to methodological aspects, but rather to a stronger need of interdisciplinary co-operation between economics and natural science where these methodologies were developed. Thus, it is assumed that agents choose between alternative locations. This may be adequate in the case of migration of persons, but is not able to explain mobility of multinational firms. However, this problem could be solved by choosing subpopulations adequately. If we take functional units of multinational firms as the smallest units of the model and model interaction between functional units within a firm correctly, this should allow good insights into the locational behaviour of multinational firms. Other forms of interaction might be integrated depending on the apt choice of subpopulations and their interaction.

To conclude:

- Sociodynamic theory is able to model changes in macrovariables as a function of individual behaviour (individual in the sense of groups of internally homogenous subpopulations that may be aggregated at different levels and according to different criteria).

- It gives a hint on the dynamic processes describing spatial evolution.

---

[45] See Weidlich, W./ Haag, G. (1988).

- As Weidlich explains, changes within the system may be combined with changes outside the system (e. g. interaction of economic, political and cultural levels). This has not been realized in the simple approach explained here, but it may be true within an extended approach that considers configurational variables in the political or cultural area that are entered into the utility function. Weidlich (2000: 234) calls this a "grand vision of an expansive modelling procedure finally integrating everything." Anyway, he admits that such a system will be characterized by strong indeterminism.

9.4.2   Modelling innovative behaviour and change

Chapter 9.1 has dealt with the relationship between novelty, mobility and change. Can sociodynamics offer useful starting-points also in this respect? Brenner applies a stochastic model to the problem of variation and imitation.[46] This being a rather general problem, it seems promising to use similar principles to model spatial behaviour of firms, e. g. choice of new locations or of interaction with agents at new locations. The approach explained below is evolutionary by nature and takes into account the features that were explained in chapter 9.1 (motivation for change, search and evaluation of new alternatives).

The explanation will progress by answering the following sequence of questions:

- How are alternative choices of behaviour evaluated? What role do experiences play in this respect?

- What is the motivation of agents for change?

- What about the role of first-movers and imitators?

- How can we derive macro developments from micro decision-making?

We start from the question: Why do agents choose new behaviours (locations) and why are there followers of this behaviour? How does this affect the macro-dynamics of the system?

a)   Evaluation of alternative choices

There are N decision-makers (i=1,...,N) and a given set of alternatives I=1,...A.[47] The choice of each location results in a stochastic utility with a given probability distribution of utilities. Information about the locations is gained from own experiences as well as others' experience. Experiences η_i describe the average utility a decision-maker expects from choosing a location. Experiences are

---

[46] See Brenner, Th. (1996).

[47] This shows that the alternatives are still predefined in the model. Novelty refers to switching from one alternative to another.

updated in the course of time and old experiences are replaced by new ones. The information gained from others depend on the amount of communication from one decision-maker to another.

$$\eta_i(I,t+\Delta t)=(1-\sum_{j=1}^{N}\delta(I=I_j(t))\times k_{ij})\times\eta_i(I,t)+\sum_{j=1}^{n}\delta(I=I_j(t))\times\kappa_{ij}\times u(I_j(t),t)$$

$\eta_i(I,t+\Delta t)$ describes the experience of a decision-maker i about the alternative I at time $t+\Delta t$. This experience results from the weighing of old experiences $\eta_i(I,t)$ and new utilities $u(I_j(t),t)$. These two factors are weighted by k_{ij}, the intensity of communication from decision-maker j to i. Depending on this parameter old experiences are partly replaced and new are added. δ has the function that only decision-makers who choose the alternative $(I=I_j(t))$ can make new experiences about an alternative. Experiences help decision-makers to judge new alternatives.

b)   Motivation for change

Change is motivated whenever decision-makers are not satisfied with their current status. Satisfaction is derived from the level of satisfaction in the last period and the outcome of new experiences. These are compared with a certain level of aspiration. The motivation for change depends on a constant motivation for change as well as the present level of satisfaction.

$$s_i(t+\Delta t)=(1-\kappa_s)\times s_i(t)+\kappa_s(u(I_i(t),t)-\alpha_i(t))$$

s is the level of satisfaction as long as the same alternative is chosen several times. κ is a weighing factor. Old satisfaction levels are updated with the direction of the update depending on the difference between realized utility and aspiration level α. Agents will desire to change their situation whenever satisfaction is below zero. Moreover, there are other reasons why behaviour may change. This is true because we may assume a constant motivation for change $m_i(t)=m_0-s_i(t)$ if $s_i<0$ or $m_i(t)=m_0$ if $s_i\geq0$.

c)   Probabilities of variation (first-movers) or imitation (followers): p_v, p_I

Variation describes the fact that from time to time firms try new alternatives by chance. v_V is a general likelihood of variation. The probability of choosing a new alternative depends on the tendency of an agent towards variation (choosing alternative J), on his motivation for change and his experiences before.

$$p_v(i,J,t) = v_v \times m_i(t) \times e^{\xi \times \eta_i(J,t)}$$

Similarly a probability for imitation (imitating decision-maker i) describing learning from others can be derived. This probability has to imply a term that secures that only satisfied pioneers are imitated.

$$p_I(i,j,t) = v_I \times m_i(t) \times e^{\xi \times \eta_i(Ij(t),t) \times Q(s_j(t))}$$

v_I is the general likelihood of imitation. Compared to the term for variation above, imitation is based on those agents that were satisfied. This is implied in Q which has the value zero, if satisfaction is negative or s if satisfaction is positive.

From these probabilities, we can derive the transition rates of changes r e. g. in locational constellations. They comprise the probability that there is one firm as a first-mover at the location and the probabilities of several others imitating locational behaviour that has been chosen by others. This is related to the idea of heterogeneity of agents.

$$r_i(J \leftarrow I,t) = p_v(i,J,t) + \sum_{j=1}^{N} \delta(I_j(t) = J) \times p_I(i,j,t)$$

Similarly to the approach described before the Master Equation may be helpful to derive the quasi-meanvalues and probabilities of different states of the system. Thus, locational choice would be assumed to have strong parallels to patterns of innovative behaviour. There are interdependencies among the micro- and macrolevel that are due to to interdependent search processes and communication.

What about the applicability of this approach for the explanation of patterns of mobility? First of all the combination of stochastic aspects with certain rules of evaluation seems to be a good starting-point to explain mobility. Furthermore, the elements included fit our ideas about the determinants of mobility very well. The fact that experiences play a role for spatial decision-making in a world of uncertainty is broadly accepted. Moreover, follower effects in the sense of firms learning from the experiences of others have been discussed. Thus, imitation should be a meaningful concept as well. Heterogeneity among agents in the sense of first-movers (choosing variation) and followers (imitators) seems to be a promising concept. Thus, even if the model presented is not taylor-made for our purpose, similar approaches might offer methodological opportunities to further develop our formal theories.

10 Geography, culture, organization and politics as determinants of distance

The basic assumption of the approaches chosen is that mobility is embedded into space and time. Space has been integrated into traditional economic models in the form of country- and city-points without extensions or regions as well as distance. Initially, the concept of geographical distance has been transferred to price concepts in international economics by using transport costs. Concerning mobility distance matters because it influences the volume of flow of goods e.g. However, transport costs do not primarily influence the direction of flows as they are often assumed to be unspecific as regards spatial direction. However, there are more determinants of distance influencing mobility. Political borders create distance because they may go along with barriers to trade and factor mobility. Thus, borders create distance in space that are discontinuous. This has been well acknowledged in the literature. Similar effects may be due to cultural distance or different organizational logics as will be shown in the next chapters. These are structures in space that are not necessarily congruent to political borders, but are often measured along them.

10.1 Culture and organization

"Culture remains generally invisible and, when visible, we usually think it causes problems." (Adler 1997: 98)

Choosing only one of the numerous definitions, culture has been defined as a

"system of widely accepted beliefs and internalized values that determines the actions and behaviour of people. Culture at a national level reflects the socio-cultural background, the historical evolution and the ideological concepts of a country." (Lang 1998: 5)

Culture can be supposed to influence interaction and locational choice strongly. A focus of the analysis will therefore have to lie on the patterns of interaction within and between members of different cultures. The following chapter will argue that there is a relationship between patterns of mobility and those elements that might be subsumed under the headline of culture. Thus, in contrast to the culture-free point of view, approaches of culturalists will be presented (culture-bound argumentation).

- It will be argued that members of one society or culture seem to be inclined to choose certain patterns of transacting and organizing. While there are some societies that tend to rely on contacts within their own group, others seem to distinguish less between insiders and outsiders.

- As regards its relationship to organization culture is about how problems are solved, how authority is exercised and how teamwork operates (Schreyögg 1994: 4), but also on whether individuals or collectives matter.

- Different cultural habits go along with different implications for mobility within and among cultures. Cultural distance may be important to explain the way members of different cultures do or do not interact.

Culture is a phenomenon that is difficult to handle as regards its spatial borders. It is usually related to societies, frequently measured for nations or countries, but nonetheless often correlated with regional, ethnic, religious and linguistic groups. Lacking availability of data and the fact that nations are – besides political entities – also historically developed groups may perhaps justify the fact that "measurements" of culture are often applied to nations. Nonetheless, we have to keep in mind that ethnic and religious groups often transcend political country borders. As Ronen and Shenkar (1985: 441) describe: "Reporting a country's internal diversity is important." There are multicultural nations as well as multinational cultures (in a double sense as will be seen later) (Schreyögg 1994: 3). And the US is a good example for a nation that was formed out of an ethnic mixture.

Considering the mobility effects of culture, some authors have pointed to the example of China's overseas people (ch. 9.3.4). They seem to form powerful informal networks that are stateless and stitched together by factors other than spatial proximity (Sender 1991: 29). They enable their members to cross borders with ease. It has been stated that - because of this common culture - overseas Chinese treat the Southeast Asian region (where their presence is strongest) as a single borderless economy. It is a "seamless web" they create. Other observations underline the importance of cultural or ethnic proximity. Kotkin's (1992: 219) statement confirms this view: "Most of Hong Kong's Indian businesses - from the tiny two man operation to the giant conglomerate – fit the classical mold with extended families providing the linkages between various national markets." Gould (1994) comes to the result that immigration into the US increases US bilateral trade with immigrants' countries of origin. Even if the power of these networks may sometimes be considered as exaggerated (Brown 1998), they may be an example that culture may affect mobility in a way that is stronger than national boundaries. Thus, we can state that whenever culture is a feature that is independent from location and borders, it may enhance mobility, change its direction, but also set borders. The mobility horizon of people may be widened to all those locations where other people resp. firms of the respective culture are located.

What is it e. g. in the case of the overseas Chinese that holds their networks together and that creates the distinction between insiders and outsiders? Redding argues that first of all family ties are of major importance. In a wider context these are complemented by perceptions of regional identities and personal networks as well as a feeling of "Chineseness" (Redding 1990). Interpersonal ties – "guanxi" – are also important. Hamilton and Biggart (1988: S85) even state that Chinese have developed special techniques to aid forward and backward linkages. Lang (1998: 37) calls this "guanxixue" or "connectionology". Even if these networks are able to enhance mobility, their functions are limited to a specific set of agents and their locations. Sometimes, it has been doubted however that the principles of Chinese capitalism will function beyond the borders of East Asia. Therefore, Chinese networks may represent a very specific example which is however interesting in the context of mobility (East Asia Analytical Unit 1995: 250).

Redding (1990: 7) states that economic culture is a set of connections between socio-cultural values and economic behaviour that create a unique constellation of features. Hall (1976) distinguishes high context and low context cultures. High context cultures deal with concrete and uncodified data in face-to face situations that are complex. Meanwhile low context cultures are oriented towards the selective use of codified abstract data in simple impersonal settings. High context actions are rooted in the past, slow to change and highly stable. The reason for this is that uncodified transactions lack a definition that facilitates abstraction. High context cultures make a greater distinction between insiders and outsiders. Codification is not necessarily a matter of what can be codified, but also what is intended to be codified. Whenever channels are preferred that rely on stable ties, interpersonal relationships and shared traditions, codification needs not be necessary. This emphasizes another time the special attention that should be paid to flows of information and the high complexity of this topic. While flows of homogenous goods may well be analyzed on markets, information exchange may make a difference between insiders and outsiders and leads to more complex and specific forms of interaction.

Thus, culture seems to be a matter of being bound into certain modes of transactions rather than a matter of political nationality or personality. However, Boisot (1995: 297f) states that we can assign dominant characteristics to certain nations. He names the Japanese society as an example of a high context culture because of the nation's marked preference for the use of restricted codes. Pre-modern societies naturally seem to stick more in the low part of the I-space that was already presented in chapter 9.3.1 (fig. 9.2) because of their particularistic cultural values and their underdeveloped communication infrastructure. Nonetheless, Boisot stresses that culture is never a unitary object with a single location in the I-space, but a scatter of points with a center of gravity that defines the culture's core value in the I-space with a certain level of cultural tolerance around it. The scatter is related to different transactions pursued regardless of the person acting. Thus, the same person can use different modes in different transactions, but also different persons may differ according to their choice. For example, the "center of gravity" of the US is – according to Boisot - grouped around the "market region", while Britain is closer to the "clan region". France with its "dirigiste" traditions is more plausibly a bureaucratic culture. There are centripetal cultures whose institutions are closely bunched together in the I-space as well as centrifugal cultures whose institutions are widely dispersed. In centripetal cultures, scatter ceases to matter, while in centrifugal cultures, it is the scatter that matters and not the centre of gravity. Thus, there may be cultures that share a common centre of gravity, but are nonetheless different because of their scatter. It is a culture's "configuration" that gives it its particular character. Sometimes, political strategies may aim at creating a centripetal cultural order as in the case of Marxism-Leninism in China for example. Nonetheless, culture and cultural centers of gravity are from the very beginning not matters of nation-state borders.

Although it may only change slowly, culture is not a static framework. As regards cultural evolution Boisot analyzes how China's state-owned enterprises seem to be stuck in a fief culture, while Japan is becoming more and more centrifugal despite the pull of fiefs and clans although both share a Confucian tradition. Boisot describes present dynamics in China's private small enterprises as a move to a network capitalism. Similarly, he states that many large Western firms are moving from an overinvestment into markets and bureaucracies to networks. Applied to China's and Japan's development we can e.g. see that it has proceeded in completely different modes. In China, resistance to outward technologies has been strong. The Chinese religion of Heaven has made the perception of rival civilizations impossible for a long time. Pressure to adopt other technologies was low. Meanwhile – according to Boisot - Japan has switched from a system of "Japanese spirit, Chinese Technique" to "Western Technology, but Japanese spirit". In Japan the necessity to learn from other cultures has always been higher than in China. Even if these hypostheses can be discussed, they imply the idea of a common dynamic development of societies. Nonetheless, forces of modernization in China have neither been equal in all parts of the country nor in all parts of society. State-owned enterprises have developed differently from private. Moreover, strong centrifugal forces can be observed in the Southern parts of China (provinces of Guangdong, Fujian and the quasi-capitalistic enclave of Shenzen) and increasingly also in other parts – a phenomenon of cultural evolution supported by political decentralization and creation of special conditions. This shows that even in a centrally led state, culture – defined in this way - is different from state borders, a phenomenon which is strengthened by the generally cellular structure of the Chinese society (Boisot 1995: 402).

Finally, this idea of culture gives us an impression about what may be happening inside a society. It leaves the question of what happens at its borders or when multinational firms move outside the culture (interaction in space and locational mobility and culture). Boisot (1995: 337) calls this transactions with strangers. According to him there may be difficulties of uncodified exchange with out-groups. Transactions may in this case evolve to the upper part of the I-space where information can be made explicit. But moreover this may mean that only some types of transactions can be done between members of different cultures.

What about the relationships between culture and networks? Networks have played an important role in many of the preceding parts. The reason for this is that networks are a form of interorganizational interaction whose spatial implications may be interesting. This is true because – in contrast to markets – networks imply a limitation of interaction in a more or less defined set of agents. They may be characterized by ties of different strength – a fact that is important for the way exchange across space is done. However, it has also become obvious that the term "network" has been subject to a certain form of misuse because it is applied to a number of different phenomena. These are industrial districts as localized networks for example or the phenomenon of ethnic networks as a cultural phenomenon. These different examples certainly have the aspects of interaction within a limited set and specificity of ties in common. Nonetheless, they are built on different motives and histories. In industrial districts it seems to be the type of transaction (exchange of knowledge that is hard to codify) that is the root of a form of organization which is first of all characterized by spatial proximity. Industrial districts seem to be a transaction-specific phenomenon that is not a characteristic feature of a set of agents. Industrial districts can be found in the US which might be considered a market-based society as well as in France or China. Meanwhile, the phenomenon of Chinese networks seems to give us information about some kind of transactional preference inherent in the Chinese society.

According to this cultural approach different cultures will shape the present and future organization of people and firms in space. Interpreting mobility as organization in space (= *where to locate, with whom to interact over which distance, which ties to develop how*) culture and cultural differences will be essential for mobility patterns. In order to understand the implications of cultural aspects for mobility we have to solve two problems:

1. the identification of cultural areas (which may – as has been explained – be different from political borders) and

2. the analysis of cultural distance (which will not be congruent to geographical distance).

Frankel (1997: 45) includes different laws, institutions, habits and languages into aspects of cultural unfamiliarity. Singh and Kogut (1988) use a composite index of cultural distance that relies on four cultural dimensions Hofstede (1980) made out in his famous study:

- power distance (PDI) measured by employees perception of their superior's style of decision-making, the fear to disagree and the types of decision-making preferred,

- uncertainty avoidance (UA) measured by rule orientation, acceptance to break the company's rules, employment stability and feeling of stress,

- individualism (IDV) as the relationship between the individual and the relevant collectivity and

- masculinity (MAS) or femininity answering the question of whether biological differences have implications for roles in society.

The following index takes these four features (i=1,...,4) into account and measures the cultural distance (CD) between a country and its trading partners. Values for the indices in the different countries can be taken from Hofstede's studies as well.

$$CD = \sum_{i=1}^{4} \left\{ \left(I_{ij} - I_{iu} \right)^2 / V_i \right\} / 4$$

CD = cultural distance

j=country towards which distance is measured

u=comparative basis, e. g. US

V= variance

Hofstede describes that in societies with a high power distance index power is the leading principle of protection against uncertainty. Power distance has its roots in the family: Large indices of power distance will go along with patterns of dependence on seniors pervading all human contacts. With low power distance uncertainty can be reduced by an inner need for living up to rules. According to Hofstede, uncertainty avoidance deals with tolerance of the unpredictable. It measures a feeling of threat by uncertain or unknown situations, but is however different from risk aversion. Cultures with high uncertainty avoidance try to reduce ambiguity which may also be done by accepting risks. They look for structures, institutions and relationships that make events predictable. Cultures with low uncertainty avoidance on the other hand accept familiar and unfamiliar risks. Because of the high uncertainty avoidance there may be an emotional need for rules and a stronger tendency to suppress new ideas. Trust against other cultures may be difficult to achieve. As stated before uncertainty is inherent in any decision about mobility. The type and degree of uncertainty avoidance may be important for the willingness of firms to cross distances and their possibility to disperse functions. Uncertainty avoidance therefore might be important for the willingness to move, while power distance may be related to intra-firm control and communication channels in the multinational enterprise.

Erramilli (1996) derives that the propensity to establish majority owned subsidiaries - in contrast to other forms of ownership - increases as power distance and uncertainty avoidance of a multinationals home country increase, which is particularly true for small multinational firms.

Hofstede states that differences in power distance are more manageable than differences in uncertainty avoidance. Managers from countries with low power distance will however be more able to adapt than those with higher power distance. On the other hand, uncertainty avoidance seems to be a key variable for the possibility to co-operate.

He groups countries according to these two dimensions and tries to derive patterns of organization for them. Table 10.1 shows some of the conclusions about the relationship between power distance, uncertainty avoidance and organizational patterns.[48] It clusters different countries according to their constellation of the two features and derives ideas about preferred forms of organization in these countries.

Table 10.1: Power distance, uncertainty avoidance and organization

■ small **power distance**   1
■ weak **uncertainty avoidance**
■ **countries**: Anglo, Scandinavian,
   Netherlands
■ **organization type**: implicitly
   structured
■ **implicit model of organization**:
   market
	■ large **power distance** 2
	■ weak **uncertainty avoidance**
	■ **countries**: Southeast Asian
	■ **organization type**: personnel
	   bureaucracy
	■ **implicit model of organization**:
	   family

■ small **power distance**   3
■ strong **uncertainty avoidance**
■ **countries**: German-speaking,
   Finland, Israel
■ **organization type**: workflow
   bureaucracy
■ **implicit model of organization**:
   well-oiled machine
	■ large **power distance** 4
	■ strong **uncertainty avoidance**
	■ **countries:** Latin, Mediterranean,
	   Islamic, Japan, some other Asian
	■ **organization type:** full
	   bureaucracy
	■ **implicit model of organization:**
	   pyramid

Source: Hofstede (1980: 319)

---

[48] Another classification of national cultures related to organization can be found in Trompenaars (1998), ch.11.

Using these criteria Hofstede comes to similar ideas about possible forms of organization as Boisot. This may be true because uncertainty avoidance will be related to the codification of knowledge and the means to reduce this uncertainty. Hofstede does not derive ideas about the spatial or interpersonal diffusion of knowledge. However, he adds information to Boisot's ideas as he points to the importance of rules as parts of organizational structures. Rules imply already some part of abstract and codified knowledge when concerning workflows. However, rules may also be related to relationships. They may concern the degree with which hierarchies are accepted as given. Whenever rules in personal relationships are strong, reducing uncertainty by other principles may not be necessary. On the other hand, building up clear and strict hierarchies related to positions may be one way – besides prescribing workflows – to avoid uncertainty.

Mintzberg (1983: 299-467) describes the first of Hofstede's organizational types as adhocracy as it is based on mutual adjustment by informal communication with people in staff roles supplying services as key agents. He characterizes the second example as a simple structure and names China as the most important example. In this society the preferred coordination mechanism is direct supervision with the top management or the head of the family as key agents. However, the idea of direct supervision may be misunderstood, if interpreted as (spatial) concentration of activities. The third type according to him relies on standardization of skills with those people doing the work as key agents. Finally, there is the fourth type of the full bureaucracy where those people in staff roles supplying ideas are most important. According to Minzberg, the US takes an intermediate divisionalized position in this diagram.

As regards uncertainty avoidance Hofstede (1991:ch 7) reports studies in Asian countries having worked with a variable called Confucian dynamism. The values of this variable were above all high in mainland China. According to him this variable expresses the strong belief in virtue rather than belief in truth (which is measured by the variable uncertainty avoidance).

Hofstede tries to design culture areas using the four functions (fig. 10.2).

Fig. 10.2: Cultural clusters I

Clusters 1 and 2:	less developed Latin (high PDI, high UA, low IDV, low MAS) 1) Columbia, Mexico, Venezuela 2) Chile, Peru, Portugal
Cluster 2:	more developed Asian (medium PDI, high, UA, medium IDV, high MAS) **Japan**
Cluster 3 and 4:	more developed Latin (high PDI, high UA, medium to high IDV, medium MAS) 3) Belgium, France, French speaking Switzerland 4) Argentina, Brazil, Spain
Cluster 5 and 6:	less developed Asian (high PDI, low to medium UA, low IDV, medium MAS) 5) Pakistan, Taiwan, Thailand 6) Hong Kong, India, Philippines, Singapore
Cluster 7:	Near Eastern (high PDI, high UA, low IDV, medium MAS) Greece, Iran, Turkey
Cluster 8 and 9:	Germanic (low PDI, medium to high UA, medium IDV, medium to high MAS) 7) Austria Israel 8) Germany, German-speaking Switzerland
Cluster 10:	Anglo (low to medium PDI, low to medium UA, high IDV, high MAS) Australia, Canada, Great Britain, Ireland, New Zealand, USA
Cluster 11:	Nordic (low PDI, low to medium UA, medium to high IDV, low MAS) Denmark, Finland, Netherlands, Norway, Sweden

Source: Hofstede (1980: 336)

The resulting groupings have several special features:

- They comprise very different numbers of countries. E. g. Japan forms an own cultural area. This may lead to the question whether it is an advantage to belong to a big cultural area.

- The countries in a group are not necessarily adjacent, although groups tend to have a common geographical basis.

- Cultural areas are not designed on the basis of a common language, although for most part the countries in a cluster share a language or a language group. Language differences seem to interact with internal political order of a country and its history. This is shown for the example of Belgium and Switzerland.

While in Belgium language is a very hot topic, the members of the two groups seem to have the same culture (orientation to France). Meanwhile, language has not that much been a topic of dispute in Switzerland. Nonetheless, the cultural differences between the different Swiss groups are large. Hofstede explains the different importance of language in the two countries by their political system which is monolithical in Belgium and federal in Switzerland.

- Technological development seems to be important: Ronen and Shenkar (1985) conclude in the case of Japan that technology and economic development may override traditional dimensions of language, geography and religion.

Culture-specific organizational patterns may be one aspect to explain mobility within and   between cultures. Between cultures differences in business habits create distance in the sense of barriers of knowledge about each other. Vahlne and Wiedersheim (1977) call this psychic distance. This factor also comprises differences in the level of economic development and education, different local and business languages, differences in political, administrative and legal systems and business habits. Vahlne and Wiedersheim show that this factor of psychic distance can be used to explain flows of goods between Sweden and other countries.

What distinguishes cultural-organizational approaches from market models is that it matters who goes where and who interacts with whom. In contrast the price-mechanism is at first hand in the same way valid for any firm. Thus, we may be able to derive a more differentiated set of patterns of mobility, if we can make the line of argumentation "culture → organization → mobility" plausible. The idea of culture as an important determinant for behavioural patterns might give us new ideas about patterns of mobility:

- as regards location: Choosing a location means being active in an environment where agents of different other cultures, but possibly also compatriots are present. Most of the time, locations will be characterized by a dominant culture of the host country and a more or less strong scatter of other cultures. Thus, choosing a location will go along with intercultural interaction. Depending on cultural features and distances some locations may be more difficult to penetrate than others. On the other hand, some cultures might be more capable of dealing with other cultures (being mobile). For example Junius (1999: 81) explains that Japanese manufacturing investment is likely to be located near other Japanese firms. It does not mimic geographical patterns of US firms. This can be observed in centers of Japanese communities like Düsseldorf in Germany. This might make us conclude that the externalities arising from interaction may in some cases be culture-bound. It also leads us to the question of possible ways for firms of dealing with intercultural differences. Is a successful strategy one where one adapts to the new culture or one where economic success is achieved by transplanting one's own culture? According to Jaeger (1983) there are type A multinationals with formal bureaucratic control that adapt to local culture and type Z firms with informal cultural control that import their cultures to host countries.

Kogut and Singh (1988) have shown that there seems to be a correlation between modes of market entry and cultural distance: The greater the cultural distance, the more probable is a joint venture rather than an acquisition. The same is true for higher values of uncertainty avoidance. Moreover Zhu and Slater (1995: 8) state that

> „whereas theories of internalisation and the firm may be culturally robust, their empirical application in a comparative setting appears to warrant the consideration of cultural differences on the costs and risks which managers consider."

- as regards interaction across distance: From an economic point of view interaction refers to exchange. Culture may with this respect play an important role because cultures of partners of interaction will have to be matched.

However, interaction across space in the form of flows of goods for example is not only a matter of "where from – where to". The influence of culture-specific preferences has been underlined in marketing strategies. In international economics however, we mostly assume that preferences may be heterogeneous in different countries, but not within one country. Rationally, we may suppose that the differences in preferences that might be prevalent across cultures are nuances. This is why from a methodological point of view, the approach to be chosen should be a market with differentiated products. In this case, two different ways of modelling preferences are dominant. Either do we assume that consumers estimate variety by itself or we start from the assumption that they have an ideal variety, so that consumption of other varieties can only be induced on the basis of a compensation (Helpman and Krugman 1986). In order to model different culture-specific preferences we might assume that domestic varieties are demanded stronger (Venables 1987) or that different societies differ according to the distribution of consumers as regards their ideal variety. However, even this assumption may not be realistic. Referring to the assumption that mobility – and also mobility in the sense of an ability to trade – differs among firms according to their capabilities, this might also imply that agents have the possibility to adapt their varieties in order to fit the foreign market better. They are able to position themselves in the market. This aspect however does not seem to have received much interest in international economic theory.

In any way, cultural aspects give a much different view of our globe than do political borders or pure geography. This is shown in figure 10.1. Deriving cultural areas and patterns of mobility we will have to draw new borders into our political map in some cases. But in others, political borders are bridged by cultural similarities.

Ronen and Shenkar choose a presentation that takes into account the different levels of development of cultural areas (fig. 10.2). It results from surveying a number of studies about cultural areas and shows that the result of these studies were consistent enough to make out widely accepted patterns of cultural areas. Countries in the center of the concentric circles are supposed to be more developed measured in terms of GNP per capita. From the point of view of mobility development levels may be important if more developed   countries possess better communication and information facilities and better resources to develop mobility and transmit information about their territories into the world. Thus, there may be centers and peripheries of mobility. However, in this case, the measurement of economic development may be more complex than measuring GNP per capita. Moreover, Ronen and Shenkar argue that economic development may be a factor to overcome traditional cultural and linguistic aspects which might explain the special position of Japan.[49]

What is very striking is the global scale of the Anglo area comprising countries from all five continents and being reinforced by common language. This phenomenon might help us to explain e.g. the significant share of investment by US firms in Britain. It might lead us to suspect that for Great Britain its belonging to such a huge cultural area together with a strong player like the US might be an advantage that no other European country possesses. On the other hand, it is striking that the US is treated as one cultural entity. Ronen and Shenkar (1985) argue that this area has developed from colonization and immigration. Hofstede (1980: 344) states that the US's cultural continuity shows that culture is learned and not inborn. This also emphasizes the longterm dynamic features of culture.

The cultural map of the world shows that cultural borders are not congruent to political borders and cultural distance is different from geographical. Some European countries still have cultural diversity despite ongoing integration. Political and economic institutional integration does not necessarily seem to lead to convergence of cultures. Sometimes, the institutional arrangements to be observed empirically even seem to be contrasted to cultural structures. An example of this is Australia's or also the US's membership in APEC, although at present observers have also talked about a growing distance between Australia and Asia.[50]

---

[49] The development status of countries (GNP per capita) would of course have to be updated. However, - as explained – this measurement does not seem appropriate for the analysis of mobility. Thus, the focus of the figure lies on the recognition of a generally accepted perception of cultural areas.

[50] See NN (2000); „Polls among Asian political decision-makers say that Australia is leaving Asia. Australia orientates itself to its old anchor USA rather than to the Asian neighbours Premier Howells is not able to communicate. " (translated from German and summarized)

However, even if cultural features are an important, but mostly neglected determinant of economic organizations, we have to be careful not to overestimate their impact and relate anything that cannot be explained by pure market thinking to cultural features. Opponents of this idea have been numerous. Organizational patterns are most probably not a deterministic result of national culture, although they may be influenced by it.

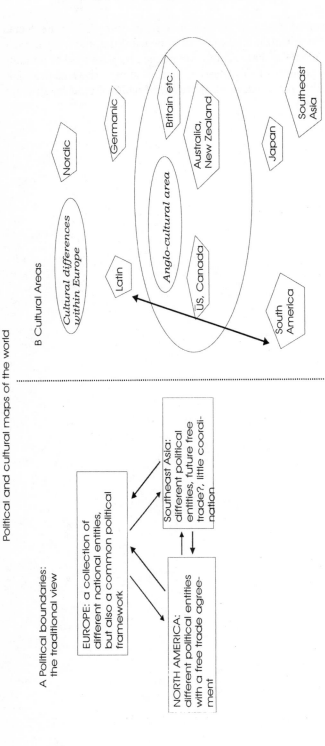

Fig. 10.1: Political and cultural maps of the world

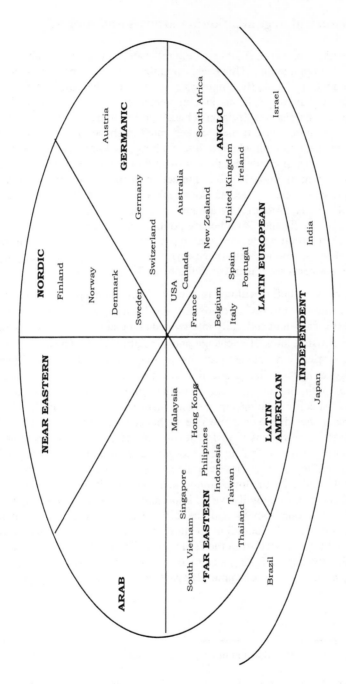

Fig. 10.2: Cultural clusters II, adapted from Rhonen and Shenkhar (1985:449)

10.2 Historical organizational patterns and mobility

The preceding chapter has linked cultural aspects with ideas about preferred patterns of organization. However, organization and mobility are strongly interdependent. It is nearly impossible to define what organization is about without talking about decisions and movements in space. Organization among other things concerns the decision whether to combine functions at one site or whether to separate them, if they are separated in space, how to coordinate them and also the question with whom to interact how. This however leads to aspects of location and flows of goods and factors (including information) in space. Thus, we can conclude that mobility is about interaction in space – interaction either with a local environment and its agents (location), but also on any other spatial scale. Space however, is structured by a number of aspects: One of them is geography and geographical distance. Another are political borders. And finally – as has been shown – intercultural borders may be important. The latter are not congruent with political borders, nor are they necessarily related to any specific geographical scale. These aspects are illustrated in figure 10.3.

As already stated before culture is a very elusive concept and lends itself to a number of interpretations.[51] Moreover, it has been argued that there are countries that are historically and culturally intertwined and that have nonetheless developed very different structures of exchange and specialization.[52] Thus, we may have to take the historically developed patterns of social organization as a direct starting point. Biggart and Guillén argue that we are able to make out certain typical patterns of authority in different countries with different actors as legitimate players and specific relationships among them (Biggart and Guillen 1999: 723). They explain that differences are due to history, collective understandings and cultural practice as well as to different roles of the state as one legitimate player. Thus, countries may differ in their organizational logics. As derived before, organizational logics are closely related to patterns of mobility. They may influence the intensity of flows among members of different societies as well as locational choices. They will give us important information about the channels of mobility within one society and the differences existing among members of different societies. In addition to this, already the traditional theories of international trade started from the assumption that the direction of trade is due to patterns of advantages. Taking a comparison of Asian economies as well as Spain and Argentina as an example Biggart and Guillén argue that different

---

[51] Anthropologists have collected more than 160 different definitions of culture, see Faure (1993).

[52] See Hamilton and Biggart (1988); they apply this argument to the example of Japan, Korea and Taiwan.

organizational logics also lead to distinctive capabilities of societies. This allows us to derive ideas about the export and import patterns of a nation. Different export patterns are among other things due to complex institutional differences that are difficult to change fundamentally in the short or medium run.

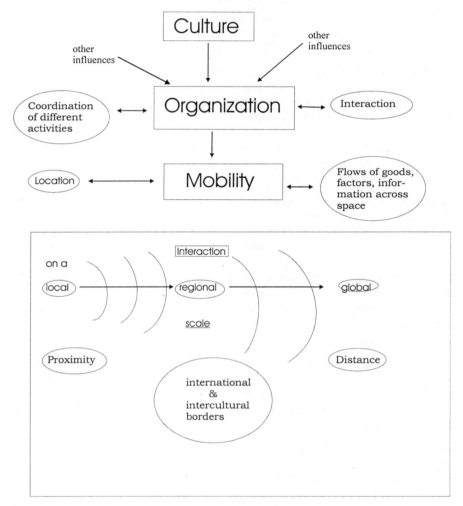

Fig. 10.3: Culture, organization and mobility

The features of different organizational patterns that may be relevant are

- the size of firms: This is related to the capital investment that is possible for these firms and for the economies of scale and scope that can be exploited.

This aspect is also related to the degree of vertical integration of firms. However, the size of firms is an endogenous variable resulting from the history of an economic system.

- the question whether ownership is primarily domestic or foreign.

- the degree to which firms establish network structures with their supplier firms. Biggart et al. show that these institutional differences have led to quite different patterns of export in different countries.

What are the sources of these different organizational logics? In the case of Taiwan and Korea e. g. the different size of firms and different degrees of intrafirm integration are e.g. due to different customs of heritage. In Korea patrimonialism is the prevalent system with the eldest son inheriting the largest share. Meanwhile the network system of small firms in Taiwan has resulted from a system of partible inheritance with all males remaining in the line of descent. There is patrilineage that quickly expands and bifurcated loyalties. Families rely on diversification into small firms.

Moreover, the state has pursued different strategies in order to legitimize its role in these countries. While in Korea, it has pushed size, concentration and top down structures, in Taiwan strategies have resulted in small firms networking among each other. Thus, the actors and their relationships are quite different: a strong state and highly vertically integrated firms in Korea,[53] families in Taiwan or as in the case of Japan strong intermediate powers of market groups. This also is decisive for the capabilities that are developed and the advantages that guide the international exchange of goods. Feenstra and Hamilton (2000) point out that these structures have persisted and developed their own dynamics even after policy modifications.

This institutional approach emphasizes that institutions are not optimal structures. They are not the result of overall valid rules of maximization, but they are object to different historical developments and source of comparative advantages. There is no organizational best practice. Nonetheless, organizational patterns influence patterns of specialization as well as national and international transactions.

Apart from the intra-firm logics of organization, exchange patterns among firms in different societies may vary. The relationships between different agents can also be interpreted as culturally different trading worlds. The classification that has been proposed by Biggart and Delbridge (1999: 12f) has already been introduced in chapter 9.3.1 (table 2). They consider the market type as the intellectual and political basis for Anglo-American style economies. Associative exchange is important in Asian economies. These economies – as Biggart and Delbridge argue

---

[53] Insiders of the Korean economic system observe that in Korea e. g. power has shifted from a strong state towards more independent chaebol. Whether their power is sustainable is however doubted; see Kim (2000).

– have never developed the conditions like individualism that support price-driven markets. Another example for associative are horizontal exchange networks like Silicon Valley. Kinship and ethnic ties may be a basis for communal exchange. Here, the value of relationships is the basis of exchange. The strong distinction between insiders and outsiders has already been reflected by the example of Chinese networks. Certainly, similar classifications have been done taking culture as a basis. However, the institutional approach described here is not relying on cultural argumentation alone. It is argued that institutional patterns and patterns of exchange develop historically with a number of determinants shaping the outcome. Common cultural understandings may only be one of these. In contrast, we may sometimes find

> "building-blocks of rationality that are located in practices which have a far greater institutional framing in the regulatory context than they do in local reserves of culture. What might appear as quite naturally a cultural matter to an outside observer, dazzled by the charms of difference, may in fact be the result of institutional arrangements which have very few roots in a specific culture." (Clegg 1992)

Certainly there will be constellations where culture plays a more important role than in others. The "extend to which local cultural resources are drawn on" may be variable. Anyways, it becomes very obvious that the path between an "undersocialized" and "economistic" and an "oversocialized" and "culturalist" point of view (Clegg 1992) is a very narrow one.

The fact that individualism is less important ideologically and institutionally in Asian countries also helps us to understand why models that primarily rely on individuals and their actions on markets rarely explain Asian economies (Biggart 1992). According to Clegg (1992: 57), "East Asia has been a test bed for much cultural theory as well as a death bed for a great deal of economic theory". Their organization is built on groups and networks of people and firms. Thus, to build more realistic models may also be a matter of aggregation. To understand the driving forces we will have to make out the dominant agents and groups and analyze their motives and rules of behaviour. Only then will we be able to understand their rationality. This is a matter of understanding the heterogeneity of agents. Traditionally, similar questions have been dealt with in international economics under the headline of integration of activities within a firm. Aggregation of activities rather than organizations has been explained as horizontal or vertical integration within firms primarily being based on economies of scale.

> However, "agents are not necessarily people. Provided there are mechanisms in place for achieving effective subordination and control of individually effective agents then the agency may take either an organizational or suborganizational form." (Clegg 1992)

Clegg also speaks of "organizational agencies".

Feenstra and Hamilton (2000, see also Feenstra et al. 2000) have applied a similar reasoning to explain the different structures of Asian business groups. They show that a price model is able to generate very similar results concerning vertical and horizontal integration as can be observed in Taiwan and Korea. Principally independent firms are in their model given the possibility to integrate in that they influence the prices of intermediate products and to coordinate intrafirm transfers. Business groups are sets of firms jointly maximizing profits. In a model of monopolistic competition firms sell intermediates at marginal costs within business groups and at higher prices on the market to unaffiliated firms (depending on price elasticities). However, it may still be doubtful whether the whole set of cultural, political and socio-economic factors influencing the organizational configuration of the economic system can be integrated into a price model. Even if this model comes to realistic results, the subtleness of determinants does not seem to be integrated adequately.

Spencer and Qiu (2000) integrate the idea of culture-specific forms of organization into a formal model in order to analyze its influence on trade patterns. They refer to the structure of the automobile sector of Japan relative to the US. The former is characterized by vertical relationships in keiretsu within which part-suppliers are assumed to make relationship-specific investments. This is only true for Japanese part-suppliers as US suppliers are assumed to lack the local presence and to be confronted with language and cultural barriers. Thus, the model reflects the empirical institutional differences between US and Japanese firms, which show that ties within Japanese keiretsu are typically relatively stable, while US firms rely stronger on spot transactions. The idea of relationship-specific investments is incorporated into the model by introducing fixed costs that are sunk costs in each following period. This concept is very similar to the ideas about the evolution of networks that were presented in chapter 9.3.1. Relationship-specific investment is a source of rents in the form of reduced assembly costs. Suppliers are assumed to decide on this investment in the first phase, while the payment of the supplier by the automobile producer is only determined after the investment has become sunk. This is done in a bargaining process which is influenced by the bargaining power of the parties as well as the marginal costs of suppliers on the market and the level of the sunk costs. The supplier of the parts is in this process able to gain a share of the rent he creates. The alternative for the automobile producer is to buy on the market. This may be a domestic market, but it may also be the world market, if trade is possible. While the model assumes that all domestic suppliers only differ as to their relationship-specific investments, there may be an efficiency gap between US and Japanese suppliers. The possibility to import parts influences the automobile producers' position in the bargaining process. They are thus able to absorb part of the efficiency gap and the payment to the supplier is reduced. The model comes to the conclusion that the parts that are imported will be those parts that have the lowest value in the production process. Moreover, there may be a range of parts for which the foreign suppliers have lower costs, but that are nonetheless produced in Japan.

Therefore, this model gives us an idea about the effects created because of insider advantages of Japanese suppliers. International mobility of goods and factors is influenced by the structures of organization in different countries and the insider-outsider patterns that are created by them. International trade is even influenced without any restrictions set at national borders. It is important that

> keiretsu "do business mainly with each other, freezing out competing buyers and sellers foreign and domestic....This system...does more than outright trade barriers or even government administrative guidance to keep out foreign products." (Church 1995)

10.3 An interplay of cultural, political and economic influences

10.3.1 Why do national borders matter?

The preceding chapter has argued that culture and institutions may be neglected dimensions in international economics. Certainly, there are a number of examples where the institutional setting seems to be a good explanation for trade and investment flows. This has been shown in the case of Chinese networks and also as regards the idea of an Anglo cultural area. However, culture is one of the dimensions that has to be taken into account and interpreted in an interplay of cultural, socio-economic, geographical and political forces. All these elements may exert an influence of varying strength depending on the special constellation of regions and agents.

Traditionally, gravity models have been "the work-horse" for empirical studies of patterns of flow mobility (Bayoumi and Eichengreen 1995: 2). These models are based on the assumption that the volume of trade between two countries should increase with their real GDP and diminish with geographical distance. A number of other variables have been added to shed more light on the determinants of trade patterns, among them e. g. a dummy variable for membership in a common preferential agreement. We may suppose that such models may be interesting for the analysis of mobility when dealing with the effect of borders. One problem in this context is the fact that coefficients or dummy variables indicating membership within a common political framework may easily become "a catch basin" for a number of different factors (Bayoumi and Eichengreen 1995: 3). This is also due to the fact that gravity models lack a "sound theoretical basis." (Brada and Mendez 1985: 549) Among other things they include of course all those effects resulting from trade impedances and formal political barriers to trade. The intention of this chapter however is to show that national borders do matter, even if these impedances are more or less absent. This is why we will have to select those studies from the broad range of empirical material where we can plausibly assume that formal barriers are not mixed with other effects national borders may have. This is true for countries that are strongly integrated, but also for subnational states.

Especially the interplay between political borders and geographical distance has puzzled economists for some time now. Empirically trade intensities between Canadian provinces and US states have served as an example to show that borders still matter and that they may matter apart from the existence of tariffs, quotas etc. On the one hand, there are strong cultural similarities between the US and Canada. As described above, both are generally counted to the Anglo-cultural area. Tariffs and border limitations have traditionally been low between these countries. There is a large degree of foreign ownership in Canada with the US being the largest source country. The US and Canada are a good example for adjacent market economies which are so large in area that there are significant distances within countries. Therefore, if borders can be neglected in a globalized world, the example of Canada and the US should be a very good example to prove this. Nonetheless, empirical analysis has shown that even in this case national borders still have a significant impact. If borders did not matter and we take geographical distance and GDP-effects into account, Canadian provinces close to the US border should be expected to export much more to California than to other Canadian provinces. But in contrast, empirical observation shows that Canadian provinces trade about twenty times as much with each other than with US states of similar size and distance (Mc Callum 1995 and also Helliwell 1996). After the Free Trade Agreement with the US border effects have decreased, but are still significant (Helliwell 1998). Thus, as Helliwell states there may be a "trade creating power" of political units. Contrastive examples are the negative effects on trade flows when countries like former Czechoslovakia break up.

One more thing that is special about the case of Canada is the separatist tendencies of Québec. In many aspects Québec seems to have a French rather than an Anglo culture. Nonetheless, none of the studies about cultural areas has counted Québec as an exception. What might be suspected is that Québec's tendencies to trade with US states rather than more distant Canadian provinces are higher than for other Canadian provinces. However, empirical analysis has shown that Québec's links with Canada relative to those with the US are at least as strong as for other provinces.

If the observation of strong border effects holds, this might have negative effects on Québec in case of a separation from Canada as those trade flows that were formerly intra-Canadian will not be substituted by Québec-US trade.

Wolf (1997) tests a similar home bias using the example of the US states. Thus, home bias on a subnational level is tested. He argues that among US states there are strong constitutional protections for inter-state commerce, exchange rate effects are irrelevant and there is a high degree of cultural and institutional homogeneity. He comes to the result that the intra-national bias is lower than the inter-national home bias, but nonetheless significant.

Of course, a theoretical explanation of this phenomenon is difficult to find from an economist's point of view. Traditionally, borders have mattered for trade whenever there were tariffs and formal trade limitations. Nonetheless, it has been shown that border effects are there even without these limitations. From the point of view of international economic theory the border between the US and Canada is nearly non-existent. Nonetheless, we can show how much it matters. Helliwell (1998: 119) therefore even suspects that neoclassical theories like the Heckscher-Ohlin-Vanek theorem might work better for trade within countries than between them:

> "There is nothing wrong with international trade theory except its title. If 'international' is taken out of the title the theory has much to contribute to the explanation of trade patterns of regions within a country."

He explains the importance of borders by stating that educational, cultural, historical, political, associational and geographical links are strong within a country. Certainly, crossing borders also implies entering a new system of regulations and norms. It influences the degree of uncertainty involved. Therefore, borders may also be lines in space where uncertainty rises discontinuously. There are migration and family ties and networks of transportation and communication within a country. However, if the argument of culture is difficult to hold and geographical aspects have been taken into account, the other aspects may have to be clarified. Today it seems improbable that networks of transportation and communication are inhibited by national borders. Moreover, currency effects might play a role. However, it has been difficult to prove significant and negative effects of exchange rate volatility on trade flows.

Therefore, the conclusion of these studies seems to be that mobility is subject to an interplay of cultural, socio-economic, political and geographical forces. Especially national borders seem to be places where a complex set of special influences is set into effect or measured. Especially the effects of culture are very hard to understand. In the case of Québec, we might suspect that the links to France are covered by the geographical distance. Culture will be more important whenever cultural areas cross borders of adjacent countries and when culture is not equated with purely separatist tendencies like e.g. in the Basque region in Spain. Moreover, cultural-economic distance to geographically closer countries may be important. Of course, it can be shown that the effects of the Anglo-cultural area are still significant. However, this may serve as an explanation that US foreign direct investment is oriented to Great Britain more than to other parts of Europe. But it will not set aside the effects of geographical proximity and a huge home market.

Altogether, if these studies indicate that national borders matter, we will have to analyze whether the effects measured are really a matter of national borders and politics and not of cultural aspects or others.

10.3.2   Borders, markets and ties

Borders matter independently from the restrictions to mobility they set. This is the main argument of the preceding chapter. Generally, we have assumed that agents on both sides of borders are related to one another by prices. However, chapter 9.3 and also 10.2 have given us an idea of other ways agents are tied to each other, e. g. networks, business groups or ethnic ties. One possibility to justify the effects of borders is to assume that national borders restrict information. While transactions within a nation may be done with full information, crossing borders creates uncertainty. On the other hand, ties within certain groups may also cross political borders and help their members to reduce uncertainty. Taking such a situation as a starting-point may be helpful to get an idea about the relationship between national borders, organizational principles and the direction and channels for mobility.

The following paragraph is based on a trade model by Rauch and Casella (1998, see also Casella and Rauch 1997). In this model incentives to do international transactions are given by higher returns which might for example be due to different wage levels. International transactions can be market transactions or transactions within a group extending across national borders. Output is generated by a joint venture between two firms. International market transactions imply uncertainty about the foreign partner. Agents are supposed to be heterogeneous. They are arranged on a line extending from −1 to 1. This position is a determinant for the gains to be realized from matching and for the bargaining position of agents. The farther agents' positions are away from each other, the more favourable is the matching. Matches with partners on different sides of zero are good matches. Matches with partners farther away from zero are more desirable. Matching on the market is random. Thus, borders are supposed to have effects that are essentially different from traditional trade barriers. Any agent acting on the international market has the possibility to revise this decision and match on the domestic market with certain information about his partners. On the other hand, a limited group of agents is able to transact within the boundaries of their group. Group ties provide perfect information even across national borders. Thus, belonging to a group in this model provides no advantage as long as transactions are domestic. Group ties however may be essential when crossing borders because they provide full information that is not available on the international market. "Prices convey incomplete information to the complete set of producers while ties convey complete information to an incomplete set of producers". (Rauch and Casella 1998: 3) Subramanian and Lawrence (1999: 5, 10) point out that search and deliberation are important in exploiting cross-border economic opportunities.

While the former refers to identifying potential exchange partners, the latter refers to assessing their reliability and trustworthiness. The uncertainties involved in this grow with spatial dispersion of economic action and irreversible investments. While "domestic vendor selection is more often a 'choice' situation....International vendor selection on the other hand often is a 'search' situation."(Lang and Parkhe 1997: 510) This is why firms may "turn to their businesses and social networks" as these alleviate the problems of search and deliberation and help them to discover and exploit cross-border opportunities (Subramaian and Lawrence 1999: 6).

The returns to be gained with complete information on domestic markets or within groups are decided in a process of competition for matching partners and bargaining between heterogeneous agents. The model shows that the probability to get a good match on the market is different for agents according to their position on the line. This is true because of the different bargaining power agents can exploit in their groups or domestically The assumption of imperfect information on markets leads to a reduced volume of trade without group ties. Agents with different positions and bargaining powers are to a different degree involved into trade. Moreover, with group ties it is possible to show that we can discern certain patterns of agents (differing in their position on the line/ their bargaining power) preferring transactions on the market or within their group. It can be shown that some group members will not use the ties that are available to them.

Another conclusion of an extended 3-country version of the model is that the distribution of group ties across space may be an important parameter to determine the direction of flows. Basically, the spatial patterns of group ties are independent from those allocative signals that are given by prices. Ties may have effects that are in opposition to price signals. This will also have strong distributional effects between group members and non-members.

Whenever interaction is limited to insiders and whenever it makes a difference whether matches are made within or outside a group, there will be a clear relationship between the spatial distribution of insiders of a group and the aggregated flows among nation states. While national borders inhibit information, ties may bridge these borders. This is illustrated in figure 10.4.

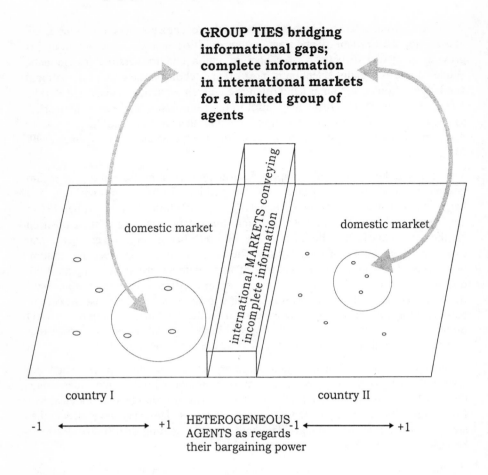

Fig. 10.4: Groups and markets

11   Spaces of multinationalization

In the preceding chapters approaches have been described to delineate cultural areas in the sense of drawing boundaries in space. However, already the phenomenon of huge Chinese diasporas has shown that culture may not only be a determinant for patterns of mobility, but also subject of mobility. Moreover, we often neglect that mobility is a process within which not only locations change, but also people and organizations may change when moving.

However, the concept of culture has opened up many ambiguities. As argued in chapter 10.1 many authors have assumed that national cultures imprint organizational behaviour and thus set external constraints. Meanwhile, recently, interest in corporate culture as an internal phenomenon has risen. This aspect has been dealt with excessively in management literature. It has been acknowledged that there are types of multinational firms that are mobile by adapting to the cultures of their host countries, while others take their culture with them.

Japanese culture has excessively been dealt with as a dominant determinant of Japanese management. Japanese firms go global without becoming local (NN 1990: 59). Jaeger (1983) distinguishes different types of firms. One of them is characterized by informal cultural control mechanisms between headquarters and subsidiaries. Multinationals of this type possess an organization-wide culture. Large Japanese organizations may be considered an example of this type. Cultural control proceeds by strong use of interpersonal interaction and expatriates and emphasis on the home language. We may conclude that these are relatively closed systems for outsiders. Culture is imported into the host country (see also Tolich et al. 1999). Jaeger argues that these multinationals are highly dependent on conformity with their surroundings. If habits in the host country are in conflict with the company culture, this might hamper its operations. From this we might derive that sticking to one's culture might limit the search and operation horizon of these firms. Moreover, it is obvious that the local embeddedness of these firms will be weak, if they do not form enclaves of firms with the same nationality as Japanese firms seem to do frequently.

Indeed studies about Japanese investment e. g. in Chinese Special Economic Zones confirm that Japanese were cautious about investing in China because of an old uneasiness about the investment environment. There was a lot of negative publicity and Japanese were often not able to cope with the inadequate legal system. They could not escape "doing things strictly by the book" which hampered their operation within China and made them in the beginning favour trade on investment there (Wu 1999: 53). Nowadays however, Japanese investors are numerous in China.

Nonetheless, there seem to be striking differences in corporate cultures within one cultural context. In management literature, adaptation to new cultural contexts has been treated as a strategic issue in multinational firms. Pluralist cultures have been distinguished from universal corporate cultures. Pluralist corporations are truly multicultural as they adopt different organizational strategies according to the cultures they operate in. These strategies may be synergetic to each other or not. Universal corporate cultures are those that either take their home country or headquarter culture with them or create a geocentric common culture for all their locations. In any case differences to host countries will be created by this strategy.[54]

A big Swedish furniture retailer e. g. has been cited as an example where a unique corporate culture created a competitive advantage.[55] It has been argued that its culture has indeed been strongly determined by the Swedish culture. Its management style has been implanted in many locations. Typically management has been described as informal, open, social and non-hierarchical (which also fits into Hofstede's characterization of Nordic countries). Today the company is active in many countries of the world. Therefore, two questions arise:

- How are such companies capable to transfer their culture?

- What is it that makes a unique organizational culture a competitive advantage and not a restriction to mobility?

Let us continue to take this company as an example. First of all, cultural transfer in this case has not been without frictions. Grol and Schoch (2000: K4) report that Germans were much more used to formally fixed written rules and French rejected informal management within its subsidiaries. In the US culture-specific aspects of furniture demand had to be considered. Thus, adaptations have been necessary which however did not destroy the firms overall common culture. This also shows that organizational culture can be a competitive advantage whenever it does not close an organization against its environment. Grol calls this open organizational

---

[54] Similar ideas have been presented by Perlmutter who distinguished ethnocentric and geocentric corporate strategies from poly- and regiocentric, see Perlmutter (1969).

[55] The following explanations are by no means intended to stress special features of this company. But however it seems to be a good example to clarify the main points of this chapter.

cultures. Open cultures do not restrict their interaction to agents who share their culture. They allow adaptation. Grol speaks of cultural capability to integrate new members/ employees. The company's culture does not intend to exclude others. In France it is well aware for example that it is necessary to employ mostly French. Thus, it is a balance of international corporation and Swedish corporation the firm seems to be searching for. However, as Grol puts it even in such a case decision-makers seem to be thinking about whether to get more multicultural. Especially the entry into Asian markets seems to pose special challenges with respect of organizational cultures.

Depending on their strategies, firms may not only be forced to manage cultural differences that are external, but also multinational cultural diversity within the firm. As firms become multinational - in contrast to multidomestic – cultural diversity enters the organization having managers from all over the world e. g (Adler 1997: 125).

Nonetheless, seeing corporate culture this way, the boundaries between culture and strategy seem to get blurred. Therefore, we clearly have to define what are the core characteristics of organizational culture. Hofstede et al. enumerate the following features (Hofstede et al. 1990: 286):

- Corporate culture is holistic.

- It is historically determined,

- related to anthropological concepts,

- socially constructed and

- difficult to change.

He concludes that organizational cultures "reflect nationality, demographics of employees and managers, industry and market; they are related to organization structure and control systems; but all of these leave room for unique and idiosyncratic elements." (Hofstede et al. 1990: 311)

It thus becomes obvious that firms that operate on an international scale not only have to adapt to new markets, but also to different cultures. There is no agreement on

- whether culture is a restricting influence on organizations and mobility,

- whether culture is nation- or firm-bound and

- in how far it is transferable to other locations.

Altogether, multinational firms nowadays seem to create their own spaces. They recognize cultural aspects as an important part in their strategy and the flexibility of corporate cultures or the special strengths inherent in it may be important sources of advantage. The spaces and structures thus created are not contiguous spaces. Depending on the international patterns of organization and control they are more or less connected. There may be an emphasis on the global framework of the multinational firm, but also on the local relationships of its subsidiaries. It has become difficult to press multinationals into a common national or cultural framework. Nonetheless, in this context corporate culture has a different meaning from the aspects implied in national culture. It is created at an individual level of the firm. What might be interesting is whether similar ideas could be relevant for political decision-makers and immobile agents. Can local cultures of innovation, openness etc. be created that are more than singular political measures? This may be strongly related to the question about the creation of regions and industrial districts that was posed earlier.

12 Novelty, capabilities and heterogeneity of agents

Chapter 9 started from the assumption that heterogeneity of agents and their capability to develop are of major importance to understand patterns of mobility. The preceding chapters have already given us some hints on the questions which may be the sources of heterogeneity of agents that are relevant and which are their distinctive capabilities and roles. In chapter 3 we have called these capabilities for mobility "motility".

Can we make out basic capabilities for mobility that induce novelty? Witt (1987) assumes that there is a basic rate of curiosity that induces novelty. Donoghue et al. (1998: 3) state that the rate at which firms have ideas is an exogenous component in the market. These arguments may be based on the difficulties arising when trying to introduce the causes of novelty into theoretical modelling. They take us back to the discussion whether novelty is predictable. Pred (1967: 19) states that "pioneering innovational acts in a locational context are no different from pioneering innovational acts in any other context in the sense that they are acts of invention, often competitively inspired."

In the following paragraphs it is intended to underline those basic features that have in the models presented before appeared as relevant characteristics of agents.

On the one hand, agents may differ as to their role as first-movers inducing change or followers reacting to this. This has been shown by game-theoretic approaches (ch. 9.2.2). Furthermore uncertainty or the availability of information as well the way it is processed seem to be important. There is an option value of waiting as was explained in chapter 9.2.3. The role of information has already been acknowledged by Pred (1967: 24f) who chose a matrix with the dimensions availability of information and ability to process it to explain the behavioural basis for locational decisions. Some authors also suggest that multinational enterprises may have informational advantages because they "are simultaneously embedded in two or more distinct social networks" (Subramaian and Lawrence 1999). Moreover, it may be rational to think of locational change being inspired not only be organizational restructuring and novelty, but also by the product lifecycle. This is an aspect that is not explicitly taken into account by neoclassical and other market theories. This is why these theories many times predict much smoother or deterministic paths than may be true in reality.

> „Neoclassical models give us images of highly constrained spatial behaviour, bounded by market clearing, perfect competition and profit equalization. The locational calculus forces us to find an optimum site within the existing bounds of market areas, transport systems and resource supplies." (Storper and Walker 1989: 72)

Why can product lifecycles influence locational choice? Early stages of the product cycle involve processes where new inputs are needed that are created rather than available at a certain location. Therefore, there may be fewer spatial ties in young industries. As Boschma and Lambooy (1999: 424) explain

> „there is likely to be a gap between the requirements of major new technologies and their local selection environment. Therefore, new industries depend on their capacity ... to produce locally their own necessary conditions of growth, such as specific knowledge, skills, input components and capital."

This kind of spatial change depends on the capacity of firms to secure what they need at a given location. Similarly to the predictions made by the approaches dealing with innovative milieus, linkages and spatial relationships can then develop simultaneously so that location does not follow given input-output coefficients (Storper and Walker 1989: 73,80). What may however be important for these industries is proximity to markets or an innovative environment. In this stage, knowledge spillovers play an important role as is shown by the example of Silicon Valley. Therefore, the forces that keep firms at a given location or pull them there may differ according to the stage in the lifecycle a product is in. This may be an opportunity for new regions to induce growth (window of locational opportunity). Storper and Walker (1989: 71,73) also call this "spatial leapfrogging". From their point of view "history is replete with cases of industries springing up in unexpected places." They explain however, that spatial change is not only a matter of the product lifecycle, but also of organizational restructuring (window of organizational opportunity).

Fine (1999) made out the idea of an industrial clockspeed. This refers to the fact that different industries may exhibit different speeds of change, innovation and adjustment. Fine states that human and financial mobility are the motor of evolution in a world of high clockspeed. He distinguishes clockspeeds as regards products, organizations and processes. As we have seen, especially the field of organization is invariably related to space as any kind of organization – be it intra- or interfirm – always has a spatial structure. Thus, to speak in Fine's words there should be a clockspeed of mobility in different industrial sectors.

The importance of location-specific learning and of experiences in internationalization have been stressed. Thus, the strategy of the individual firm will consist of a complex mix of mobility and immobility.

Finally, chapter 10 has shown that individual capabilities are also due to the ability to cross cultural borders. Many times, we do not only deal with multinational firms, but also with multicultural firms or firms that are able to build "bridges" between different logics of organization prevalent in different societies.

Thus, it seems to be a mosaic of different characteristics and conditions that might at least help us to understand the different roles of firms in dynamic spatial developments.[56] However, we probably will have to stay at this level of basic characteristics as any deeper explanation may lead us to an infinite regression. More empirical research will moreover be necessary in this field. What may have become obvious is that those firms may have advantages that are able to perceive and overcome barriers and borders in space, be it informational, cultural or institutional barriers. While political borders seemed to be more or less objective for everyone, other types of barriers and borders may pose much more subtle problems. Overcoming borders however is not only a problem of individual capabilities, it is a matter of interpersonal relationships.

In addition to this, the approaches presented have underlined that capabilities for mobility are by no means a matter of "the more the better". They imply finding an "optimal" relationship between flexibility and ties and considering immobility as a temporary decision rather than a given restriction. It seems to be the capability to build up specific relationships to agents and/ or space and to use these relationships in a way that balances the decision between mobility and immobility. To say it in the terms already introduced in the chapter about Evolutionary Economics: The possibility space we have taken as a methodological starting-point is a matter of agents' capabilities to shape and use their scope of action.

---

[56] A study dealing with the capabilities of firms to export has been done by Koch (1994). He makes out global market research and intelligence, strategic analysis, cultural empathy, linguistic skills and intimacy with law, customs and habits, motivation of employees and management commitment, reaction time, delivery periods, consistent product quality as major aspects of such capabilities. These capabilities have up to now been analyzed in management literature rather than economic theory.

13 A new understanding of a complex matter – space and time

13.1 Mobility in time

The following chapter is to give a short summary concerning the different aspects that relate mobility to time and space. This is done because it is assumed that both dimensions are much more complex matters than they appear to be at first sight. Moreover, especially the relationship between space and agents' scope of action deserves interest. Chapter 13.1 will therefore start with aspects related to the question of time, chapter 13.2 deals with the dimension of space. All the aspects to be approached can be derived from the preceding chapters so that no completely new ideas are introduced. The aim is to make many of the points that have been implicit in the approaches more evident.

Time is constituted by aspect of change, by durations of different length, more or less continuous changes as well as the perception of history and future relative to the present. This is illustrated by figure 13.1.

These aspects have repeatedly been relevant in the previous chapters. Novelty and change are related to evolution and innovation. Chapter 9.4.2 has tried to offer a theoretical approach for dealing with innovation. Path-dependence has already been inherent in more traditional models of New Economic Geography, but is also relevant in any case where learning is important. As has been shown learning can have location-specific features. Similarly, lock-in effects have been illustrated by the non-linear dynamics of the models of New Economic Geography. Moreover, it should have become obvious that mobility is more than decision-making at a point in time. Different decisions about mobility have different time horizons. Certainly, locational decision-making has a longer time horizon than flow mobility whose adaptation to changes often is assumed to be possible instantaneously (although ch. 9.3 has pointed to the importance of relatively stable ties). Locational decisions are binding for a certain period in time. However, locational mobility and flow mobility are interdependent concepts. Therefore, the long time horizon of locational mobility (which is often explained by the existence of sunk costs) strongly influences flow mobility. E. g. Frankel (1997: 115f, 126) comes to the result that the influence of colonial ties persists even after this ties have been resolved. This is reflected by the trade flows between the respective countries. He explains this with the stock of capital that has been invested in these countries and the networks that have been established. However, the importance of these ties seems to be declining in time.

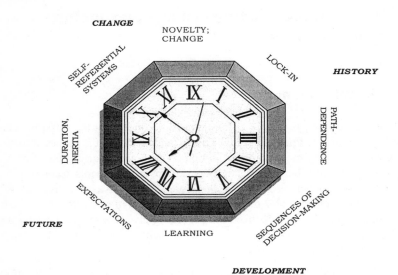

Fig. 13.1: Aspects of time

Moreover, current decisions do not only affect future scopes of action, but also the present is influenced by the past. Ties existing today have taken time to develop. The history of migration is important which is to a large degree due to processes of learning.

Although at first sight these aspects of time seem to be relatively independent from each other, it can be shown that it is their interplay that shapes the trajectories of regional and locational development (fig. 13.2) For example, the establishment of industrial locations may be due to the initiative of economic agents (first-movers), but also to political initiatives. However, it has been doubted whether political planning alone can initiate regional or local development or only support it as a catalytic function. First-movers that are successful tend to be followed. Moreover, regional and local development will be determined by the degree with which economic and political agents learn and adapt themselves to new conditions. As has been shown before, regional trajectories will also differ

- depending on the embeddedness of agents in networks,

- depending on the global, national and regional relationships on the political and economic level.

Whenever such processes in time are important, path dependence and lock-in effects may have to be taken into account. Knowledge about these paths of regional development, their determinants and dynamics may be important from the point of view of political decision-makers.

Finally, the spatial economy can be understood as a self-referential system. This becomes even more clear when taking into account other determinants of mobility than political borders. While international mobility does not change political borders, intercultural mobility and mobility between different institutional frameworks may change these structures although probably slowly. While political borders are objective borders that are true for everybody in the same way and whose abolition is a matter of decision-making, intercultural borders can only be overcome by learning and adaptation of behaviours. Those agents that have the capability to be mobile within such a heterogeneous framework may be the critical agents that are able to change the basic structures of the system in the long run.

Thus, mobility indeed is a matter of different time scales. It creates change and is determined by changes.

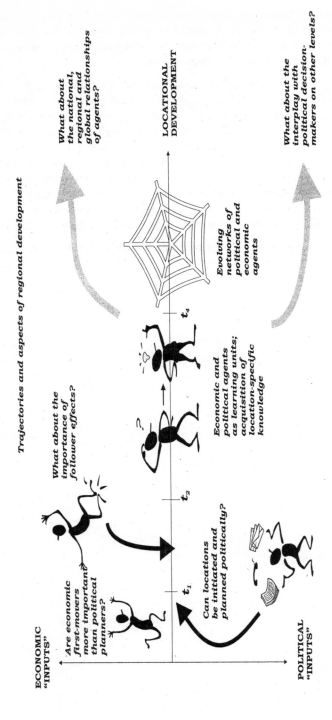

Fig. 13.2: Trajectories and aspects of spatial development

13.2 Mobility in space – spaces of mobility

Everybody would easily agree at first sight that international economics must refer to space-related approaches of economic theory. However, part B started from a space- and also timeless point of view of traditional theories dealing with flows between borders. This represented some kind of a paradox. Step by step we came to the conclusion that mobility might be a much better starting point to have a look at the aims and achievements of these theoretical approaches. Mobility however is in fact inherently related to space. This was in the past acknowledged in theoretical approaches by a more or less geographical point of view. Methodologically space was taken into account by introducing transport costs. Moreover, space was understood as political borders which was recognized by analyzing the effects of trade policies. The previous chapters in part C however have come to the result that mobility is also determined by cultural and institutional aspects. These structures in space however cannot be analyzed without taking into account heterogeneous agents that are more or less mobile. In addition to this, in many senses mobility as an economic phenomenon cannot be analyzed without having a look at interpersonal or interfirm relationships. The spaces and spatial structures that were in this way defined were different from absolute space measured in kilometres. Space seemed to be the result rather than a determinant of mobility. From an economic point of view *there is no space without economic agents and their interaction.* Many of the reflections made in the previous chapters assumed that the outcomes to be derived in the different approaches were due to agents' scopes of action. Capabilities of agents – immobile and mobile – described the extent to which they were able to shape and use their "possibility spaces". This also implies that space is no absolute and given concept: It is determined by agents' capabilities and their relationships, but it is also due to the evolution of these capabilities and relationships. And of course, agents do not only comprise mobile economic agents, but also political decision-makers that open up their territories for economic actions by foreigners.

This is a point of view that emphasizes the importance of a deep analysis of the meaning of space which is however a space that is defined differently than commonly done. It is a space related to the interaction and perceptions of agents, a space that is a "playing field" rather than a given dimension. It is however also a space that is much more complex to describe, measure and even the more to analyze.

Having a look at the title and starting-point "mobility in space and time", the ideas of the last chapters round off our understanding of the relationship between these keywords. Starting from a search for space and time in order to understand mobility we reached a theoretical concept where mobility gives us a new understanding of space and time.

14 A formal model of mobility

"I think the most striking joint implication...is that ... we can no longer go back to any single simple explanation of trade. Out new findings have been pushed to the point where we are now irreversibly aware of several basic real life causes operating in combination."
(Keesing 1970: 274)

The preceding chapters have tried to complete our understanding of mobility (above all of firms), its determinants, expressions and effects. Most certainly, this more complex picture also renders it difficult to press it into one integrated theoretical framework. However, some conclusions about the aspects that have to be introduced and their relationships can be derived.

First of all, it has been shown that spatial structures will have to be analyzed in a more detailed way, structures of locations, regions and nations. A formal model to deal with international mobility will have to derive structures in space from the different types of boundaries influencing mobility:

1. Political borders: These are state-level borders that create discontinuities in spatial mobility, but that also design areas where special rules and advantages can be fostered. Furthermore, there are political decision-makers on the regional and local level. These do hardly have the possibility to influence political borders, but they can shape the conditions in their territories and attract economic agents.

    Political borders may create discontinuous distances in space that are not related to geographical distance (fig. 14.1). The political distance that is created most of all depends of the intensity of political intervention at borders. Engel and Rogers (1996) have tried to measure the importance of borders relative to geographical distance: How much distance creates the same effects as borders? By studying the variability of consumer prices in 23 Canadian and

US cities they have shown that borders can be equated to significant distances – borders are wide.

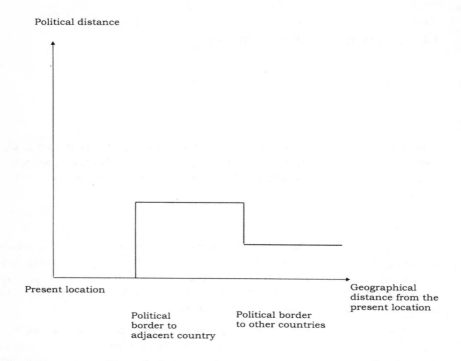

Fig. 14.1: Borders and political distance

2. Cultural distance indices: Cultural (institutional) distance affects the way transactions are done and the structure of organizations and exchange. Cultural distance furthermore decreases the transferability of insider knowledge. Insiders may in this context be people who have developed ties to the territory of their location, but also people who are part of interpersonal relationships and networks of agents.

For cultural distance, a very similar picture to the one of political distance can be created with few exceptions. The spatial scale of cultural communities may be of variable size – which is also true for political entities – and the borders created by culture depend on the distribution of agents in space, which may be a very flexible parameter in a time when agents are mobile. Culture furthermore may be an ambiguous feature because principally it is related to the members of a society as a collective. What is not certain is whether culture changes with location. If it does, cultural distance is a matter of absolute and relatively stable given space. If it does not, it is a matter of relative locations of agents.

3. The more or less objective filter due to the way agents and firms perceive space and partners of interaction: Concerning the locational choice of agents, a number of studies have shown that firms have mental maps and search horizons and that there may be spatial biases when evaluating possibilities in space (Hayter 1997: ch. 6). Furthermore, choice will be influenced by past and present relationships and interaction.

4. Finally, as discussed above locational changes may bring about a change of partners of interaction. The costs of this change can be incorporated in cultural distance and/ or attractivity of a location. But it may also mean that distance sensitive ties are extended in space. In that case geographical distance will matter as a determinant. We thus have three aspects to be integrated into the calculus of the firm: geographical distance, cultural and political distance as costs and attractivity as an advantage. Empirical studies have moreover shown that even geographical distance is a relative concept. Frankel (1997: 143) illustrates that remoteness of a country from the rest of the world has a positive effect on the bilateral trade volume with a specific trading partner. Geographical distance and aspects of subjective evaluation are illustrated in figure 14.2.

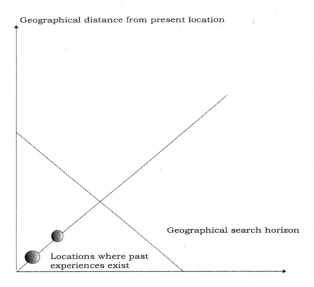

Fig. 14.2: The subjective and individual perception of the firm

What we learn from this is that the relevant constellations regarding agents and locations are much more complex than political structures and possible general laws may be much more difficult to derive.

Combining these ideas, we can - in a stylized way - try to describe any location as regards the geographical, political and cultural distance it reflects from the point of view of an agent and his individual perception and historical experience. While political distance is combined with the geographical position of locations in the second quarter of figure 14.3, geography and individual evaluations are intended to be illustrated in the third. Cultural aspects are added in the fourth quarter in their relationship to geographical space. Quarter I cumulates the information about political and cultural distance. Together with quarter III which has two equal axes (and is therefore presented as a 45° line), we get information about political, cultural and geographical distance at any location relative to the present location that is considered. The fact that the different types of distance are measured from such a reference position in space reflects that space is no absolute concept. The perception of distance depends on the position of the decision-maker and the position of agents he interacts with. Moreover, this is always an evaluation that is given at a point in time. Learning and new capabilities may change the perception in future periods.

Space and time relationships have in physics been subject to a revolution when Einstein made up his theory of the universe (relativity theory). In relativity theory we are able to define distance time and the velocity of light (Hawking 1999: ch. 2). This makes it possible for different observers to come to a unique conclusion about distance. Whether a similar thing is possible as regards economic space and distance is still an open question. Presently, we can only try to give an understanding of the synthesis of different types of distances that is necessary. This is done in figure 14.3.

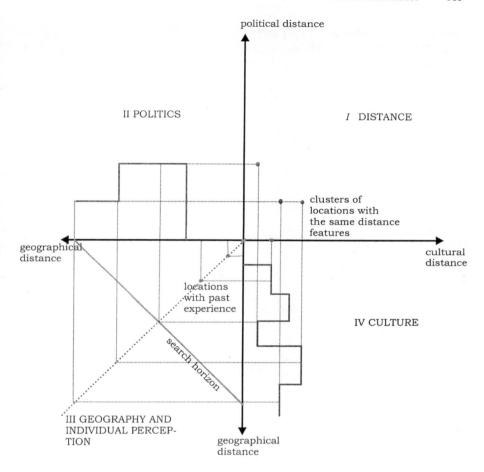

Fig. 14.3: Combining political and cultural distance and individual perception

What is derived in quadrant I are clusters of locations with the same features of political and cultural/ institutional distance relative to the present location of a firm. To get information about the geographical locations we have to combine quadrant I with quadrant III. Of course, the complex filter of a firm's perception and experiences can only be introduced in a very simple manner in this figure as they consist of a whole set of information and relationships.

Up to now we have only been dealing with the restrictions agents face when choosing their location. What is missing is the attractiveness of a location as a positive factor. Attractiveness in a point of time may be created by political decision-makers, it may be due to the endowment of a territory with resources or it may be due to the number and type of other agents located there. Thus, any of the geographical points in space can be assigned an attractiveness from the point of view of an individual agent in the sense of the pay-offs to be gained at a location given the location of all other agents. This dimension is added in figure 14.4 as a vertical axis.

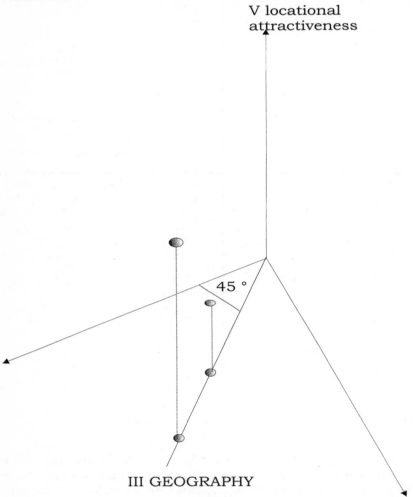

Fig. 14.4: Introducing locational attractiveness

Altogether, we get three vectors which can be aggregated to describe the calculus of a firm: geographical, cultural/ institutional and political distance as well as attractiveness (fig. 14.5). Depending on the type of the firm and its calculus, the types of costs may have to be weighed in a different way.

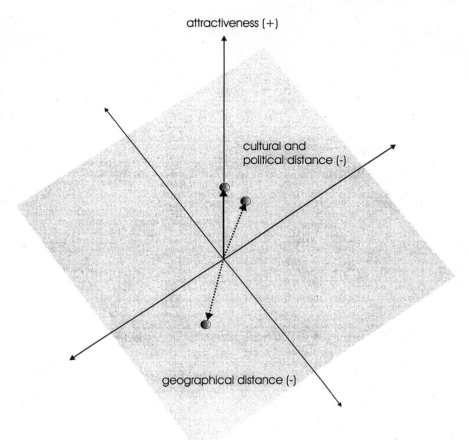

Fig. 14.5: Locational calculus of a firm

Even if this graphic presentation is strongly simplified, it expresses that a number of determinants may shape mobility that may have different weights in different constellations of decision-making.

Part D   Between given knowledge and new challenges

15 Conclusion

„If everything occurred at the same time, there would be no development. If everything existed in the same place, there could be no particularity. Only space makes possible the particular, which then unfolds in time...[T]he question how the economy fits into space not only opens a new field, but leads in the final analysis to a new formulation of the entire theory of economics." (Lösch 1954)

15.1 What do old and new theories tell us about mobility?

The following table 15.1 is intended to summarize the most important ideas about mobility that have been presented in various approaches. As it is assumed that this schematic presentation is much more illustrative so that a verbal description does not seem necessary.

Table 15.1: Some ideas about mobility

Assumptions	Ideas about mobility
A Traditional theory of international trade	
• Agents and resources are tied to a country. • The nationwide distribution of productive factors and agents is not too unequal. • Flows of goods react to price differences.	• The direction and intensity of international flows of goods can be derived from a given distribution of productive factors, technology and preferences.

Table 15.1: continued

B New Trade Theory	
• The national distribution of consumers and productive factors is given. • Firm-specific advantages are important. • Firms are able to split their production at different locations (horizontally, vertically integrated firms). • Decision-making about locations is maximizing behaviour depending on transport-costs, factor-costs and fixed costs of a new plant. • Structures of interaction are given by monopolistic competition market structures.	• Flows of goods and locational choice are interdependent concepts. Different production regimes with varying shares of multinational and national firms can be derived from the given assumptions.
C1 Core-Periphery Models and New Economic Geography	
• The relevant spatial entity is not necessarily a nation-state; introduction of the concept of regions. • The supply of productive factors and consumers in each region is given. • Upstream and downstream firms are mobile between the regions. • There are transport costs for intermediates and final products. • Locational choice is maximizing behaviour depending on the advantages of agglomeration vs. disadvantages of transport costs and factor price differentials.	• Centrifugal and centripetal forces in a market model make it possible to derive central and peripheral regions.

Table 15.1: continued

C2 City Agglomerations and New Economic Geography	
• Locations and their size (number of firms) are not given. • Firms and workers are mobile. • Agricultural production is immobile. • There are transport costs. • The size of the population is a variable and an important determinant for the number and distribution of cities in space.	• City agglomerations (number, size, as well as distribution and distance of cities in space) can be derived from the given assumptions.

Summary of the traditional models:

AGENTS: representative, fully informed, maximizing behaviour

INTERACTION: markets, prices   →market models

SPACE: countries, regions, cities

TIME: comparative statics versus non-linear dynamics and simulations

D Evolutionary Economics	
• Mobility is invariably linked to *novelty* and *evolution*, if we accept that agents' information is incomplete. • Difficulties to deal with novelty are still high as novelty can by definition not be predicted. • Novelty is linked to the idea of *heterogeneity of agents*.	• Interest has to be paid to - the development of new organizational capabilities that are relevant for mobility, - the ways agents are "trying-out" new locations, - the way innovations shape locational choice. • Rules of evolution may be related to - learning, - the way agents acquire information, - the stimuli that make them more daring or dissatisfied with existing situations. • Adequate method: Sociodynamic approaches?

Table 15.1: continued

E Heterogeneity and Sequences of Decision-Making	
<ul><li>Agents are *heterogeneous* as regards</li><li>- their locational preferences and needs,</li><li>- their willingness to make decisions and to take risks,</li><li>- their migratory biography,</li><li>- the amount of information available to them.</li></ul><ul><li>Models have to be dynamic by nature.</li></ul><ul><li>Availability of information and learning play an important role.</li></ul><ul><li>Uncertainty is not equally high for all locations.</li></ul><ul><li>Agents to be taken into account do not only comprise mobile economic agents, but also immobile (political/economic) agents which have a developing task.</li></ul>	<ul><li>Attention has to be paid to the question of the sources of spatial changes and to whether there is a logic of sequential decision-making among heterogeneous agents.</li></ul><ul><li>If locational changes bear uncertainties in them, these can be reduced by "wait and see behaviour" and observing the experiences of others.</li></ul><ul><li>Depending on the characteristics of the location and the agent, ties or location specific assets may be built up in the course of time. These may be difficult or impossible to transfer and may render locational changes costly.</li></ul><ul><li>Adequate method: game theory?</li></ul>

Table 15.1: continued

F Networking, Industrial districts and innovative milieus	
• Agents are linked in a number of ways that are *different from pure price-linkages* and that go beyond spot-interactions. • *Ties* and interaction have a value of their own which is built up in the course of time. • Interaction is subject to *decision-making*.	• Ties may be distinguished as regards their strength and their spatial scale. • Networking may be related to places and spatial proximity (industrial districts and innovative milieus). • In localized networks, stimulation from outside will be important (combinations of local and global ties). • Comparisons of different types of networks show that networks can be a basis for mobility or immobility depending on their type.
G Culture and organization	
• Apart from national political borders, there are other structures that influence mobility.	• Culture may matter for organizational and exchange patterns. Thus, intra- and intercultural mobility may be of interest. • However, other influences of logics of organization and exchange will have to be taken into account.
H Multinational firms	
• Idea of a "corporate culture"	• Multinational firms create their own spatial structures. They can hardly be pressed into any political, cultural or institutional framework.

Table 15.1: continued

I National borders and territorial developers	
• National borders are more than just places where tariffs are paid or entrance of goods/ agents / factors is denied or at least can we measure effects along them that are not due to formal political instruments.	• A number of effects measured at national borders are not due to the traditional instruments of trade policies that are taken into account by international economics.
	• Spatial development may be led by a developer (political entrepreneur) who internalizes "market failures" and develops a "strategy for locational development".
J Time	• Mobility and trajectories of regional development are subject to complex temporal structures.
	• Mobility takes place within a self-referential system. Mobility is effect and determinant of change at the same time.
K Space	• Space is about interpersonal / interfirm relationships.
	• Agents and their interaction define space.

These ideas can be structured into aspects of the role of individual agents and their decisions, their relationships, ties and interaction as well as the importance of space and time. This is illustrated in figure 15.1.

Fig. 15.1: Aspects of mobility and spatial structures and dynamics

spatial structures and dynamics

given, stable for some time   outcome of mobility

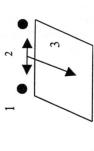

Σ =

1 INDIVIDUAL AGENTS: THEIR FEATURES AND LOCATIONS

⇑ *starting-point of locational mobility: exogenous stimuli vs. intrinsic drive, heterogeneity of agents*
⇑ *direction of locational mobility: prices in space (factor prices), prices across space (transport costs, tariffs) and costs of mobility (fixed costs of new plants), cultural and institutional borders*
⇑ *evolution of agents' capabilities*

2 RELATIONSHIPS AMONG AGENTS & FLOWS

⇑ *price interaction vs. non-price interaction and evolution of ties*
⇑ *culture-specific types of organization and interaction*
⇑ *special role of multinational firms*
⇑ *direction of interaction: prices in space (price differences of goods and factors of production), distribution of social capital, ethnicity, cultural & institutional borders*
⇑ *timing of interdependent decisions: sequences of decision-making*
⇑ *intensity of interaction: sensitivity to different types of distance*

3 RELATIONSHIPS OF AGENTS TO SPACE

⇑ *creating location-specific assets*
⇑ *transferability of this knowledge to other locations?*
⇑ *uncertainty in space   ⇒ spatial dimensions of ties and ties of networks to space*
⇑ *role of immobile agents in creating an innovative atmosphere*

"(B)orders are a point of reference, a physical and cognitive element of order, signification and identity...economic necessity, environmental pressures and basic human curiosity guarantee (however) that borders are permanently transcended, perforated "spiritualized" or otherwise disregarded." (Scott 1996)

15.2   Achievements and open questions of the new approach

International economics has traditionally been the economics of transactions across borders set by political/ state-level decision-makers. The effects of some actions of these decision-makers (measures of liberalization or protection) have been broadly examined by international economic theory.

The preceding chapters have questioned, but also complemented many of the concepts that have been considered as vital parts of international economic theory. It has been shown that there are gaps between the way international economic theory traditionally deals with mobility and the idea of mobility pursued here.

- First of all, the exclusive importance of national borders as politically defined units for economic processes has been examined. Countries have by definition always been the basic object of research in international economic theory. Nonetheless, it has also been shown that national borders are still important and more important than traditional international economic theory might make us believe in a time when formal restrictions by political borders are decreasing. Borders and national structures seem to matter even without tariffs. Nonetheless, further empirical research will be needed to make sure whether the effects measured at national political borders are due to these borders or just measured along them. *Thus, the approach makes us rethink our ideas about borders in economic theory.*

- Secondly, it has been discussed whether - apart from political structures - cultural and institutional aspects might be important structures that determine mobility. Introducing culture as one determinant of mobility, we have recognized that culture is a much more elusive concept than political borders. It is usually related to societies. Culturalists have treated it as a restricting variable for patterns of organization. Others have started at the level of different institutional patterns to explain organizational and exchange logics. Moreover, the idea of a corporate culture has received much interest. Today this may be just as encompassing from a spatial point of view as the cultural structures of societies because multinational corporations may have an enormous size. The example of ethnic networks has shown that some aspects of culture are not necessarily a matter of immobility. They may be related to people rather than places. According to O'Toole (1998: 61) culture "is the shape a place takes when it's inside the heads of its people: all the habits, attitudes and values they take for granted". Some authors have argued in favour of the existence of regional cultures. These comprise according to Weiss (1989: 3) the "environmental influences that have particular historical, political, economic and social characteristics" and "patterns of shared beliefs observations, expectations, and traditions whose participants have similar ways of viewing space, time, things and people." This definition reflects many of the key terms that have been used in the preceding chapters very well.

- Thirdly, the influence of microeconomic diversity and heterogeneity of agents has been emphasized. This point of view may be rejected by economists as a topic of research arguing that economic theory is interested in macro-phenomena leaving microeconomic behaviour for business economics. Empirically, it becomes obvious that the capability to act as a global player or to develop successful strategies of mobility has become a major competitive advantage. *Dynamics are fundamentally shaped by the intrinsic drive of firms to find new alternatives of economic action.* This is also true for spatial behaviour of economic agents. Certainly, it will not be useful to disaggregate down to the smallest unit of the individual agents in economic theory. Nonetheless, the fact that agents are heterogeneous and striving for new alternatives will have to be recognized, if we want to derive knowledge about spatial dynamics. Therefore, we will have to think about the elements that make up firms' heterogeneity as regards mobility.

- Finally, the importance of non-price interaction has been underlined. Traditionally, however, economic theory is pure market theory. It acknowledges that decisions about locations, flows of goods and factors and interaction are interdependent. Business practice also shows that interaction is not only guided by the anonymous market. Personal ties, experiences and trust are clearly important. These are social aspects that will add to a theory that is closer to reality. Furthermore, they might be a starting-point for a better understanding of the importance of distance in a globalized world. It has been shown that there are aspects like mobility of information, creation of an innovative atmosphere or social capital that are much less physical than traditional lows of goods and factors and might be described as soft factors of mobility.

These facets of interaction and ties towards space show different degrees of stability or immobility that are due to the fact that

- there are social insider advantages like in ethnic groups or advantages that are related to social capital,

- there are advantages of intra-firm transactions rather than market transactions, which is especially true for knowledge and capabilities,

- there are place-specific insider advantages (location-specific assets).

Thus, we get aware that we may have to revise our ideas about "economic" and "non-economic" aspects of societies.

- Moreover, a richer image of political and economic decision-makers and their interaction has been painted. Thus, spatial dynamics are determined by a number of different agents all of which have certain competences to shape what happens inside and outside national borders. Locational choice is not an automatic reaction. It happens within a scope of action and it cannot be analyzed within a comparative-static framework. It is a choice rather than a change at a point in time.

Faist (1997b: 252) describes the concept of a migratory space that does not only consist of a number of geographical locations, but also of politically and culturally relevant ties, individual perceptions and images and the structure of opportunities all of which may be linked by intermediate mechanisms like networks. Park and Markusen (1995) underline the complex nature of locational decision-making with *multiple agents* in *multiple locations* participating (political agents at different levels, multi-locational firms, local boosters, scientific and engineering labour, universities, small entrepreneurial firms).

- The notion of inside (intra-)-outside (inter-) considerations has been dominant in all the approaches explaining the different facets of mobility. However, we have seen that inside and outside are concepts that are much more flexible than traditional economic theory suggests. Intra-analysis (e.g. analyzing structures within a network) may be as important as inter-analysis (e. g. analysis of international trade). This is why we get an understanding of point-economies/ -regions/ -cities that acknowledges not only that there is a space between the points, but also the possibility to disaggregate them into smaller parts that may be heterogeneous.

The following figure 15.2 illustrates that the new ideas developed in part C are mainly related to

- the importance of heterogeneity and development of agents,
- the inter- and intrafirm relationships and relationships between and to other agents,
- the importance and relationship to space,
- evolution of all the levels in time.

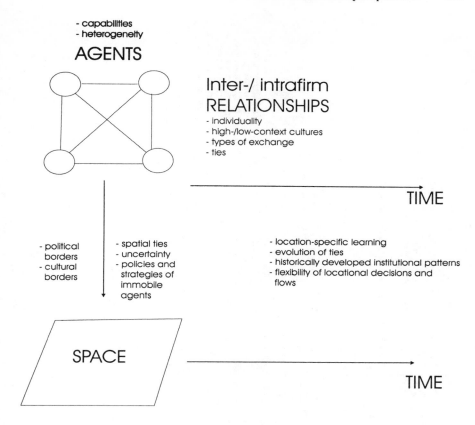

- capabilities
- heterogeneity
AGENTS

Inter-/ intrafirm
RELATIONSHIPS
- individuality
- high-/low-context cultures
- types of exchange
- ties

TIME

- political
  borders
- cultural
  borders

- spatial ties
- uncertainty
- policies and
  strategies of
  immobile
  agents

- location-specific learning
- evolution of ties
- historically developed institutional patterns
- flexibility of locational decisions and
  flows

SPACE

TIME

Fig. 15.2: Agents, relationships, space and time

The proposal of a broader framework is based on the assumption that

- there is an urgent need to modernize the theory of international economics;

- this modernization can only be done within a broader framework whose key term might be the idea of mobility; possibilities for theoretical development from within the existing theory seem to be rather limited.

This certainly does not mean that "old" theories are criticised or should be discarded. All of them shed light on certain important aspects of the international economic system. And all of them have been developed within a certain configuration in space and time. Thus, in a time when national borders are prevalent, models will have a different shape than nowadays. Also the strong interest into Asian economies is a relatively new phenomenon that has brought culture-related aspects into the focus of our interest. Many more examples for such a space-time-relatedness of theoretical approaches can be found.

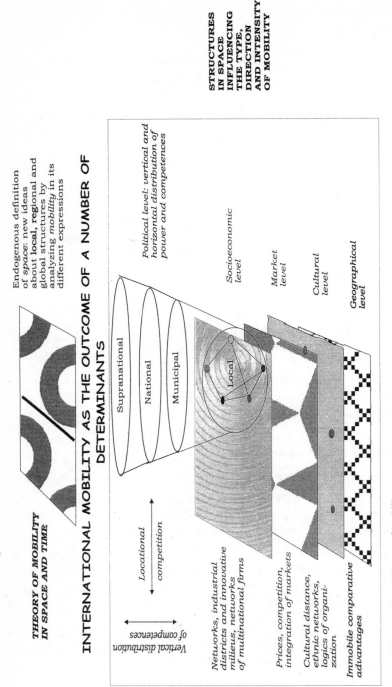

Fig. 15.3: A multilevel theory of mobility

The point of view offered here in any way is more encompassing than traditional ones. Not only has it been shown that the determinants of mobility are diverse, but also that mobility is more than mobility of goods and factors across national borders. As regards the determinants a multidimensional framework is necessary to fully understand mobility (fig. 15.3).[57]

What remains of the basic idea of *international* economics? Clearly, we have to have a more differentiated understanding on spatial structures. Even if we have a look at small scale agglomerations or subnational regions, we always have to be aware that these are embedded into a wider national and international context. Regions and locations cannot be considered isolated entities. Their position in the global context will be decisive for their success. Thus, it will be the interplay between local conditions, national framework and global position that shapes economic (spatial) structures. This has been shown in the case of industrial districts for example. Traditional approaches to international economics do only have a look on what crosses borders. Thus, what is considered is what happens in between nations. In effect, these approaches neither worry about the "where from" nor about the "where to" of flows. The origin of flows is entirely local. It vanishes within the concept of the national point economy. This idea is taken up in figure 15.4.

---

[57] The recognition of the importance of seemingly „non-economic" determinants may also be relevant in other fields. E. g. Heiduk and Pohl (1999) apply this to the analysis of the boundaries and stability of regions.

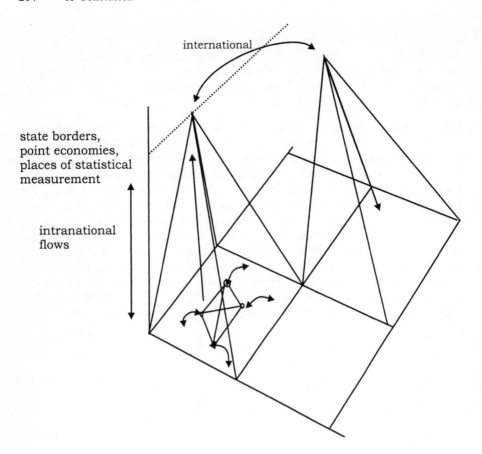

Fig. 15.4: International mobility, origins and destinations of flows

In the case of multinational firms, a final product that crosses borders may be the result of a number of transborder transactions preceding its trade. This may e. g. concern the exchange of information and people among the subsidiaries of a multinational corporation. These are flows that are not made visible by traditional approaches of the theory of international economics, but that may nonetheless be decisive for those flows that can be seen (fig. 15.5). Similar things may be true in the case of ethnic networks that cross borders.

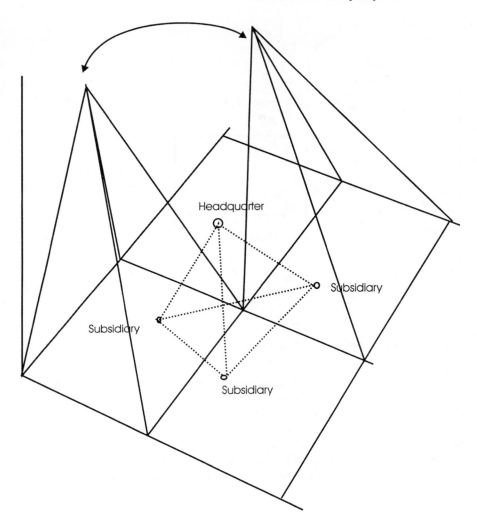

Fig. 15.5: Invisible international flows

The destination of flows may not only be a matter of national preferential structures, but also of cultural differences. Thus, an analysis of the origins and destinations of the flows measured between countries is a matter of special configurations of political, cultural, institutional and possibly other aspects. While in some cases, political and other borders may be strongly congruent (fig. 15.6), a number of examples for more interesting constellations can be found (fig. 15.7).

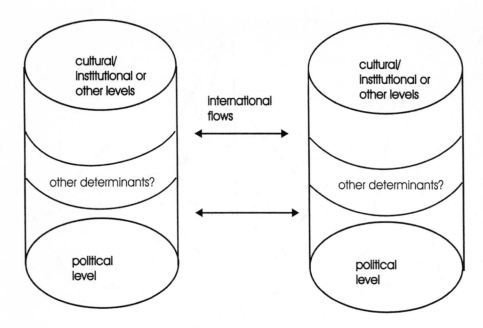

Fig. 15.6: Congruence of different determinants

One of these more difficult examples might be the case of Québec with its cultural ties to France, but which is situated within the borders of Canada, a country being integrated into NAFTA. These relationships are reflected in figure 15.7. Trade and transactions between these countries and regions (the content of the matrix) are a matter of a complex constellation as regards culture, regional integration and geographical distance. One of the most interesting points will be to get a better idea of the interplay and the importance of these different aspects.

Empirical observation of flows among different nations: What are their determinants? What can be said about the interplay of determinants?

	Canada	France	Great Britain	USA
Canada	✕			
France		✕		
Great Britain			✕	
USA				✕

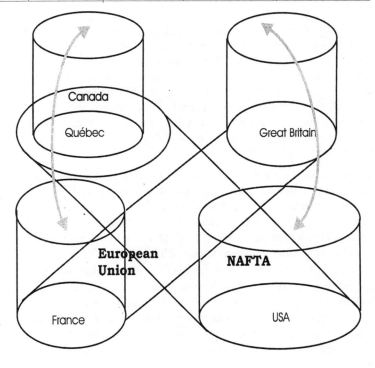

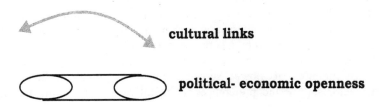

Fig. 15.7: Mobility as the result of a complex set of determinants

On the other hand, dealing with questions of culture and different institutions, we are frequently confronted with examples within the Asian region. Why is this the case? We might propose that culture plays a much more important role whenever "high context" cultures are involved. This seems to be reasonable because these cultures make a stronger distinction between insiders and outsiders. It is important with whom to deal and on the basis of which norms that may be shared or contrasting norms. This makes us conclude that from a theoretical point of view more attention has to be paid to the selection of relevant agents and their aggregation as well as to the rules and norms governing their behaviour. This is related to Hofstede's notion that some cultures are more individualistic than others (ch. 10.1).

These examples show that in different constellations different levels or different determinants may be decisive for transactions between nations. The flows measured are the results of these determinants. Traditionally, we only dealt with single causal relations. Thus, the flows measured were interpreted as a result of the openness of countries that was politically determined or within which we assumed that homogeneity as regards different aspects was given. The broader approach gives us a better awareness for the fact that flows are a result of constellations consisting of a set of different levels that may to a different and varying degree be decisive.

Of course, dealing with such a complex set of determinants of mobility makes it nearly impossible to derive general deterministic laws. We will be forced to examine specific configurations more detailed to understand which are the dominant agents and influences. Most certainly, many of the concepts and influences discussed do not lend themselves easily to mathematical modelling. But - as Boulding states - mathematics is a bad master, although it may be a wonderful servant.[58] And finally, economics is a social science and not a branch of the natural sciences. Mathematical modelling often goes along with the need to reduce human behaviour to a degree of uniformity in space and time that may not exist. Clearly, reductions of a similar kind are necessary to reduce complexity and deduce "laws". However, we have to look for the degree of reduction that minimizes the trade-off between methodological complexity and valuable realistic insights.

However, if we still operate within a framework of international economics, we have to come to the conclusion that mainstream theories have only shed light on one part of the determinants of international economic transactions. Traditionally, "inter"national has been defined by a common political framework within borders and heterogeneous structures or impediments of mobility among states. The incentives for mobility of flows were set by international differences in technology, factor supply and preferences, competitive aspects or the fact that

---

[58] Quoted according to Higgins and Savoie (1995: 162)

consumers estimated variety. Implicitly however, political homogeneity seems to have been transferred on other features that shape a nation (culture, norms, business practices), but that are normally not defined by political borders. What has been neglected is that "nation" does not mean "state". An important question to define the tasks of international economics will thus be: Which features of a nation can be pressed into framework of political borders? Most certainly this will not be true for culture. Even closed economies comprise different cultures. Within an open economy culture is a feature that is even more difficult to define in a spatial context. Goods, people and firms with different cultural backgrounds operate in the same spatial context. They take their cultures to new locations and adapt partly to new environments. The degree to which adaptation takes place may itself be a matter of culture. Corporations acting on a global scale may even create new corporate cultures. On the other hand, host nations' cultures may be penetrated to a different degree. This is impressively illustrated by the influence of the Chinese culture in Singapore, Indonesia and other Asian regions or the Latin American influence in parts of the US. It shows that culture is not bound by national borders.

International is thus a concept that is more than "interstate" or even "interpolitical". From an economic point of view there is not reason why international should not be "intercultural", if we accept that culture may have an influence on economics that is in some cases just as strong as political borders. Thus, international is a concept that is by far less simple than political borders make us think. In the past a number of aspects have been neglected which may be much more difficult to deal with theoretically. There may be an interplay among political borders and other features of a nation. There may be overlaps, but not necessarily congruence.

Nonetheless, we have to be careful because political rule is not given by nature. It may change in time as shows the example of the former Soviet Union or also Hong Kong. While Hong Kong has been under British rule for a long time, it has now been given back to China, while retaining a number of special rights as a special administrative region. Even if these rights had not remained, we may doubt whether transactions between Hong Kong and Mainland China would have become truly national. On the other hand, Macao has long been ruled by the Portuguese. Nonetheless, we hardly had the impression that Macao was Portuguese. Intuitively, we are most of the time well able to distinguish different nationalities, although different criteria may be relevant in different cases.

Political borders have in international economic theory mostly denoted openness and outward strategies of a country. Nonetheless, there are examples where even in this respect countries are not homogenous. A good example are open zones in countries like China. These territories offer much better conditions for foreign investors to enter the Chinese market. They are in many senses completely different from the rest of China and have in many senses experienced a much faster development. Although these areas are definitely Chinese, if we start from their political rule, the economic and innovative culture is different from the rest of the country.

Moreover, frequently economic forces seem to be much stronger than any political or historical resentment. This is reflected e.g. by the strong engagement of Taiwanese investors in China. In some cases cultural differences seems to be relative insignificant from an economic point of view as is shown in the US where political entities have been created from diverse cultures. In others, a lot of skills are needed to keep different cultures together in one political framework as is shown by the example of countries like Spain and Belgium. This may also be due to historical evolution: Have borders been built around cultures and economic facts or have culture and the economy developed within borders?

The way international transactions are dealt with theoretically in many ways seem to correspond to their statistical measurement, which is of course done along national borders. However, the importance of borders for measurement should not lead us to conclude that flows across national borders are exclusively determined by political features or boundaries of the nation state. The determinants for mobility, its incentives, but also the barriers to mobility are much more complex. Some of the aspects that have to be taken into account may facilitate international transactions (e. g. transnational networks), others may impede them (cultural distance e. g.). Moreover, the effects of these structures are diverse. Not only do they affect the intensity of interaction and flows, but also the way transactions are done and their direction. This higher complexity also explains why the slogan of the decreasing importance of nation states in the sense of a declining relevance of national borders is too simple. Not only are the determinants for mobility more complex, but also the distribution of the relevant aspects in space is not necessarily congruent to political borders. Moreover neither nations, nor borders are points in space. They have an extension in space where diverse constellations may lead to different influences on international mobility. It is the whole set of determinants of mobility that may help us to explain what or who is mobile, the direction of mobility and the intensity of flows.

What about the future of international economic theory? Most certainly, this field of research will be interesting and valuable in the future as well. Its insights remain valid and important, although maybe in a much broader context where the aspect of political borders as important structures is only one line of research. The concept of mobility in space and time offers many more possibilities, but is nonetheless different from other economic fields because of its spatial perspective. It is also different from geographic points of view because it is centered around economic argumentation and economic agents are in the center of interest. It is expected to underline those spatial aspects that are relevant from an economic point of view, even if it takes other aspects into account. It starts from the idea that territory as the basis for economic action is defined as a "sedimentation of specific and interrelated historical, social and cultural factors in local areas" (Garofoli 1991: 122). Structures bind together space and time (Neuberger 1995: 300).

Therefore, we should not forecast an end for international economic theory, but rather a new beginning within a broader context.

15.3 Empirical and theoretical research agenda

Altogether the achievements of the preceding chapters lie in proposing a new framework for research while at the same time giving ideas about existing theoretical approaches that can be useful to achieve these aims. However, we have also come to the conclusion that the research agenda for the future is broad. This is above all true with respect to the empirical side and even more as regards methodological questions of modelling.

To broaden the empirical basis of understanding mobility has been beyond the scope of the agenda of this book. It has been shown however that even if we rely on plausible basic assumptions about the determinants and relevant aspects of mobility, the gap between empirical observation and theoretical modelling is already huge. Nonetheless, a more detailed empirical research on the causes and determinants of mobility will have to be one of the points on the future research agenda. Above all the following points will deserve interest:

- How do firms conceive and develop their possibilities for mobility?

- How does interaction among agents influence their spatial behaviour? In this context special attention will have to be paid to the role of spatially immobile political decision-makers and other agents that might boost local, regional and national development.

- New ideas about spatial structures: Which aspects are important determinants for the type, direction and intensity of mobility apart from political borders?

From a methodological point of view we will have to choose our methods according to the degree to which they are open to integrate elements of heterogeneity, interaction and above all space and time. Interaction results in flows between agents. Some of these flows are expressions of the traditional transactions considered in international economic theory (e.g. trade flows). But frequently, interaction is a matter of information, its exchange and circulation. Models dealing with market transactions are related to those actions agents on both sides of the market pursue. Between them is the market matching them without any uncertainties or mismatches. Direct *interaction* however does not occur in these models. Empirically structures of interaction are however results rather than starting-points. The search for partners of interaction and the evolution of ties as well as the matching of agents are sequential and uncertain steps in *time* shaped by agents perceptions of *space* and distance. It has been shown that especially features of heterogeneity, interaction and time may be well dealt with in game-theoretic approaches. The approach presented in chapter 9 was only a very simple example of a co-operative dynamic game. Evolutionary game theoretic models might however deal with agents learning from their experiences as to which strategy to play. In these models the macro-environment might evolve according to the success of the strategies. Dealing with endogenous networks, Kirman emphasizes two main problems: [59]

- finding out which structures are stable and not subject to endogenous pressures to change them;

- dealing with links that are reinforced over time; thus, we get the picture of an economy whose structure changes over time.

Modelling of interaction has been done by random matching of agents. However, we will have to distinguish those theoretical aspects that are indeed random events happening by chance and the randomness resulting from the possibility of agents to decide as well as randomness that is assumed because we do not know what is behind the things we observe. Only in the first case does randomness have its justification. In the second case, there are scopes of action and we may not be able to work with deterministic approaches, but we may be able to develop ideas about the relevant probability distribution. The third aspect is a methodological weakness rather than a justified method. These problems related to randomness are very similar with the idea of introducing exogenous stimuli into models. This may be justified, if these stimuli are indeed external to the system that is analyzed. However, it often also seems to express an ignorance of relevant interdependencies. Thus, a better understanding of agents, their development and their capabilities may give us a better understanding of the background of those elements that are methodologically taken as random or exogenous.

Accepting that interaction is much more than only price interaction, we will have to complement our market models by more flexible concepts. One promising approach in this context might be stochastic models like sociodynamics and synergetics as presented in chapter 9.4. Much of this work will be and is already done by computer simulations. The models might also be able to deal with the analysis of evolving interaction. Thus, they might help us to understand how the probabilities that links between agents are used evolve. Thus, the macro pattern we conceive may be an evolving probability distribution. In a more complicated version, we might also deal with agents that have different types of links. "However the analysis of this sort of multi-layered graph seems to be rather intractable." (Kirman 1999: 33) Especially sociodynamic models moreover have shown a bigger degree of openness as regards the aggregation and disaggregation of agents into meaningful groups and entities. Aggregation will also matter as regards the spatial dimension of the economic system. Even when dealing with

---

[59] Kirman (1999) gives a very good overview about possible approaches and their problems.

international transactions, we will have to take intranational structures into account. Concerning time, it seems plausible to assume that the time of comparative statics is over and that an evolutionary point of view may be more adequate.

Certainly, formal models to deal with such questions have been developed. However, also the conscience of the many remaining problems is high. Against the background of the preceding chapters especially two problems seem to be prevalent:

- to cope with the trade-off between mathematical feasibility, mathematical elegance and reasonable economic argumentation;

- to get better insights on the special aspects arising when dealing with international transactions.

To conclude we may state that the phenomenon of mobility nowadays not only needs better explanations, but is also a good starting point to give us ideas about restrictions of traditional approaches of (international) economics that may be relevant for other fields as well.

List of figures

List of tables

References

Adler, N.: International dimensions of organizational behaviour. Cincinnati: South-Western College Publ. 1997

Allen, P.: Why the future is not what it was. New models of evolution. Futures, July/ Aug., pp. 555-570 (1990)

Allen, A.: Modelling complex economic evolution. In: Schweitzer, F., Silverberg, G. (eds.): Selbstorganisation, Jahrbuch für Komplexität in der Ökonomie. Berlin: Duncker & Humblot 1998

Allen, P. M., Phang: Evolution, creativity and intelligence in complex systems. in: Haken, H., Mikhailov, A. (eds.): Interdisciplinary approaches to non-linear complex systems. Berlin Heidelberg New York: Springer 1993

Amin, A. (1993): The globalization of the economy. An erosion of regional network. In: Grabher, G. (ed.): The embedded firm. On the sociodynamics of industrial networks. London: Routledge 1993

Amin, A., Robins, K.: These are not Marshallian times. In: Camagni, R. (ed.): Innovation networks: spatial perspectives. London: Belhaven Press 1991

Amin, A., Thrift, N.: Neo-Marshallian nodes in global networks. International Journal of Urban and Regional Research, Vol. 16, pp. 571-587 (1992)

Amin, A., Thrift, N.: Holding down the global. In: Amin, A., Thrift, N. (eds.): Globalization, institutions and regional development in Europe. Oxford: Oxford University Press 1994

Andersson, A. E.: The four logistical revolutions. Papers of the Regional Science Association, Vol. 59, pp. 1-12 (1986)

Arthur, B.: Industry location patterns and the importance of history. CEPR Publication No. 84, Stanford 1984

Audretsch, D. B., Feldman, M. P.: R+D spillover and the geography of innovation and production. American Economic Review, Vol. 86, No. 3, pp. 630-640 (1996)

Audretsch, D. B., Weigand, C.: Innovation, Raumstruktur und Internationalisierungs-strategien. In: Mayer, O. G., Scharrer, H.-E.(eds.): Internationale Unternehmens-strategien und nationale Standortpolitik. Baden-Baden: Nomos 1999

Ayadalot, P., Keeble, D.: High technology industry and innovative environment in Europe. In: Ayadalot, P., Keeble, D. (eds.): High technology industry and innovative environment in Europe. London: Routledge 1988

Baker, W. E.: Market networks and corporate behaviour. American Journal of Sociology, Vol. 96, No. 3, Nov., pp. 589-625 (1990)

Baker, W. E.: The network organization in theory and practice. In: Nohria, N., Eccles, R. G. (eds.): Networks and organizations: structure, form and action. Boston: Harvard Business School Press 1992

Barnes, T. J.: Rationality and relativism in economic geography, an interpretative review of the homo oeconomicus assumption. Progress in Human Geography, Vol. 12, No. 4, pp. 473-496 (1988)

Bartlett, C. A., Goshal, S.: Managing across borders: the transnational solution. Boston: London: Random House Business Press, 2nd edn. 1998 (Copyrights for U. S. and Canada are held by Harvard Business School Press)

Batten, D. , Casti, J., Thord, R. (eds.): Networks in action. Berlin: Springer 1995

Bayoumi, T., Eichengreen, B.: Is regionalism simply a diversion? Evidence from the evolution of the EC and the EFTA. National Bureau of Economic Research, Working Paper No. 5283, Cambridge/ Mass. 1995

Belussi, F.: Some theoretical foundations of the industrial district model: accumulation of tacit knowledge, decentralization and division of cognitive labour, paper presented at the conference "Evolution of Industrial Districts", Max-Planck-Institut, Jena, 7-9 Oct. 1999

Bergmann, R.: Interkulturelles Lernen als Organizational Capability. In: Nolte, H. (ed.): Aspekte ressourcenorientierter Unternehmensführung. München: Hampp 1998

Bergman, E. M., Maier, G., Tödtling, F.: Introduction. In: Bergman, E. M., Maier, G., Tödtling, F. (eds.): Regions reconsidered. London: Mansell 1991a

Bergman, E. M., Maier, G., Tödtling, F.: Reconsidering regions. In: Bergman, E. M., Maier, G., Tödtling, F. (eds.): Regions reconsidered. London: Mansell 1991b

Bertuglia, C. S. et al.: The interacting choice processes of innovation, location and mobility: a compartmental approach. In: Bertuglia, C. S., Fischer, M. M., Preto, G. (eds.): Technological Change, Economic Development and Space. Berlin: Springer 1995

Biggart, N. W.: Institutional logic and economic explanation. In: Marceau, J. (ed.): Reworking the world. Berlin: de Gruyter 1992

Biggart, N. W., Delbridge, R.: Trading worlds: A typological analysis of systems of exchange. Paper presented at the American Sociological Association meetings, Aug., Chicago 1999

Biggart, N. W., Guillén, M. F.: Developing difference: social organization and the rise of the auto industries of South Korea, Taiwan, Spain and Argentina. American Sociological Review, Vol. 64, pp. 722-747 (1999)

Blaut, J. M.: Space and process,. Professional Geographer, Vol. 13 (1961)

Blotevogel, H. H.: Auf dem Wege zu einer „Theorie der Regionalität": Die Region als Forschungsobjekt der Geographie. In: Brunn, G. (ed.): Region und Regionsbildung in Europa, Baden-Baden: Nomos 1996

Blotevogel, H. H., Heinritz, G., Popp, H.: Regionalbewußtsein. Zum Stand der Diskussion um einen Stein des Anstoßes. Geographische Zeitschrift, Vol. 77, 2, pp. 65-88 (1989)

Boisot, M. M.: Information space. London: Routledge 1995

Boschma, R. A., Lambooy, J. G.: Evolutionary economics and economic geography. Journal of Evolutionary Economics, Vol. 9, pp. 411-429 (1999)

Brada, J. C., Méndez, J. A.: Economic integration among developed, developing and centrally planned economies: A comparative analysis. The Review of Economics and Statistics, Vol. 67, 4, pp. 549-556 (1985)

Brainard, L. S.: A simple theory of multinational corporations with a trade-off between proximity and concentration. NBER Working Paper No. 4269, Cambridge/ Mass. (1993)

Brenner, Th.: Learning in a repeated decision-process: A variation-imitation-decision model. Papers on Economics & Evolution, No. 9603, Max-Planck-Institut zur Erforschung von Wirtschaftssystemen, Jena (1996)

Brockfeld, H.: Regionen im Wettbewerb unter dem Gesichtspunkt der Standortqualität. Dissertation, München 1997

Brown, C.: Overseas Chinese business in South East Asia. In: Sheridan, K. (ed.): Emerging economic systems in Asia. St. Lenards: Allen & Unwin 1998

Burda, M. C.: Migration and the option value of waiting. The Economic and Social Review, Vol. 27, No. 1, Oct. , pp. 1-19 (1995)

Burt, R. S.: Structural holes: the social structure of competition. Cambridge: Harvard University Press 1992

Buzan, B.: The Asia-Pacific: what sort of region in what sort of world?. In: McGrew, A., Brook, Ch. (eds.): Asia-Pacific in the new world order,.London: Routledge 1998

Camagni, R.: The urban milieu, precondition for innovation and economic success. Paper presented at the annual congress of the Wissenschaftszentrum NRW "Laboratorien der Moderne, 27th, 28th of September 1999

Capineri, C., Romei, P.: Telecommunication and territorial innovation: the experience of the metropolitan area network and high technology network in Tuscany. In: Reggiani, A., Fabri, D. (eds.): Network developments in economic spatial systems. Aldershot: Ashgate 1999

Casella, A. Rauch, J. E.: Anonymous markets and group ties in international trade. Centre for Economic Policy Research, Discussion Paper, No. 6186, Cambridge/ Mass. 1997

Castells, M.: High technology, space and society. Beverly Hills: Sage Publ. 1985

Church, G. J.: Launch of an economic cold war. TIME Domestic, Vol. 146, July 3rd (1995)

Clegg, S.: French Bread, Italian Fashions and Asian Enterprises: Modern Passions and Postmodern Prognoses. In: Marceau, J. (ed.): Reworking the World. Berlin: de Gruyter 1992

Coleman, J.: Social capital and the creation of human capital. American Journal of Sociology, Supplement zu Vol. 94, pp. S95-S120 (1988)

Colletis, G., Pecquer, B.: Die französische Diskussion der Industriedistrikte. In: Krumbein, W. (ed.): Ökonomische und politische Netzwerke in der Region. Hamburg: Lit 1994

Cooke, Ph.: Reinventing the region: firms, clusters and networks in economic development. In: Daniels, P. W., Lever, W. F. (eds.): The global economy in transition. Essex: Harlow 1996

Cooke, Ph., Morgan, K.: Crisis and renewal: corporate and institutional change in German and Italian regions. Cardiff 1994

Courant, P., Deardorff, A. V.: International trade with lumpy countries. Journal of Political Economy, Vol. 100, No. 1, pp. 198-210 (1992)

Dalle, J. M.: Rationality and heterogeneity in stochastic aggregation models. In: Cohendet, P. et al. (eds.): The economics of networks. Berlin Heidelberg New York: Springer 1998

de la Mothe, J., Paquet, G.: Local and regional systems of innovation as learning socio-economies. In: de la Mothe, J., Paquet, G. (eds.) (1998): Local and regional systems of innovation. Boston: Kluwer 1998a

de la Mothe, J., Paquet, G. (eds.): Local and regional systems of innovation. Boston: Kluwer 1998b

de Vet, J.: Globalization and Local and Regional Competitiveness. STI Review, Vol. 13, pp. 89-121 (1993)

Dicken, P, Forsgren, M., Malmberg, A.: The local embeddedness of transnational corporations. In: Amin, A./ Thrift, N. (eds.): Globalization, institutions and regional development in Europe. Oxford: Oxford University Press 1994

Dirlik, A.: Globalisation and the politics of place. In: Olds, K. et al. (eds.): Globalisation and the Asia-Pacific. London: Routledge 1999

Drennan, M. P.:The dominance of international finance by London, New York and Tokyo. In: Daniels, P. W., Lever, W. F. (eds.): The global economy in transition. Essex: Harlow 1996

Dunn, M. H.: Die Unternehmung als soziales System. Berlin: Duncker & Humblot 1998

Dutta, M.: Economic regionalization in the Asia-Pacific. Cheltenham: Edward Elgar 1999

East Asia Analytical Unit: Overseas Chinese business networks in Asia. Canberra: Department of Foreign Affairs and Trade 1995

Ekholm, K., Forslid, R.: Agglomeration in a core-periphery model with vertically and horizontally integrated firms. CEPR Discussion Paper, No. 1607, London 1997

Engel, Ch., Rogers, J. H.: How wide is the border? American Economic Review, Vol. 86, No. 5, pp. 1113-1125 (1996)

Erdmann, G.: Elemente einer evolutorischen Innovationstheorie. Tübingen: JCB Mohr 1993

Erramilli, M.: Nationality and subsidiary ownership patterns in multinational corporations.: Journal of International Business Studies, Vol. 27, pp. 225-248 (1996)

Fagiolo, G.: Spatial interactions in dynamic decentralized economies: a review. In: Cohendet, P. et al (eds.): The Economics of Networks. Berlin Heidelberg New York: Springer 1998

Faist, Th.: The crucial meso-level. In: Hammar, T. et. al. (eds.): International migration, immobility and development. Oxford: Berg 1997a

Faist, Th.: From common questions to common concepts. In: Hammar, T. et al. (eds.): International migration, immobility and development. Oxford: Berg 1997b

Faure, G. (ed.): Culture and negotiation. London: Sage 1993

Feenstra, R. C. / Huang, D.-S./ Hamilton, G. G.: A monopolistic competition model of business groups, mimeo 2000

Feenstra, R. C. / Hamilton, G. G.: The organization of the Taiwanese and South Korean economies: a comparative analysis of networked equilibria. Forthcoming in: Rauch, J. E. (ed.): Integrating Networks and Markets. New York: Russel Sage 2000

Fei, X.: From the soil: the foundation of Chinese society. Berkeley: University of California Press 1992

Fine, Ch.: Clockspeed. Reading/ Mass: Perseus Book 1999

Fischer, J., Gensior, S.: Was sind Netzwerke, wie entstehen sie und wie werden sie zusammengehalten. In: Heinze, R. G., Minssen, H. (eds.): Regionale Netzwerke – Realität oder Fiktion. Fakultät für Sozialwissenschaften, Ruhr-University Bochum, 98-4, pp. 33-40 (1998)

Fischer, P. A. , Martin, R., Straubhaar, Th.: Should I stay or should I go? Institut für Wirtschaftspolitik, Discussion Papers in Economic Policy, No. 49, Hamburg, also in Hammar, T. et al. (eds.): International migration, immobility and development. Oxford: Berg 1997

Fischer, P. A. et al.: Why do people stay? Insider advantages and duration dependence of immobility. Paper presented at the Duisburg Volkswirtschaftliches Forschungsseminar, 30. 06. 99

Franz, P.: Soziologie der räumlichen Mobilität. Frankfurt: Campus-Verlag 1984

Frankel, J. A.: Regional trading blocks. Washington, Institute for International Economics 1997

Fuchs, G., Krauss, G., Wolff, H.-G.: Einleitung. In: Fuchs, G./ Krauss, G., Wolff, H.-G. (eds.): Die Bindungen der Globalisierung. Marburg: Metropolis Verlag 1999a

Fuchs, G., Wolff, H.-G.: Regionale und globale Bindungen. In: Fuchs, G., Krauss, G./ Wolff, H.-G. (eds.): Die Bindungen der Globalisierung. Marburg: Metropolis Verlag 1999b

Fujita, M.: On the self-organization and evolution of economic geography. The Japanese Economic Review, Vol. 47, March, pp. 34-61 (1996)

Fujita, M., Krugman, P. R.: When is the economy monocentric? Von Thünen and Chamberlin unified. Regional Science and Urban Economics, Vol. 25, pp. 505-528 (1995)

Fujita, M., Krugman, P. R., Venables, A.: The spatial economy. Cambridge: MIT Press 1999

Fujita, M., Mori, T.: The role of ports in the making of major cities, self-agglomeration and hub-effect. Journal of Development Economics, Vol. 49, pp. 93-120 (1996)

Fujita, M., Smith, T.: Additive interaction models of spatial agglomeration. Journal of Regional Science, Vol. 30, No. 1, pp. 51-74 (1990)

Fujita, M., Thisse, J.-F.: Economics of agglomeration. Journal of the Japanese and International Economies, Vol. 10, pp. 339-378 (1996)

Garofoli, G.: Local networks, innovation and policy in Italian industrial districts. In: Bergman, E. M., Maier, G., Tödtling, F.(eds.): Regions reconsidered. London: Mansell 1991

Gibson, R.: Rethinking the future. London: Brealey 1997

Gillespie, A., Robbins, K.: Geographical inequalities: the spatial bias of the new communications technologies. Journal of Communications, Summer, Vol. 39, pp. 7-18 (1989)

Gillespie, A., Williams, H.: Telecommunications and the reconstruction of regional comparative advantage. Environment and Planning A, Vol. 20, pp. 1311-1321 (1988)

Göbel, E.: Theorie und Gestaltung der Selbstorganisation. Berlin: Duncker & Humblot 1998

Goldstein, H.: Growth center vs. endogenous development strategies: The case of research parks. In: Bergman, E., Maier, G., Tödtling, F. (eds.): Regions reconsidered. London: Mansell 1991

Gould, D. M.: Immigrant links to the home country: Empirical implications for US bilateral trade flows. Review of Economics and Statistics, Vol. 76, May, pp. 302-316 (1994)

Granovetter, M.: The strength of weak ties. American Journal of Sociology, Vol. 78, pp. 1360-1380 (1973)

Granovetter, M.: Economic action and social structure: the problem of embeddedness. American Journal of Sociology, Vol. 91, No. 1985, pp. 481-510 (1985)

Grol, P., Schoch, Ch.: Kultur als Wettbewerbsfaktor. Handelsblatt, 17.03.2000, p. K4 (2000)

Grossman G. M., Helpman, E.: Innovation and growth in the global economy. Cambridge/ Mass.: MIT Press 1992

Hakansson, H.: Developing relationships in business networks. London: International Thomson Business Press 1995

Hakansson, H., Lundgren, A.: Paths, in time and space - path-dependence in industrial networks. In: Magnusson, L., Ottoson, I. (eds.): Evolutionary economics and path dependence. Cheltenham: Edward Elgar 1997

Haken, H.: Synergetics – An Introduction; Nonequilibrium Phase Transitions and Self-Organization in Physics, Chemistry and Biology. Berlin Heidelberg New York: Springer 1977

Hall, E.: Beyond culture. New York: Anchor Press 1977

Hamilton, G. G.: Introduction. In: Hamilton, G. G. (ed.): Asian Business Networks. Berlin: de Gruyter 1996a

Hamilton, G. G.: The theoretical significance of Asian business networks. In: Hamilton, G. G. (ed.): Asian Business Networks. Berlin: de Gruyter 1996b

Hamilton, G. G., Biggart, N. W.: Market culture and authority – a comparative analysis of management and organization in the Far East. American Journal of Sociology, Vol. 94, Supplement S 52-S94 (1988)

Hawking, S.: Eine kurze Geschichte der Zeit. Reinbek: Rowohl 1997 (A brief history of time)

Hayek, F.: Wirtschaftstheorie und Wissen, In: Hayek, F. (ed.): Individualismus und wirtschaftliche Ordnung. Erlenbach/ Zürich: Rentsch 1937/52

Hayter, R. : The dynamics of industrial location. Chichester: Wiley 1997

Heiduk, G., Pohl, N.: Managing technology in space and time – theoretical aspects and empirical evidence from China's open zones. Forthcoming in Journal of the Asia-Pacific Economy, Vol. 6, June (2001)

Heiduk, G., Pohl, N.: The 21st century - a „Pacific Age"? Paper presented at the conference "The XXI Century in Asia – Scenarios for the Next Millenium" at INSEAD, Fontainebleau, February 4-5, 2000

Helliwell, J. F.: Do national borders matter for Québec's trade. Canadian Journal of Economics, Vol. 29, No. 3, pp. 507-522 (1996)

Helliwell, J. F.: How much do national borders matter? Washington: Brookings Institution Press 1998

Helpman, E., Krugman, P. R.: Market structure and foreign trade. 2nd ed., Cambridge: MIT Press 1986, ch. 12,13

Herrmann-Pillath, C.: Kritik der reinen Theorie des internationalen Handels. Marburg: Metropolis 2000 forthcoming

Heuß, E.: Allgemeine Markttheorie. Tübingen: JCB Mohr 1965

Higgins, B., Savoie, D. J.: Regional development theories and their application. New Brunswick: Transaction Publ. 1995

Hinterberger, F.: On the evolution of open socio-economic systems. In: Mishra, R. K., Maaß, D., Zwierlein, E. (eds.): On self-organization. Berlin Heidelberg New York: Springer 1994

Hodgson, G.: Economics and institutions. Philadelphia: University of Pennsylvania Press

Hofstede, G.:Culture's consequences. Beverly Hills: Sage Publ. 1980

Hofstede, G.: Cultures and organizations – software of the mind. London: Mc Graw Hill 1991

Hofstede, G., Neuijen, B., Chayv, D. D., Sanders, G.: Measuring organizational cultures: A qualitative and quantitative study across twenty cases. Administrative Science Quarterly, Vol. 35, pp. 285-316 (1990)

Holland, S.: The regional problem. London: Macmillan 1976

Iwer, F., Rehberg, F.: Mythos Region? In: Fuchs, G., Krauss, G. , Wolff, H.-G. (eds.): Die Bindungen der Globalisierung. Marburg: Metropolis 1999

Jaeger, A. M.: The transfer of organizational culture overseas. Journal of International Business Studies, fall, pp. 91-114 (1983)

Jansen, D.: Theoretische Annäherung an den Netzwerkbegriff. In: Heinze, R. G., Minssen, H. (eds.): Regionale   Netzwerke – Realität oder Fiktion. Fakultät für Sozialwissenschaften, Ruhr-University Bochum, 98-4, pp. 41- 54 (1999)

Johansson, B.: Economic networks and self-organization. In: Bergmann, E. M., Maier, G., Tödtling, F. (eds.): Regions reconsidered. London: Mansell 1991

Johansson, B.: The dynamics of economic networks, in: Batten, D., Casti, J., Thord, R. (eds.): Networks in action. Berlin Heidelberg New York: Springer 1995

Johansson, J., Vahlne, J. E.: Management of internationalization. Institute of International Business, Stockholm School of Business Studies 1992

Johansson, B., Westin, L.: Affinities and frictions of trade networks. The Annals of Regional Science, Vol. 28, pp. 243-261 (1994)

Junius, K.: The Economic Geography of Production, Trade and Development. Kieler Studien 3000, Tübingen (1999)

Kamann, D.-J. F.: The distribution of dominance in networks and its spatial implications. In: Bergman, E. M., Maier, G., Tödtling, F.(eds.): Regions reconsidered. London: Mansell 1991

Keesing, C. P.: Comment. In: Vernon, R. (ed.): The technology factor in international trade. New York: NBER 1979

Keynes, J. M.: The Scope and Method of Political Economy. Partially reprinted in: Hausman, D. M. (ed.): The philosophy of economics: An Antropology, Cambridge: Cambridge University Press 1984

Kim, C.: On the origins of Korean financial crisis. Paper presented at the Duisburger Volkswirtschaftliches Forschungsseminar, 19.04.2000

Kirman, A.: Whom or what does the representative individual represent? Journal of Economic Perspectives, Vol. 6, No. 2, pp. 117-136 (1992)

Kirman, A.: Economies with interacting agents. Rheinische Friedrich-Wilhelms-Universität Bonn, Projektbereich A, Sonderforschungsbereich 303, Discussion Paper A-500 (1995)

Kirman, A.: Interaction and markets. In: Gallegati, M., Kirman, A. (eds.): Beyond the representative agent. Cheltenham: Edgar Elgar 1999

Kirzner, I. M.: Wettbewerb und Unternehmertum. Tübingen, JCB Mohr 1973/78

Koch, A.: Does success in international business require specific capabilities: an Australian perspective. Swinburne University of Technology, Business Working Papers, Serial No. 108, Hawthorn (1994)

Kogut, B.: Foreign direct investment as a sequential process. In: Kindleberger, C. P.. Audretsch, D. B. (eds.): The multinational corporation in the 1980s. Cambridge/ Mass.: MIT Press 1983

Kogut, B., Singh, H.: The effect of national culture on the choices of entry mode. Journal of International Business Studies, Vol. 19, pp. 411-432 (1988)

Kotkin, J.: Tribes: How race, religion and identity determine success in the new global economy. New York: Random House 1993

Krugman, P. R.: History versus expectations. Quarterly Journal of Economics, pp. 651-667 (1991)

Krugman, P. R.: The self-organizing economy. Cambridge: Blackwell 1996

Krugman, P. R., Venables, A. J.: The seamless world: a spatial model of international specialization. NBER Working Paper, No. 5220, Cambridge 1995

Krugman, P. R., Venables, A.: Integration, specialization and adjustment. European Economic Review, Vol. 40, pp. 959-967 (1996)

Kulke, E.: Faktoren industrieller Standortwahl - theoretische Ansätze und empirische Ergebnisse. Geographie und Schule, No. 63, p. 4 (1990)

Kunzmann, K. R., Wegener, M.: The pattern of urbanization in Western Europe. Ekistics, Vol. 350, Sept./ Oct., pp. 281-291 (1991)

Lang, N. S.: Intercultural management in China. Wiesbaden: Deutscher Universitäts-Verlag 1998

Läpple, D.: Die Ökonomie einer Metropolregion im Spannungsfeld von Globalisierung und Regionalisierung - das Beispiel Hamburg. In: Fuchs, G., Krauss, G., Wolff, H.-G. (eds.): Die Bindungen der Globalisierung. Marburg: Metropolis 1999

Liang, N./ Parkhe, A.: Importer behaviour: the neglected counterpart of international exchange. Journal of International Business Studies, 3rd quarter, pp. 495-530 (1997)

Lie, J.: Sociology of markets. Annual Review of Sociology, Vol. 23, pp. 341-360 (1997)

Loasby, B.: Industrial Districts as Knowledge Communities. Paper presented at the conference „Economics and space", CREUSET Université de Saint-Etienne, 12-13 Oct. 1996

Lösch, A.: Epilogue, in: Lösch, A.: The economics of location. New Haven: Yale University Press 1954

Maggi, R.: European integration and the role of transport related barriers at national borders. In: Nijkamp, P. (ed.): New borders and old barriers in spatial development. Aldershot: Ashgate 1994

Maillat, D., Crevoisier, O., Lecoq, B.: Innovation Networks and Territorial Dynamics: A Tentative Typology. In: Johansson, B., Karlsson, Ch., Westin, L. (eds.): Patterns of a Network Economy. Berlin et al.: Springer 1994

Marengo, L., Willinger, M.: Alternative methods for modelling evolutionary dynamics. Journal of Evolutionary Economics, Vol. 7, pp. 331-338 (1997)

Markusen, A.: Sticky places in slippery space: A typology of industrial districts. Economic Geography, Vol. 72, No. 3, pp. 293-313 (1996)

Markusen, J. E.: Multinationals, multi-plant economies and the gains from trade. Journal of International Economics, Vol. 16, pp. 205-226 (1984)

Markusen, J. R, Venables, A. J.: Multinational Firms and the New Trade Theory. NBER Working Paper No. 5036, Cambridge/ Mass. (1995)

Markusen, J. R., Venables, A. J.: The theory of endowment, intra- industry and multinational trade. NBER Working Paper No. 5529, Cambridge/ Mass.1996

Marshall, A.: Industry and trade. London, 3rd. ed.: Macmillan 1920

Marshall, A.: Principles of Economics. 8th ed., London: Macmillan 1922

Martin, P., Ottaviano. G. I. P.: Growth and agglomeration. CEPR Discussion Paper, No. 1529, London 1996

Martin, R.: The new "geographical turn" in economics: some critical reflections. Cambridge Journal of Economics, Vol. 23, No. 1, Jan., pp. 65-91 (1999)

Mayer, S.: Relationale Raumplanung. Marburg: Metropolis Verlag 1999

Mc Callum, J.: National borders matter: Canada – US regional trade patterns. The American Economic Review, Vol. 85, No. 3, June, pp. 615-623 (1995)

Meyer, M.: Die Dynamik der Regionen. Baden-Baden: Nomos Verlag 1997

Mintzberg, H.: Structure in fives: designing effective organizations. Englewood Clives: Prentice Hall 1979

Mises, L. van: Human action: a treatise on economics. New Haven: Yale University Press 1949

Mori, T.: A modelling of megalopolis formation: the maturing of city systems. Journal of Urban Economics, Vol. 42, pp. 133-157 (1997)

Mosdorf, S.: Digitale Revolution führt zur globalen Wirtschaft. Das Parlament, Vol. 48, No. 40, p. 1 (1998)

Nelson, R. R.: Why do firms differ and how does it matter? Strategic Mangement Journal, Vol. 12, pp. 61-74 (1991)

Nelson, R. R., Winters, S. G.: In search of a useful theory of innovation. Research Policy, Vol. 6, 1, pp. 36-76 (1997)

Nelson, R. R.. Winters, S. G.: An evolutionary theory of economic change. Cambridge/ Mass.: Belknap Press 1982

Neuberger, O.: Mikropolitik. Der alltägliche Aufbau und Einsatz von Macht in Organisationen. Stuttgart: Enke 1995

Nicol, L. Y.: Communications, economic development and spatial structures. Institute of Urban and Regional Development, University of California Berekeley, Working Paper No. 405 1983

Nijkamp, P.: Towards a network of regions: the United States of Europe. European Planning Studies, Vol. 1, No. 2, pp. 149-169 (1993)

NN: The stateless corporation. Business Week, May 14th, pp. 52-60 (1990)

NN: Asien läßt Australien außen vor. Handelsblatt, 10./11.03.2000

Nordstrom, K. A., Vahlne, J. E.: Is the globe shrinking? Psychic distance and the establishment of Swedish sales subsidiaries during the last 100 years. Paper presented at the International Trade and Finance Association Annual Conference April 22-25, Laredo, Texas 1992

O'Donoghue, T., Scotchmer, S., Thisse, J.-F.: Patent Breadth, Patent Life and the Pace of Technological Progress. Journal of Economics & Management Strategy, Vol. 7, No. 1, pp. 1-32 (1998)

O'Driscoll, G. P., Rizzo, M.: The economics of time and ignorance. Oxford: Blackwell Publ. 1985

Ohmae, K.: The rise of the region state.Foreign Affairs, Vol. 72, pp. 78-87 (1993)

Oi, J. C.: The role of the local state in China's transitional economy. The China Quarterly, pp. 1132-1149 (1995)

Oinas, P.: Types of enterprises and local relations. In: van der Knaap, B., Le Heron, R. (eds.): Human resources and industrial spaces. Chichester: Wiley 1995

Orrù, M.: Practical and theoretical aspects of Japanese business networks. In: Hamilton, G. G. (ed.): Asian Business Networks. Berlin: de Gruyter 1996

O'Toole, F.: The meaning of union.The New Yorker, April 27th/ May 4th, pp. 54-62 (1998)

Park, S. O., Markusen, A.: Generalizing new industrial districts: a theoretical agenda and an application from a non-Western economy. Environment and Planning, A, Vol. 27, pp. 81-104 (1995)

Parkes, D., Thrift, N.: Time, spaces and places. New York: Wiley 1980

Perlmutter, H. V.: The tortuous evolution of the multinational corporation. Columbia Journal of World Business, Vol. 4, No. 1, pp. 9-18 (1969)

Perroux, F.: Economic space, theory and applications. Quarterly Journal of Economics, Vol. 64, pp. 89-104 (1950)

Piore, M. J., Sabel, C. F.: Das Ende der Massenproduktion. Studie über die Requalifizierung der Arbeit und die Rückkehr der Ökonomie in die Gesellschaft. Berlin: Wagenbach 1989

Pohl, N.: Die Rolle der Unternehmung in der Realen Außenwirtschaftstheorie, Ausgewählte Volkswirtschaftliche Diplomarbeiten des Fachbereichs Wirtschaftswissenschaft der Gerhard-Mercator-Universität Duisburg, Vol. 32 (1998)

Ponsard, C.: History of spatial economic theory. Berlin Heidelberg New York: Springer 1983

Pred, A.: Behaviour and location, Vol. I. Lund, Lund Studies in Geography 1967

Pred, A. : Behaviour and location, Vol. II. Lund, Lund Studies in Geography 1969

Pred, A.: Systems of Cities and Information Flows. Lund: Gleerup 1973

Puga, D., Venables, A.: Preferential trading arrangements and industrial location. CEPR Discussion Paper, No. 1309, London 1995

Puga, D., Venables, A.: Agglomeration and economic development - import substitution versus trade liberalization. CEPR Discussion Paper No. 1782, London 1996

Puga, D., Venables, A.: Trading arrangements and industrial development. The World Bank Economic Review, Vol. 12, No. 12, pp. 221-249 (1998)

Rauch, J. E.: Does history matter only when it matters little? The case of city-industry location. Quarterly Journal of Economics, Aug., pp. 843-867 (1993)

Rauch, J. E.: Networks versus markets in international trade. NBER Working Paper, No. 5617, Cambridge/ Mass.1996a

Rauch, J. E.: Trade and search: social capital, sogo shosha and spillovers. NBER Working Paper No. 5618, Cambridge/ Mass. 1996b

Rauch, J. E., Casella, A.: Overcoming informational barriers to international ressource allocation: prices and group ties. National Bureau of Economic Research, Working Paper No. 6628, Cambrige/ Mass. 1998

Rauch, J. E., Trinidade, V.: Ethnic Chinese networks in international trade. NBER Working Paper No. 7189, Cambridge/ Mass. 1999

Redding, S. G.: Weak organizations and strong linkages: managerial ideology and Chinese family business networks. In: Hamilton, G. G. (ed.): Asian Business Networks. Berlin Heidelberg New York: Springer 1996

Redding, S. G.: The spirit of Chinese capitalism. Berlin: de Gruyter 1990

Reiner, R., Munz, M., Weidlich, W.: Migratory dynamics and interacting subpopulations. System Dynamics Review, Vol. 4, pp. 179-199 (1988)

Reszat, B.: Evolution, spatial self-organization and path dependence: Tokyo's role as an international financial center. Paper presented at the conference "Japan and Germany in a globalizing economic environment: saving insitutional strengths or radically converging on international standards? Duisburg University 13-14th of April, 2000

Ronen, S., Shenkhar, O.: Clustering countries on attitudinal dimensions. The Academy of Management Review, Vol. 10, pp. 435-454 (1985)

Sassen, S.: The impact of the new technologies and globalization on cities. Paper presented at the annual congress of the Wissenschaftszentrum NRW "Laboratorien der Moderne", 27th and 28th of September 1999a

Sassen, S.: Telematik und Globalisierung: Neue Zentralisierung des Raums. Das Magazin, Wissenschaftszentrum NRW, Vol. 10, No. 2 & 3/99, pp. 10-13 (1999b)

Schmutzler, A.: On the stability of geographical production patterns - the role of heterogeneity and externalities. Heidelberg University, Discussion Paper No. 225, Heidelberg (1995)

Schmutzler, A.: Changing places – the role of heterogeneity and externalities in cumulative processes. International Journal of Industrial Organization, Vol. 16, pp. 445-461 (1998)

Schreyögg, G.: The dual cultural challenge: Towards understanding the role of corporate culture in multinational corporations. Diskussionsbeitrag des Fachbereichs Wirtschaftswissenschaft der FernUniversität Hagen, No. 216, Hagen (1994)

Schumpeter, J. A.: Essays on entrepreneurs, innovations, business cycles and evolution of capitalism. ed. by R. V. Clemence, 2nd print, New Brunswick 1991

Scott, J.: Dutch-German euroregions: A model for transboundary cooperation? In: Scott, J., Sweedler, A., Ganster, P., Ebenwein, W.-D. (eds.): Border regions in the functional transition. European and North American perspectives. Regio Series of the IRS, No. 9, pp. 83-103 (1996)

Sender, H.: Inside the Overseas Chinese network. Institutional Investor, Aug. (1991)

Siebert, H.: Locational competition in the world economy. Tübingen: JCB Mohr 1994

Singapore Economic Development Board: http://www.sedb.com.sg/home.html, 28-05-2000

Smith, A.: Inquiry into the nature and causes of the wealth of nations, Vol. I, Book IV. ed. by E. Cannan, London 1961

Spencer, B. J., Qiu, L. P.: Keiretsu and relationship-specific investment: a barrier to trade? National Bureau of Economic Research, Working Paper No. 7572, Cambridge/ Mass. 2000

Steiner, M.: How different are regions? An evolutionary approach to regional inequality. In: Peschel, K. (ed.): Infrastructure and the space economy. Berlin Heidelberg New York: Springer 1990

Storper, M.: The resurgence of regional economies, ten years later. European Urban and Regional Studies, Vol. 2 (3), pp. 191-221 (1995)

Storper, M.: The regional world. New York: Guilford 1997

Storper, M., Walker, R.: The capitalist imperative. New York: Blackwell 1989

Streitfeld, D.: Virtuelle Ratgeber. Handelsblatt, 21./22.01.2000

Subramanian, R., Lawrence, R. Z.: Search and Deliberation in International Exchange: Learning from multinational trade about lags, distance effects and home bias. NBER Working Paper No. 7012, Cambridge/ Mass. 1999

Swedberg, R., Granovetter, M. (1992): Introduction. In: Granovetter, M., Swedberg, R. (eds.): The sociology of economic life. Boulder: Westview Press 1992

The Competitiveness Institute, http://www.competitiveness.org/about/about.htm, 28-05-2000

Thimann, Ch., Thum, M.: Investing in terra incognita, waiting and learning.Economic System, Vol. 22, pp. 1-22 (1998)

Thurow, L.: Changing the nature of capitalism. In: Gibson, R. (ed.): Rethinking the future. London: Brealey 1997

Tödtling, F.: Innovation, Raumstruktur und Internationalisierungsstrategien. In: Mayer, O. G., Scharrer, H.-E. (eds.): Internationale Unternehmensstrategien und nationale Standortpolitik. Baden-Baden: Nomos 1999

Tolich, M., Kenney, M., Biggart, N. W.: Managing the managers: Japanese management strategies in the USA. Journal of Management Studies, Vol. 36, No. 5, pp. 587-608 (1999)

Töpfer, K.: Regionalpolitik und Standortentscheidung. Zentralinstitut für Raumplanung an der Universität Münster, Beiträge zur Raumplanung, Vol. 6, Bielefeld 1969

Trompenaars, F.: Riding the waves of culture,.New York: Mc Graw Hill 1998

Ulrich, H., Probst, G. I. B.: Anleitung zum ganzheitlichen Handeln. Bern: Haupt 1988

Uzzi, B.: The sources and consequences of embeddedness for the economic performance of organizations: the network effect. American Sociological Review, Vol. 61, pp. 674-698 (1996)

Vahlne, J.-E., Wiedersheim, P.: Psychic distance – an inhibiting factor in international trade. Department of Business Administration, University of Uppsala, Working Paper 1977/2

Venables, A. J.: Trade and trade policies with differentiated products: a Chamberlin-Ricardian model. The Economic Journal, Vol. 97, pp. 700-717 (1987)

Venables, A.: Equilibrium locations of vertically linked industries. CEPR Working Paper, No. 802, London 1993

Venables, A. J.: International location of economic activity. American Economic Review, Vol. 85, No. 2, Papers and Proceedings, pp. 296-300 (1995)

Venables, A. J.: Geography and specialization: industrial belts on a circular plain. In: Baldwin, R. E. et al. (eds.): Market integration, regionalism and the global economy. Cambridge: Cambridge University Press 1999

Voelzkow, H.: Die Governance regionaler Ökonomien. In: Fuchs, G., Krauss, G., Wolff, H.-G. (eds.): Die Bindungen der Globalisierung. Marburg: Metropolis 1999

Wagner, A.: Forschungstransfer in evolutionsökonomischer Perspektive - einige empirische Befunde. In: Witt, U. (1992): Studien zur Evolutorischen Ökonomik. Berlin: Duncker & Humblot 1992

Weidlich, W.: Das Modellierungskonzept der Synergetik für dynamisch sozioökonomische Prozesse. In: Witt, U. (ed.): Studien zur Evolutorischen Ökonomik II. Berlin: Duncker & Humblot 1992

Weidlich, W.: Sociodynamics - a systematic approach to mathematical modelling in social sciences. Amsterdam: Harwood Academic Publishers 2000

Weidlich, W., Haag, G. (eds.):Interregional migration. Berlin Heidelberg New York: Springer 1988

Weisbuch, G., Kirman, A., Herreiner, D. K.: Market organization. University of Bonn, Projektbereich B, Discussion Paper, No. 391, Bonn (1996)

Weiss, J. W.: Introduction. In: Weiss, J. W. (ed.): Regional cultures, managerial behavior and entrepreneurship: an international perspective. Westport: Quorum Books 1988

Windler, A.: Zum Begriff des Unternehmensnetzwerks – Eine Strukturationstheoretische Notizz. In: Heinze, R. G./ Minssen, H. (eds.): Regionale Netzwerke – Realität oder Fiktion, Fakultät für Sozialwissenschaften, Ruhr-University Bochum, No. 98-4, pp. 18-32 (1998)

Witt, U.: Coordination of individual economic activities as a an evolving process of self-organization. Economie appliquée, Vol. XXXVII, No. 3/ 4, pp. 569-595 (1985)

Witt, U.: How transaction rights are shaped to channel innovativeness. Journal of institutional and theoretical economics, Vol. 143, pp. 180-195 (1987)

Wolf, H.: Patterns of intra- and inter-state trade. National Bureau of Economic Research, Working Paper No. 5939, Cambridge/ Mass. 1997

Wu, W.: Pioneering economic reforms in China's Special Economic Zones. Aldershot: Ashgate 1999

Yeung, W.-C.: Transnational corporations and business networks. London, Routledge 1998

Zhu, Y., Slater, J. R. : National culture characteristics as a determinant of FDI. University of Birmingham, Working Papers in Commerce, Birmingham 1995

Zimmermann, J. B.: Dynamiques industrielles: le paradoxe du „local". In: Rallet, A., Torre, A. (eds.): Economie industrielle et économie spatiale. Paris: Economica 1995